SOARING

private/commercial

Flight
Manual

ii

SS315254-010
ISBN 0-88487-248-3

Introduction

The text of the *Soaring Flight Manual* is divided into two parts. The first part covers the academic areas required by FAR Part 61 for the written examination. The second part of the text section contains a review of glider operations, including assembly, pre-flight, launch, flight maneuvers, traffic patterns, and landings. The last two chapters provide a preview of advanced soaring and cross-country flight.

A workbook section follows the text, to reinforce the knowledge gained from reading the text. For best results, it is suggested that you study on a regular schedule, allotting enough time to read a chapter in the manual and then answer the workbook questions.

A final examination is provided, so that on completion of the course you can again check your readiness to take the FAA written examination. An answer sheet and answer key provide practice in working with the FAA format and allow quick, easy grading of the exam.

This course has been prepared under the sponsorship of the Soaring Society of America, some of whose members have given generously of their time and talents to make it the most authoritative soaring course yet published. Special thanks are due to Mr. Charles T. McKinnie, the SSA Technical Representative, who served as liaison between the publisher and the Review Committee. The many hours he has spent in reviewing and evaluating committee comments have contributed immeasurably to the authenticity of the course.

The Review Committee members are among the most famous names in soaring. Deep appreciation is hereby expressed to the following members of the committee:

Joe Bennis	Gene Hammond	Charles Lindsay
Forrest W. Blossom	Lazlo Horvath	Paul Schweizer
Sam Fly	Dick Johnson	Dr. Harner Selvidge
Sam Francis	Tom Knauff	Don Slotten

You're now on the threshold of one of the most exhilarating, yet relaxing experiences possible. Learn it well, and enjoy it to the fullest. *Happy Soaring!*

Table of Contents

PART I principles of soaring

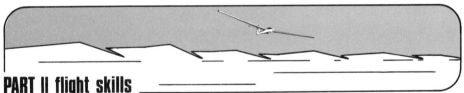

PART II flight skills

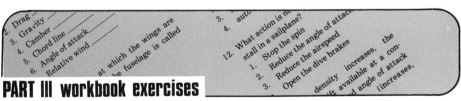

PART III workbook exercises

SOARING

Sailplane Aerodynamics

INTRODUCTION "Aerodynamics" is an impressive word. It calls up visions of formulas, slide rules, engineers hunched over drawing boards, and white-scarved test pilots. Yes, all of these visions and more are associated with the word. This chapter, however, uses no formulas, no slide rules, and no super-scientific words. It simply states what makes a sailplane stay up as long as it does and how it is controlled so precisely that even a novice pilot can land within a few feet of a designated spot.

It is the purpose of this chapter to inform the reader about the natural forces and how they are used to enable a sailplane, without any power of its own, to soar far longer than a light airplane and achieve heights above even some jet-powered aircraft. With this awareness a sailplane pilot can enjoy soaring to the utmost, serene in the knowledge that soaring is based not on some mystery, but on easily understood natural principles.

Chapter One

THREE FORCES

Three direct forces constantly act on a sailplane in flight. The result of the interaction of these forces — lift, drag, and gravity (sailplane weight) — produce the flight path, as illustrated in figure 1-1. Lift opposes gravity to give the sailplane a gentle rate of descent, so that even mild upward currents of air enable it to hold a constant altitude, while stronger updrafts make it possible to climb. Drag is a combination of forces, one of which is induced in the production of lift (induced drag); the other (parasite drag) is caused by resistance to the sailplane's passage through the air.

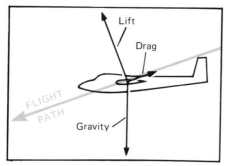

Fig. 1-1. The Three Forces

LIFT

Figure 1-2 presents a summary of the terminology associated with airfoils as an aid to understanding the basic forces involved in *lift* production. The *camber* of an airfoil is the curvature of its upper and lower surfaces. The upper surface normally has a greater camber than the lower surface.

The *chord line* is an imaginary straight line drawn from the leading edge to the trailing edge. This line is significant in determining the angle of attack of an airfoil.

The *angle of incidence* is the angle formed between the chord line of the airfoil and the longitudinal axis of the fuselage. This angle is fixed by the manufacturer, and is not adjustable by the pilot.

The *relative wind* is the motion of an airfoil with respect to the surrounding airmass. In undisturbed air, it represents the forward velocity of a sailplane and is parallel to, but opposite, the flight path.

The *angle of attack* is the angle formed by the chord line of the airfoil and the direction of the relative wind. This angle should not be confused with the sailplane's pitch angle, which is the angle between the longitudinal axis and the natural horizon.

Only one condition must be present for an airfoil to produce lift — the air pressure above the wing must be less than the air pressure below the wing. The lower air pressure above the wing in flight is a result of the differential airflow velocity above and below the wing. This pressure differential is explained by Bernoulli's Principle which states that, when a fluid or gas is in motion, the pressure it exerts decreases as its speed increases. To illustrate this, examine the airflow as it passes through the venturi tube shown in figure 1-3.

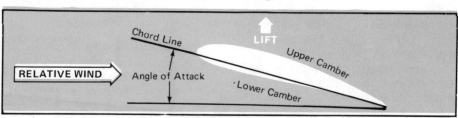

Fig. 1-2. Airfoil Terminology

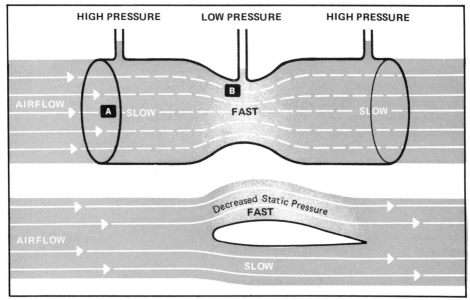

Fig. 1-3. Bernoulli's Principle

The airflow at point A has a given velocity, static pressure, and density. As it approaches the constriction at point B, a change in the velocity, pressure, or density must occur to maintain the original mass flow of air. As the airflow reaches point B, the velocity increases, resulting in a decrease of the static pressure. The upper wing surface corresponds with the lower half of the tube and the decrease in static pressure above the wing results in the lifting action.

From Bernoulli's Principle, it is known that an airfoil must create an acceleration in the airstream to produce a decrease in static pressure above the airfoil. As the angle of attack is increased, the decrease in pressure above the airfoil becomes greater. At the same time, additional pressure is created on the bottom of the airfoil due to the airflow striking the lower surface. This factor contributes approximately 25 to 30 percent of the total lift at angles of attack near maximum lift. This additional *dynamic*

pressure varies considerably as the angle of attack and airfoil velocity change, resulting in a variation of its contribution to the total lift.

The required angle of attack is affected by airspeed, the total weight of the sailplane, density of the air, and load factors imposed by flight maneuvers. It is possible for the wing to pass through the air at a high angle of attack while descending in a level flight attitude. Conversely, the angle of attack may be near zero in a steep dive.

STALL

In level flight attitudes, the flow of air over the surface of a wing is nearly uniform and smooth. The lift produced by the wing depends on the reduced pressure above it and the downward force it imparts on the air through which it moves. Any flight situation in which the wing fails to "hold" the flow of air against its upper surface produces very little lift.

Every airfoil shape (wing section) has an angle of attack beyond which the airstream tends to tear away from its upper surface. This is true at any airspeed within the normal flight range.

A stall is the most obvious effect of a high angle of attack. Stalls are caused by the turbulent airflow as the smooth flow of air breaks away from the surface of the wing at the "separation point." The separation point moves forward as the angle of attack increases, as shown in figure 1-4. A full stall occurs if the angle of attack is increased beyond the critical angle of attack, or point where the lift produced by the wing is no longer sufficient to support the weight of the sailplane. A wing can be stalled in any flight attitude or at any airspeed. The *only* thing that causes a wing to stall is exceeding its critical angle of attack.

SPINS

A spin can be defined as an aggravated stall which results in the sailplane descending in a helical, or cork screw path. Although it may appear to be violent when viewed from outside the sailplane, the stresses actually are minimal, since the sailplane cannot spin until it is fully stalled.

In a full stall condition, the flight control surfaces lose their effectiveness due to the turbulent air flow. When a wing drops, its angle of attack increases and further aggravates the stalled condition. Conversely, the rising wing has a reduced angle of attack, and continues to produce some lift. The rolling movement which results is called auto-rotation. The nose pitches downward as a result of the stall and the rotation of the wings, causing the sailplane to descend in a nose-low at-

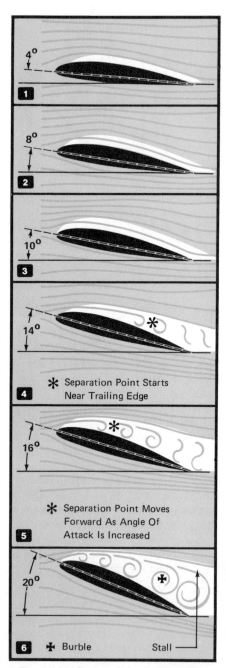

Fig. 1-4. Airflow and Angle of Attack

titude with a rolling and yawing motion in the same direction. This is shown in figure 1-5.

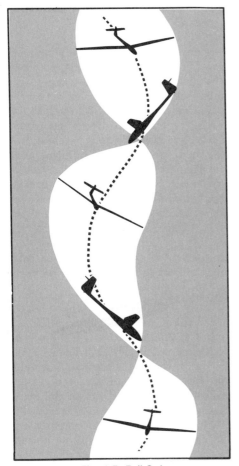

Fig. 1-5. Full Spin

Most training sailplanes have very gentle stall characteristics and must actually be forced into a spin. When the angle of attack is reduced, the stall is broken and the spin stops.

AIR DENSITY

The nature of the airmass surrounding a sailplane also affects the lift the wing is able to produce. Air density decreases as altitude increases, because there are fewer particles of air flowing over the surface of the wing. To maintain constant lift, either the angle of attack or the velocity of the sailplane must be increased.

DRAG

The second flight force is *drag*. Total drag is the sum of two components — induced drag and parasite drag. Since it is a retarding force, much of the initial design effort is aimed at reducing total drag.

INDUCED DRAG

The portion of the total drag force created by the production of lift is called induced drag. Because induced drag is a byproduct of lift, it is greatly affected by changes in airspeed. As indicated airspeed decreases at a constant lift value, induced drag increases, varying inversely with the *square* of the airspeed. For example, if the indicated airspeed decreases by one-half, the induced drag increases four times.

A slight change in the actual relative wind results from a portion of the airmass being deflected around the wing. The lift produced by the wing acts perpendicular to the modified relative wind, while the vertical lift component directly opposes the aircraft's weight. Figure 1-6 illustrates how the rearward acting component of the total lift results in the retarding force of induced drag.

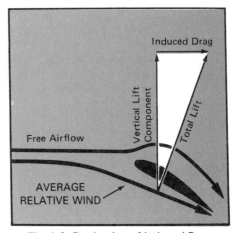

Fig. 1-6. Production of Induced Drag

PARASITE DRAG

Parasite drag includes any drag which is not associated with the production of lift. It is created by the sailplane's resistance to passage through the air. Profile drag is that portion of the resistance caused by the shape of the object moving through the air. For example, a cube creates a great deal of resistance, while a round object creates less. The streamlined shape found on high performance sailplanes, creates the least profile drag. The remainder of parasite drag is caused by the sailplane's surface as it displaces the airmass, generates turbulence, and retards smooth airflow. Parasite drag varies directly with the square of the airspeed, so that doubling the airspeed causes four times as much parasite drag.

TOTAL DRAG

The total drag of a sailplane in flight is the sum of induced and parasite drag. Figure 1-7 illustrates the variation of total drag with indicated airspeed for a given sailplane at a constant weight and configuration. For example, the parasite drag *increases* with velocity, while induced drag *decreases* with velocity. Induced drag is predominant

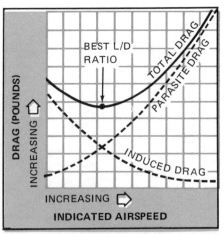

Fig. 1-7. Airspeed vs. Drag

at low airspeeds, while parasite drag is most common at high speeds.

Figure 1-7 illustrates that minimum total drag occurs at the airspeed where the induced and parasite drag curves intersect. This is the speed where the sailplane is operating with the best *lift-to-drag ratio, or L/D.* In other words, the sailplane is producing the least drag for the constant amount of lift required for support. A practical application of this ratio is the glide. The maximum horizontal distance through the air can be obtained during the glide by using the airspeed which produces the maximum lift-to-drag ratio. Any movement of the air alters this ratio with respect to the ground.

GRAVITY

The third force affecting flight is *gravity,* or the actual weight of the sailplane acting downward toward the center of the earth. The pull of gravity provides the forward motion necessary to move the wings through the air in the same way a car coasting downhill receives its forward momentum through the pull of gravity on its own weight. As the wings move forward through the air, they produce lift which, in turn, supports the weight of the sailplane.

WING PLANFORM

The shape, or planform, of the wing affects the lift and drag produced. The four most common planforms used on sailplanes are elliptical, rectangular, tapered, and sweptforward, as shown in figure 1-8. These are the basic shapes, but various combinations may appear on different sailplanes.

The elliptical wing produces the least induced drag for a given wing area; however, this kind of wing has certain

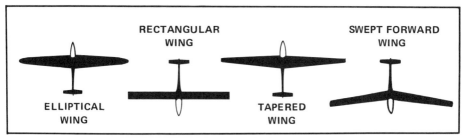

Fig. 1-8. Wing Planforms

drawbacks. It is difficult to manufacture and it transitions quickly from maximum lift to a stall without the normal stall warning. The rectangular wing has more drag than a similar size elliptical wing, but it is easier to build and has very gentle stall characteristics. In addition, it usually gives a warning by causing the plane to buffet gently before stalling.

The tapered wing, most frequently found on sailplanes, is almost as efficient as the elliptical shape, but is much easier to build. It has very good stall characteristics when designed with a slight twist or "washout." With washout, illustrated in figure 1-9, the wing root has a greater angle of attack and tends to stall before the tip. This provides ample warning of the impending stall, a gentle pitch-down, and good aileron control.

A designer may sweep the wings forward as a means of moving the lifting area forward while keeping the mounting point aft of the cockpit. This configuration is used on several tandem two-seaters to allow for a small change in center of gravity whether flying solo or with the rear seat occupied.

ASPECT RATIO

The aspect ratio of a wing is another factor affecting lift and drag. This ratio is determined by dividing the wing span (from tip to tip) by the average wing chord. Figure 1-10 shows examples of different aspect ratios. Wings with high aspect ratios have less high pressure airflow around the wingtips than those with low aspect ratios. The airflow over a wing has a tendency to move outward from the wing root to tip, as well as from the leading edge to the trailing edge. This

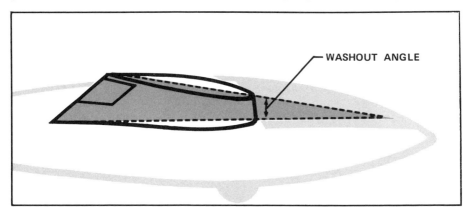

Fig. 1-9. Washout

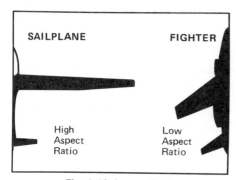

Fig. 1-10 Aspect Ratio

causes the cyclonic airflow around the wingtip, called vortices.

A high aspect ratio wing generates a comparable amount of lift at smaller angles of attack with less induced drag. For this reason, the high aspect ratio of a sailplane's highly tapered wing generates maximum lift with minimum drag at the relatively low airspeeds of normal operation.

The efficiency of a wing in any flight configuration is dependent on the maintenance of the smooth flow of air over its surface. Anything which alters the shape of the wing and disturbs this airflow, such as raindrops, snow, ice, or frost reduces the lift creating capability of the airfoil and may drastically affect the sailplane's flight and stall characteristics. Therefore, wings and tail surfaces should be completely clear prior to flight.

HIGH LIFT DEVICES

To derive maximum lift from a given wing, high lift devices can be incorporated into the wing design, thereby altering the shape and, in some cases, the area of the wing. The effect of high lift devices is to increase the camber of the wing, which produces a higher coefficient of lift for a given angle of attack and results in a slower stalling speed. At the same time, drag is increased, so the sailplane is able to make steeper, slower landing approaches with a shorter roll-out after landing. The use of high lift devices allows the wing to be designed for optimum gliding efficiency while still allowing for comfortable landing performance.

TRAILING EDGE FLAP

The most common high lift device used on sailplanes is the trailing edge flap. There are many variations, but the four basic types are illustrated in figure 1-11.

PLAIN FLAPS

The flap most commonly found on high performance sailplanes is the plain flap. When deflected, it increases the camber of the airfoil and produces an increase in lift with an accompanying increase in drag. Approximately the first 20° of flap extension, with most flap types, results in increased lift. The last portion of flap extension yields a greater proportion of drag.

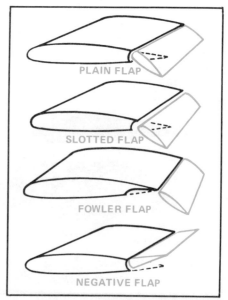

Fig. 1-11. Trailing Edge Flaps

SLOTTED FLAP

The slotted flap produces a greater increase in lift than the plain or split flap by allowing the high pressure air below the wing to flow over the upper surface of the flap. This delays airflow separation at high angles of attack and reduces the stalling speed.

FOWLER FLAP

The fowler flap is the most efficient of the four basic types. In the early portion of its extension, the flap moves rearward and increases the lift area. The rearward motion also creates the effect of a slotted flap, so stall speed is greatly reduced with only a small portion of flap extension. With this type of flap, there is very little increase in drag until it is extended beyond about 25°.

NEGATIVE FLAP

Some flap installations allow for a slight upward, or negative, deflection. The effect is to reduce drag at high speed by allowing the wing to remain at its most efficient angle of attack.

HIGH DRAG DEVICES

Just as flaps may be incorporated into some modern sailplane wings to increase lift, other devices may be installed to decrease lift or create drag. These devices are used primarily to control the glide path, or angle of approach to a landing.

Deployable spoilers can be added to the upper wing surface to "spoil" lift, as shown in figure 1-12. Spoilers also increase drag, although usually not as much as flaps or dive brakes.

Dive brakes normally are located on both upper and lower wing surfaces. They spoil lift and increase drag. For this reason, they are very effective in controlling speed at steep glide angles.

A typical drogue chute (tail parachute), is shown in figure 1-13. The high drag created by the chute results in a much steeper gliding angle and pitch attitude. The drogue chute, unlike spoilers or dive brakes, does not affect stalling speeds.

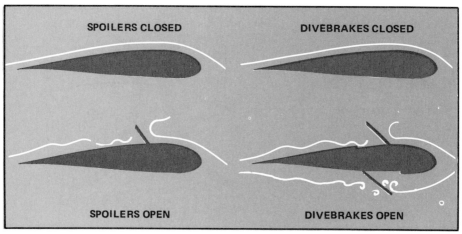

Fig. 1-12. Spoilers and Dive Brakes

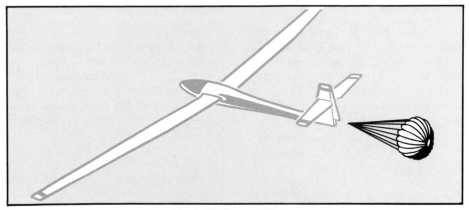

Fig. 1-13. Drogue Chute

THE THREE AXES

Flight involves operation within a true three-dimensional environment. In addition to movement forward and to the side, there is vertical motion. There is one point in the sailplane, regardless of its attitude, about which it can be balanced perfectly. This point is the center of the sailplane's total weight and is called *center of gravity*, or "CG." The location of this point varies with the loading of the sailplane. For example, it is located further forward in sailplanes loaded with two persons than it would be with only one seat occupied.

All movements of the sailplane in flight revolve around the center of gravity. Movements can be further classified as being made about one or more of three axes of rotation. These axes are called vertical, lateral, and longitudinal, and all pass through the sailplane's center of gravity. An axis is defined as a line passing through a body and about which the body rotates. As shown in figure 1-14, a yaw maneuver rotates the sailplane about the *vertical axis*; pitch changes produce movement around the *lateral axis* and banking right or left rotates the sailplane around the *longitudinal axis.*

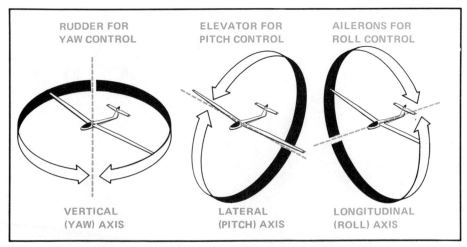

Fig. 1-14. The Three Axes

Figure 1-15 shows the relationships between the control surfaces and motion about each of these axes. Although rotation about the lateral, or pitch axis, is affected by several factors, the control of pitch is primarily the function of the *elevator*. This surface is controlled by fore and aft movement of the control stick. When forward pressure is applied to the control stick, the elevator moves downward, increasing the camber on the upward surface and producing an upward force on the horizontal tail. This raises the tail and, therefore, lowers the nose. When back pressure is applied to the stick, the elevator moves upward, resulting in a downward tail movement.

The *ailerons* create movement known as *roll* about the longitudinal axis. The ailerons are controlled by moving the control stick to the left or right. A downward deflected aileron produces additional lift, and the wing to which it is attached rises. The wing with the aileron deflected upward produces less lift and descends.

Movement about the vertical axis is referred to as *yaw*. The *rudder* is a movable control surface on the fin and is responsible for control around the vertical axis. Movement of the rudder is to the left and right and is controlled by pressure on the rudder pedals mounted on the floor of the cockpit. Pressure applied to the right rudder pedal displaces the rudder to the right. This increases the camber on the left side of the vertical tail components, creating a low-pressure area on the left side and a high-pressure area on the right side of the tail. The resulting pressures cause the tail to move left and the nose of the sailplane to move right. Applying pressure to the left rudder pedal provides an opposite reaction.

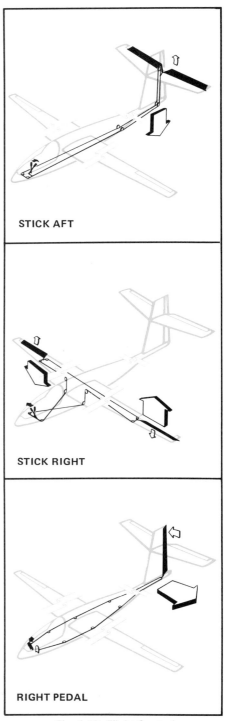

STICK AFT

STICK RIGHT

RIGHT PEDAL

Fig. 1-15. Flight Controls

The "V" tail seen on many sailplanes offers a low drag configuration. The movable surfaces on each side of the "V" operate together with control stick motion and in opposite directions with rudder pedal movement to provide both pitch and yaw control.

STABILITY

Stability defines a sailplane's tendency to maintain a uniform flight condition, and to return to that condition when disturbed. An excessively stable sailplane would strongly resist any attempts to change its attitude or direction, and would make it difficult to control. The design of an aircraft takes into consideration the kind of operation for which it will be used, so the proper balance is reached between stability and controllability. An airliner, for example, is quite stable, so it can be flown on precise flight paths without excessive workload on the part of the pilot. On the other hand, aerobatic airplanes are more responsive to controls to permit easy and rapid maneuvering. The stability designed into any given sailplane or airplane can be altered by its balance when loaded. This is especially true of longitudinal stability. Loading a sailplane outside its allowable CG limits can have a very adverse effect on pitch stability.

STATIC STABILITY

Static stability is the initial tendency to return to a state of equilibrium following a displacement from that state. Figure 1-16 illustrates in item A that *positive* static stability exists when there is a tendency to return to the original position. If an object tends to move farther away from its original position following displacement, as in item B, it is demonstrating *negative* static stability. Item C illustrates *neutral* static stability — the ball tends to remain in the displaced position.

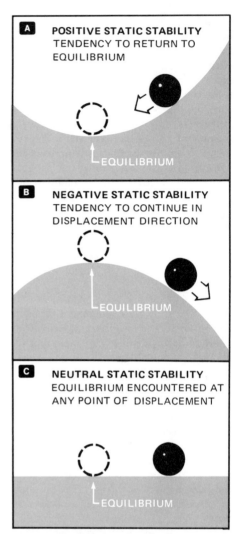

Fig. 1-16. Static Stability

DYNAMIC STABILITY

The ball in figure 1-16, item A would not return immediately to rest at the bottom of the bowl when the force is removed but, rather, would oscillate from one side to the other. These oscillations would decrease in amplitude until the ball eventually came to rest at the bottom of the bowl, demonstrating positive dynamic stability. Dynamic stability, then, describes the motion and time required for a response to static stability. For a sailplane, *positive* dynamic stability is demonstrated by the decreasing oscillations in its flight path, as shown by sailplane A in figure 1-17. *Neutral* dynamic stability is exhibited by sailplane B, where oscillations remain at the same amplitude. In the case of sailplane C, *negative* dynamic stability exists since the oscillations increase in amplitude.

Regardless of the stability inherent in any aircraft, *flutter* may develop in certain high speed situations. Flutter is the rapid vibration of the control surfaces caused by a reaction between the aerodynamic loads and the control surfaces which results in a partial or complete loss of control.

Flutter tendencies are evaluated during the wind tunnel and flight testing of a new design, and a safe margin is provided beyond the normal flight envelope. Several factors, however, can

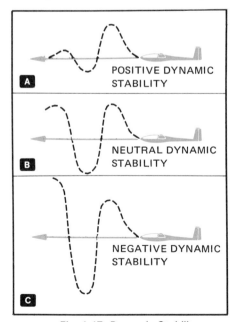

Fig. 1-17. Dynamic Stability

lower the flutter speed of a sailplane; for example, a few extra coats of paint, disturbing the balance of a control surface, or a change in aerodynamic properties. Also, if there is any looseness in the flight control linkage or attachments, flutter can result while flying near maximum speed in turbulence. If a vibration is felt in any flight control, an airspeed reduction should eliminate it.

STABILITY ABOUT THE SAILPLANE AXES

Any aircraft certified under the Federal Aviation Regulations must be stable about all three axes. This requirement assures safe flight characteristics in addition to making a pilot's workload much easier.

LONGITUDINAL STABILITY

The elevator control forces can be adjusted to maintain a desired pitch attitude by means of a trim control. If disturbed, a sailplane with positive static and dynamic longitudinal stability tends to return to the trimmed pitch attitude when the displacing force is removed.

To obtain longitudinal stability, the sailplane is designed so it is slightly nose-heavy. During normal flight, it has a continuous tendency to dive. However, this tendency is offset by the horizontal tail surfaces (stabilizer) being set at a negative angle of attack, as shown in figure 1-18. This position produces a downward or negative lift so that the downward force on the tail exactly counteracts the nose heaviness at a predetermined speed.

When the nose is pulled up, the sailplane loses speed. Thus, the speed of the air over the tail decreases and results in less downward force on the tail. This permits the nose to drop and allows gravity to act as a thrust force.

As the sailplane dives, its airspeed increases. This, in turn, provides more downward force on the tail and pushes the nose up, causing the sailplane to go into a climb. As the climb continues, the speed again decreases, and the downward force on the tail becomes gradually less until the nose drops once more. This time, if the sailplane is dynamically stable, the nose does not drop as far as it did the first time, and enters a much shallower dive. The speed then increases until the plane again goes into a shallower climb, as before. After several such oscillations, the sailplane finally settles down to a speed at which the downward force on the tail exactly offsets the tendency to dive.

Loading the sailplane so that its CG exceeds the aft limits destroys this stability, since the tail has to produce upward lift. A loss of airspeed then causes the nose to rise, further aggravating the situation. A control correction is required to return the nose of the sailplane to its original position. Each time the pitch attitude is disturbed, a control input is required. In extreme circumstances, there might not be adequate control to stop the nose from pitching up; the result would be a spin from which there would be no possibility of recovery. Thus, it can be seen that proper loading is of the utmost importance.

LATERAL STABILITY

Lateral stability refers to a sailplane's tendency to return to wings-level flight following a displacement. As illustrated in figure 1-19, position A, stable rolling moments result when a wing drops and a side slip is introduced. When the relative wind strikes the sailplane from the side, the lower wing experiences an increased angle of attack and increased lift. The higher wing has a reduced

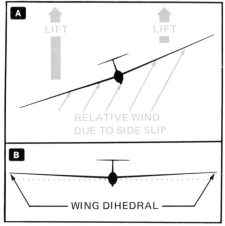

Fig. 1-19. Lateral Stability

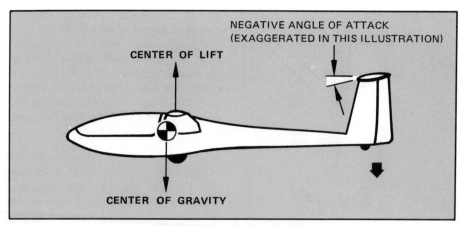

Fig 1-18. Longitudinal Stability

angle of attack and decreased lift. The lift differential results in a rolling moment, which tends to raise the low wing.

Dihedral, as illustrated in position B, is a major wing design consideration used to obtain lateral stability. It increases the stabilizing effect of side slips by increasing the lift differential between the high and low wing during the slip.

DIRECTIONAL STABILITY

Directional stability is the tendency of the sailplane to remain stationary about the vertical, or yaw, axis. When the relative wind is parallel to the longitudinal axis, the sailplane is in equilibrium. If some force yaws the sailplane and produces a slip, a positive yawing moment is developed and the sailplane returns to equilibrium. To obtain this stability, the side area of fuselage ahead of the center of gravity must be counterbalanced by the vertical tail and rear fuselage side surfaces.

The vertical stabilizer is an airfoil, capable of producing lift in either direction. Figure 1-20 shows how a slip angle causes the relative wind to meet the vertical stabilizer at an angle,

resulting in a side force on the tail which turns the sailplane's nose back into the relative wind. In the illustration, the sailplane is in a slip to the right, resulting in a side force which moves the tail to the left, causing the longitudinal axis to align with the relative wind.

TURNING FLIGHT

Turns are made by inclining the lift of the wings to produce a force which turns the aircraft. This lift force can be subdivided and represented as two component forces — one acting vertically and one acting horizontally, as shown in figure 1-21. The horizontal component is the part that makes the sailplane turn, while the vertical component is the part that opposes gravity.

In a turn, there are pairs of opposing forces in balance. The centrifugal force acting outward is opposite and equal to the inward turning force. The vertical component of lift is opposite the force of gravity. The resultant force is equal and opposite the total lifting force, and is composed of centrifugal force and gravity.

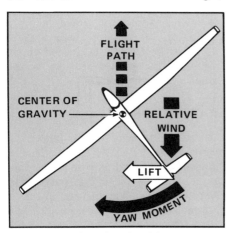

Fig. 1-20. Directional Stability

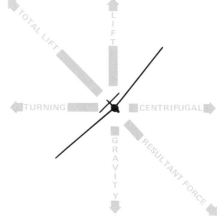

Fig. 1-21. Forces In A Turn

As the bank steepens, the vertical lift decreases and the sink rate increases. The steeper the bank, the greater the increase in sink rate.

The force opposing total lift is the resultant of gravity and centrifugal force, and represents the *equivalent* weight which, divided by actual weight, equals the load factor, expressed in multiples of gravity (G). Load factor increases rapidly as the bank increases, being equal to 1.4 times aircraft weight, (1.4G) in a 45° bank, and twice the aircraft weight, (2.0 G) in a 60° bank, as shown by the graph in figure 1-22.

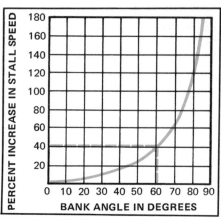

Fig. 1-23. Stall Speed in Turns

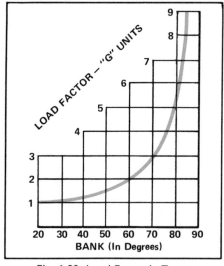

Fig. 1-22. Load Factor in Turns

STALL SPEED IN TURNS

In a turn at constant speed, the increased lift must be developed by increasing the angle of attack. As the bank angle increases, angle of attack must also increase to provide the required lift. At some point, however, the stall angle of attack is reached. Figure 1-23 illustrates the percent of increase in stall speed with increasing bank angle. For example, the dotted line shows that stall speed increases 40 percent in a 60° bank.

DRAG IN TURNS

Induced drag also is increased as a result of the increased lift required in a turn. The increased induced drag results in an increased rate of sink in a turn, as compared with level flight.

RADIUS OF TURN

The radius of turn at any given bank angle varies directly with the square of the airspeed. Therefore, if the airspeed is doubled, the radius of turn is multiplied by four. In figure 1-24, for example, sailplane A in a 30° bank would have a turn radius of 185 feet, sailplane B's turn radius would be 417 feet, and sailplane C would require a radius of 740 feet at a bank angle of 30°. As the bank is steepened at any airspeed, the radius of turn is substantially decreased.

RATE OF TURN

The rate of turn for a given bank angle varies inversely with airspeed. That is, if speed is doubled at a constant bank angle, the rate of turn is cut in half. Rates of turn for the three sailplanes in figure 1-24 in a 30° bank are 18° per second for sailplane A, 12° per second for B, and 9° per second for C. The

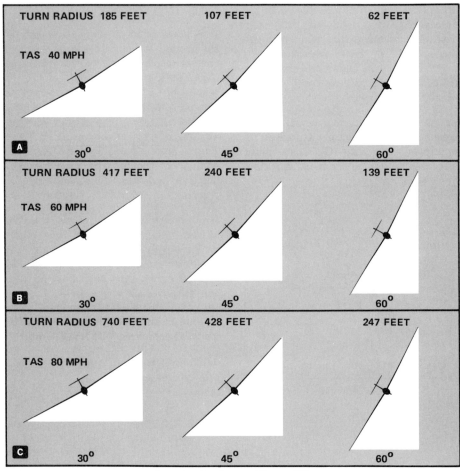

Fig. 1-24. Radius and Rate of Turn

slower the sailplane's airspeed, the less distance and time required to complete a turn.

SLIPS AND SKIDS

To maintain maximum sailplane performance, coordination of rudder and aileron is necessary in the turn. Too little rudder, or rudder applied too late in a turn will cause a slip. Too much rudder, or rudder applied before aileron, results in a skid. In both slips and skids, the fuselage of the sailplane is swung into the relative wind. This creates additional parasite drag which, in turn, reduces lift and airspeed. Intentional slips, however, are useful in a landing approach to steepen the approach path and to counteract a crosswind.

ADVERSE YAW

As a turn is entered, the aileron on the rising wing is deflected downward, changing the wing camber and increasing the angle of attack and the lift of that wing. Simultaneously, the aileron on the descending wing is deflected upward, changing the effective camber and decreasing the angle of attack and the lift of that wing. As lift decreases on the descending wing, induced drag also decreases, allowing that wing to move through the air faster than the raised wing. Figure 1-25 shows how these differences in induced drag cause the sailplane to yaw toward the slower, raised wing in a direction opposite to the turn. Proper rudder usage (coordination) corrects for adverse yaw or aileron drag.

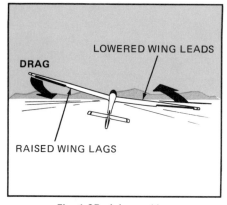

Fig. 1-25. Adverse Yaw

GROUND EFFECT

It is possible to fly a sailplane just off the ground at a slightly slower airspeed than that required to sustain level flight at higher altitudes. This is the result of a phenomenon known as ground effect. Ground effect is due to the interference of the surface with the airflow patterns about a wing in flight. The compression of air between the wing and the ground increases the positive pressure below the wing, increasing lift and reducing induced drag.

Ground effect is measurable at a higher altitude above the ground than might be expected. As a general rule, the results of ground effect can be detected and measured up to an altitude equal to one wingspan above the surface.

It is ground effect which causes the sailplane to float without any control input as it approaches the touchdown point. Awareness of this factor will help prevent excessive float just before landing.

SOARING

Performance Considerations

INTRODUCTION The performance of a sailplane basically means how well it does the job for which it was designed. When soaring pilots speak of performance, they talk about lift-to-drag ratios, climb and speed capabilities, and overall responsiveness.

This chapter introduces the atmospheric conditions, including density altitude and temperature, which influence a sailplane's performance. Also covered are performance curves and recommended airspeeds to fly for maximum efficiency. It includes the importance and ease of keeping the sailplane within proper weight and balance limitations, and explains how to control and check sailplane loading. Finally it provides a section on placarded airspeeds and sets the parameters for safety and structural integrity during all flight operations.

Chapter Two

DENSITY ALTITUDE

The nature of the earth's atmosphere varies with barometric pressure, temperature and, to a lesser degree, humidity. Chapter 1 briefly discussed air density — the higher the altitude, the thinner or less dense the air becomes. Temperature affects air in the same manner. The warmer the temperature, the less dense the air becomes. Standard temperature is considered to be 59° Fahrenheit at sea level, but standard conditions seldom exist. On a 76° day with a barometric pressure of 29.92 in. Hg., the air at a sea level gliderport has the density of air normally found at 1,400 feet. Figure 2-1 illustrates this point.

Density altitude is not a height reference and cannot be read from an altimeter; rather, it is an index of expected performance. The sailplane performs as though it is soaring higher than its actual altitude.

At high density altitude and a given indicated airspeed, true airspeed and groundspeed increase. This means the ground roll will be slightly longer on landing.

Since high density altitude also affects the power output of the towplane, it can be anticipated that its takeoff roll will be longer. Climb performance of the towplane also suffers with increasing density altitude, so it will probably take longer to climb to a planned release altitude.

WIND

The motion of the airmass, as well as its density, affects sailplane performance. The all-important L/D, or glide ratio, never changes in relation to the airmass, because L/D is determined by the design of the sailplane. Glide angle with respect to the ground, however, reflects the direction and velocity of the airmass in which the sailplane flies. Figure 2-2 shows an extreme example of wind effect. A sailplane gliding into a 40 m.p.h. headwind at the best L/D airspeed of 40 m.p.h., would move vertically downward. The forward movement of the plane across the ground would be cancelled out by the headwind.

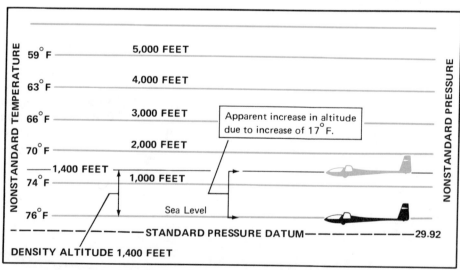

Fig. 2-1. Low Pressure — High Temperature

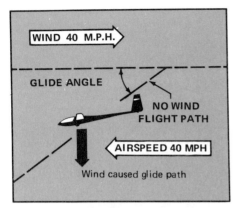

Fig. 2-2. Wind Effect on Glide Path

The reverse would be true if the sailplane were gliding at best L/D speed with a 40 m.p.h. tailwind. Groundspeed would increase to 80 m.p.h.

WEIGHT AND BALANCE

A sailplane must be stable to fly safely. Stability, as discussed in Chapter 1, means the sailplane tends to return to a trimmed flight attitude when disturbed by a control input or an outside force such as turbulence. Maximum and minimum weights must be adhered to in order to preserve the safe flying qualities designed into the sailplane.

In general, the sailplane's center of gravity is ahead of the aerodynamic center of the wing. This condition is inherently stable and is a configuration used when pitch stability is a requirement.

The exact distance the CG is ahead of the aerodynamic center varies for all sailplanes and different loadings but, usually, it is only a matter of inches. A CG located too far forward may cause a nose-down pitching moment which the elevators are unable to correct at slow airspeeds. An excessive aft CG may cause a condition of neutral stability or instability, by requiring up loading on the tail surfaces to maintain level

flight. In this event, additional forward stick movement may not be available to recover from a stall/spin situation. Either way, as the sailplane becomes difficult to control, performance suffers.

Two criteria must be met in the loading of a sailplane — weight and position of the weight with respect to the aerodynamic center of the wing. Neither parameter may be violated without undesirable results. If the pilot weighs less than the specified minimum, ballast must be added. Ballast must never be placed haphazardly in the cockpit, but always secured in the location recommended by the manufacturer. If the pilot and equipment are heavier than the specified maximum, the sailplane is not safe to be flown.

A sailplane can be fully within weight limitations, however, and still be out of balance. In two-seat sailplanes, the rear-seat passenger sits near the center of gravity so that the balance is not appreciably affected.

EFFECTS OF BALLAST

Some high-performance sailplanes use water ballast in the wings or fuselage to increase cruise speed. This ballast can impose additional restrictions on pilot weight, but it also can be extremely useful. The water is carried near the center of gravity for minimum effect on CG and handling characteristics.

Since the L/D ratio is solely a function of aerodynamic parameters, it is independent of weight, and the ratio is the *same* with or without water ballast. With greater weight aboard, the sailplane obtains greater lift by flying faster, rather than by increasing the angle of attack. Water ballast, therefore, improves the cruise performance of a sailplane, allowing higher cruise speeds at the same L/D. It should be noted that some sailplanes require any water ballast be jettisoned before landing.

Weight and balance papers are provided for each individual sailplane and loading limitations should be placarded in the cockpit. A typical cockpit placard is illustrated in figure 2-3. To compute weight and balance, several constants must be known. The center of gravity range limits usually are specified in inches from a *datum*. As shown in figure 2-4, a datum is an imaginary location in a vertical plane from which all pertinent horizontal measurements are made.

The distance weight is located from this datum also affects the balance condition. This distance is called the *arm* in weight and balance calculations.

An arm is defined as the horizontal distance in inches from the datum line to an item. When this distance is multiplied by the weight of the item, the product is called *moment* and usually is expressed in pound-inches. The empty weight of the sailplane and its arm, as well as the arm for each of the weights, such as pilot and ballast,

Fig. 2-3. Limitations Placard

can be found in the sailplane weight and balance papers.

The two basic methods used to check the weight and balance of the sailplane are the graph method and computation method. The graph method is the simplest to use to determine proper loading for a sailplane.

To find the CG using this method, refer to figure 2-5, which is a sample weight and balance graph for a typical trainer sailplane. For this problem, assume the pilot weighs 250 pounds and the passenger weighs 150 pounds.

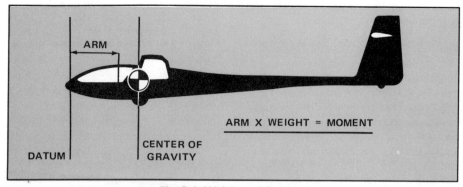

Fig. 2-4. Weight and Balance

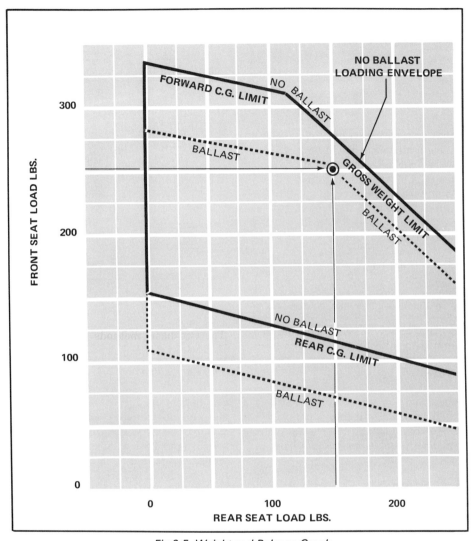

Fig 2-5. Weight and Balance Graph

1. Project a horizontal line at forward seat weight (250 lbs.).

2. Project a vertical line at rear seat weight (150 lbs.).

3. If the intersection of the lines is within the envelope, the CG is within limits.

4. Gross weight must not exceed the certificated maximum, or 1,040 lbs. in this example.

Figure 2-6 shows this same sample loading problem worked by the computation method. Weights are inserted in the proper column and multiplied by the arm to determine moments. Total weight and total moment are added; then, total weight is divided into total moment to determine the number of inches aft of the datum the loaded CG is located. Here, total weight is less than the gross maximum of 1,040

WEIGHT AND BALANCE CALCULATIONS

	Example Sailplane			My Sailplane — Serial Number _____		
ITEM	WEIGHT	ARM	MOMENT	WEIGHT	ARM	MOMENT
Sailplane empty weight & empty C.G.	612	96.12	58,825	612	96.12	58,825
Front Pilot Weight	170	43.80	7,446	250	43.80	10,950
Rear Pilot Weight	150	74.70	11,205	150	74.70	11,205
Ballast, if used	0	14.75	- 0 -	0	14.75	0
Total Moment			77,476			80,980
Total Weight	982			1012		

Example: $\dfrac{\text{Total Moment}}{\text{Total Weight}} = \dfrac{77,476}{932} = 83.13$

My Sailplane: Actual flying CG $\dfrac{\text{Total Moment}}{\text{Total Weight}} = \dfrac{80,980}{1012} = 80.02$

This CG is between the limits of Sta. 78.20 and 86.10, and gross weight is less than 1,040 lbs., so this sailplane has a proper flight weight and balance loading.

1. Is this between the CG limits?

2. Is total weight less than 1,040 lbs.?

Fig. 2-6. Weight and Balance Computation

pounds, and the new CG arm (80.02) is located between the fore and aft CG limits of 78.20 and 86.10. The sailplane is within allowable weight and balance limits.

PERFORMANCE SPEEDS

Sailplane performance is defined in terms of lift over drag (L/D), or glide ratio, a measurement of horizontal distance traveled per foot of altitude lost, and sink rates which correlate altitude lost to a given period of time. Each sailplane has a predetermined performance at specific weights and airspeeds. Charts showing these performance curves usually are contained in the flight manual.

Figure 2-7 illustrates performance curves for L/D ratios and airspeeds. For this particular sailplane, the best L/D

can be obtained solo at an indicated airspeed of 45 m.p.h. and dual at 52 m.p.h. The best L/D, regardless of weight is 22.25:1. Gliding solo with an indicated airspeed of 68 m.p.h., the L/D ratio is reduced to 16:1.

The lower half of the chart, shown in figure 2-8, plots airspeeds and corresponding sink rates. Minimum sink speed is that speed which permits the least loss of altitude in a given time period. Unlike best L/D, minimum sink does not correlate to horizontal distance covered but rather to remaining airborne for as long as possible. Minimum sink speed solo is 38 m.p.h. and the sink rate is 2.6 feet per second or 156 feet per minute. At an indicated airspeed of 66 m.p.h., the sink rate for the solo sailplane increases to 6 feet per second, or 360 feet per minute.

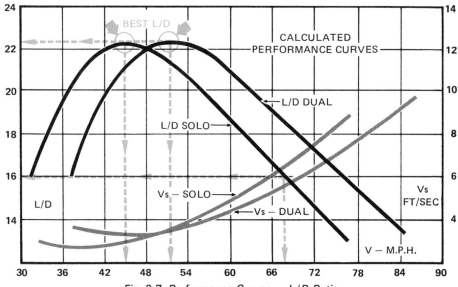

Fig. 2-7. Performance Curves — L/D Ratio

If maximum distance over the ground is desired, the airspeed for best L/D should be used. When gliding into a headwind, maximum distance will be achieved by adding approximately one-half of the estimated headwind velocity to the best L/D speed. However, when circling within a thermal or prolonging flight in still air, minimum sink speed should be used.

Performance charts for some sailplanes are presented as a comparison of speed vs. rate of sink, and may be plotted in

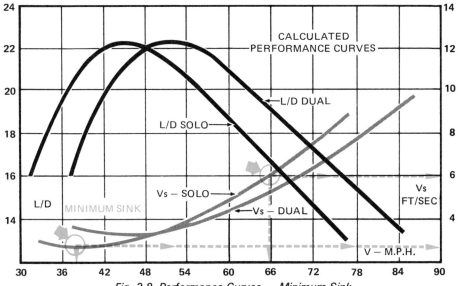

Fig. 2-8. Performance Curves — Minimum Sink

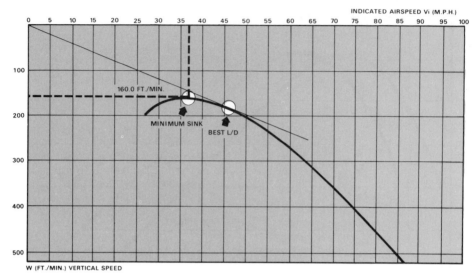

Fig. 2-9. Sailplane Performance Polar

such units as km/meters per second, m.p.h./feet per minute (or feet per second), or knots/knots of sink. In figure 2-9, the $V_{min\ sink}$ (apex of the curve) is approximately 160 f.p.m. at 37 m.p.h., and Best L/D (tangent line) is about 185 f.p.m. at 46 m.p.h. The polar curve is used to predict the best speeds to fly under specific lift conditions, and the results are frequently displayed on a "speed ring" mounted on the variometer.

STALL SPEED AND LOAD FACTOR

Operational speeds are posted in the sailplane and in the flight manual. To safely and efficiently utilize these recommended speeds, it is helpful to review the factors affecting them.

ANGLE OF BANK

Figure 2-10 illustrates the relationship between angle of bank and stall speed. Note that there is a progressive increase in stalling speed as the angle of bank is increased from zero. The stall speed increases due to the additional load factor or weight supported by the wings. As load factor increases, the total lift also must increase. This additional lift is generated by increasing the angle of attack. Therefore, in a turn, the critical or stall angle of attack is reached at a higher airspeed than in level flight. For example, the stall speed is approximately 40 percent greater in a 60° bank turn than when the sailplane is in straight-and-level flight. The stall speed shown in the flight manual is normally for a wings-level flight attitude.

LOAD FACTOR

Load factor is the ratio of the load supported by the wings to the actual weight of the sailplane. With the bank required to produce a load factor of two G's (twice the force of gravity), the wings support twice the weight of the sailplane; at a load factor of four G's, they support four times its weight.

INDICATED AND TRUE AIRSPEEDS

Indicated airspeed (IAS) is the direct instrument reading the pilot obtains

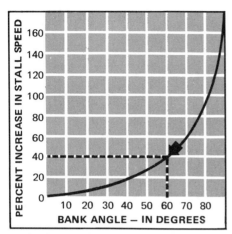

Fig. 2-10. Stall Speed and Bank Angle

from the airspeed indicator. It is uncorrected for variation in atmospheric density or any installation and instrument errors.

True airspeed (TAS) is the actual speed of the sailplane through the airmass. This speed cannot be read from the airspeed indicator. Because air density decreases with an increase in altitude, the sailplane flies faster at higher altitudes for the same indicated airspeed. Thus, for a given indicated airspeed, as altitude increases, true airspeed increases approximately two percent per one thousand feet.

MINIMUM CONTROL AIRSPEED

Minimum control airspeed is the speed at which an increase of either the angle of attack or load factor would result in an immediate stall. Minimum control speed is, therefore, only a few miles per hour above the stall speed, nearly coinciding with minimum sink speed.

The steep angles of bank often necessary to remain within a thermal radius may cause minimum control airspeed to coincide with minimum sink speed. An increase in load due to a gust, turbulence, or excessive bank angle could cause a stall.

PLACARD SPEEDS

All sailplanes carry operating limitations, either on a cockpit placard or in the flight manual. In addition to advising of weight and balance tolerances, the limitations placard states maximum airspeeds which may be used in flight. Exceeding the placarded airspeed parameters can cause structural damage or failure.

MANEUVERING SPEED

The speed at which full abrupt control travel at maximum gross weight may be used without exceeding the load limits is called maneuvering speed. This speed may be stated in the flight manual, or may be depicted on a chart similar to the one shown in figure 2-11. In the example shown, the speed area which is not cross-hatched is the area within which neither abrupt control inputs nor turbulence will impose damaging structural loads on the sailplane. The hatched area requires caution in maneuvering and in turbulence. The area marked "NO" should never be entered intentionally. From this flight envelope it can be seen that maneuvering speed is 65 m.p.h., the dividing line between limited maneuvering and no limitations.

If severe turbulence is encountered, the airspeed should be reduced to the maneuvering speed and the aircraft held in as constant an *attitude* as possible. If maneuvering speed is not specified for a particular sailplane, it can be safely estimated by multiplying the normal stall speed by two.

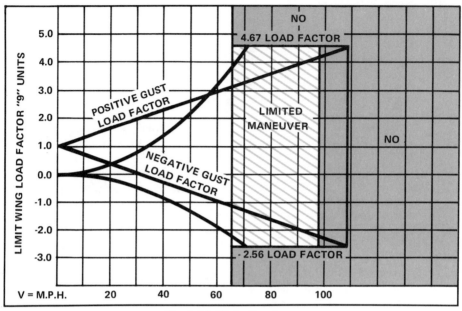

Fig. 2-11. Flight Envelope

AERO TOW AND GROUND LAUNCH SPEEDS

Maximum aero tow and ground launch speeds are posted on a placard in the cockpit. Maximum speeds usually are above the sailplane's normal operating speed, but provide a safe margin below stress limits.

FLAPS EXTENDED SPEED

Flaps extended speed, or VFE, is the maximum airspeed at which flaps can be extended without the possibility of causing structural damage. When the flaps are used for a rapid descent, care should be exercised to avoid exceeding this speed. The speed range with flaps extended may be depicted by a white arc on the airspeed indicator.

NEVER EXCEED SPEED

Never exceed speed, or VNE, is the "red line" maximum indicated airspeed at which the sailplane should be flown in calm air. If turbulent air is encountered, the sailplane should be slowed to maneuvering speed.

This chapter has presented the factors which affect the performance of sailplanes in general. Thorough knowledge of the performance speeds for the particular sailplane being flown will provide increased confidence, enjoyment, and the ability to extract all the performance designed into it. In addition, the knowledgeable soaring pilot will be aware of the design stress limitations of a sailplane and ensure safe and efficient operation by adhering to them.

Flight Instruments

INTRODUCTION One of the important areas of aeronautical knowledge is flight instruments and their respective systems. Acquiring such a knowledge enables pilots to visualize what takes place behind an instrument panel and what makes each of the instruments function. In addition, with this knowledge, pilots are much more capable of interpreting the different types of information displayed on the instruments during the various conditions of flight.

This chapter introduces the basic instruments and systems found in most sailplanes as well as communications equipment which is becoming more prevalent in modern soaring.

SOARING

Chapter Three

MAGNETIC COMPASS

A magnetic compass, such as illustrated in figure 3-1, is essential for cross-country flying or for competition. When leaving a thermal over strange territory, the compass provides quick orientation without having to search for landmarks.

Fig. 3-1. Magnetic Compass

Since the compass is a magnetic device, it tends to align with the earth's magnetic field. The magnetic poles are displaced from the geographic poles; therefore, an angular correction, called *variation*, must be made to follow a true course on an aeronautical chart.

Lines on charts which connect points of equal magnetic variation are called *isogonic lines*. They are labeled in degrees east and west of the earth's geographic North Pole, as can be seen in figure 3-2. An isogonic line representing zero degrees variation is called an *agonic line*.

COMPASS CONSTRUCTION

The compass card is graduated in five-degree increments, and the magnetic headings (without the last zero) are printed every 30°. The card is attached to a float to keep it in a horizontal position in the compass fluid. The pivot below the card rests on a jeweled

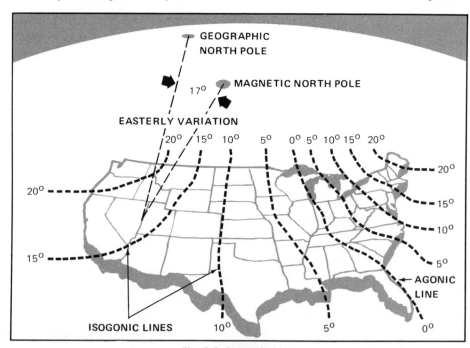

Fig. 3-2. Isogonic Lines

bearing, while two long magnets, mounted underneath, give the compass its directional quality.

The float assembly is sealed in a chamber filled with acid-free, white kerosene, which serves as a lubricant for the pivot and dampens oscillations of the compass card. The float assembly is balanced on the pivot, allowing free rotation of the card and a tilt of up to 18°. Behind the glass window is a *lubber* or reference line to designate the compass indication.

DEVIATION

Deviation is the deflection of the compass from a position of magnetic north by a magnetic disturbance in the aircraft. It is important to avoid placing metallic objects near the compass during flight, since this practice may induce large errors. Two small compensating magnets, adjustable by screws, are located in the top or bottom of the compass case. Adjusting the screws to correct for deviation is known as *swinging the compass,* a procedure which should be performed periodically by maintenance personnel.

Any uncorrectable deviation should be recorded on a correction card attached to the compass. The pilot should refer to this card and make the appropriate adjustment for the desired compass heading.

COMPASS ERRORS

Although the compass is a very reliable instrument, it is subject to errors which must be recognized. These errors are caused primarily by the vertical component, or dip, in the earth's magnetic field.

TURNING ERROR

Northerly turning error is the most pronounced of the inflight errors and is most apparent when turning to or from headings of north and south. When the sailplane is banked, the vertical components of the earth's magnetic field cause the earth-seeking ends of the compass to dip to the low side of the turn, giving the pilot an erroneous turn indication, as shown in figure 3-3.

When making a turn from a heading of north in the Northern Hemisphere, the compass briefly gives an indication of a turn in the *opposite* direction. If this turn is continued east or west, the compass card will begin to indicate a turn in the correct direction, but will *lag* behind the actual turn until within a few degrees of east or west.

The same set of forces is in effect when making a turn from a heading of south, but the indications are quite different. The compass gives an indication of a turn in the correct direction, but at a much faster rate than is actually being experienced. As the turn is continued toward east or west, the compass indications continue to precede the actual turn, but in a diminishing amount until within a few degrees of west or east.

ACCELERATION/DECELERATION ERRORS

Acceleration errors can occur during airspeed changes and are most apparent on headings of east and west. Because of its mounting, the compass card tilts during speed changes. The momentary tilting of the card from its horizontal position results in an error. When accelerating on either an east or west heading, the error is in the form of an indication of a turn to the north; when decelerating, the error is in the form of an indication of a turn to the south.

OUTSIDE AIR TEMPERATURE GAUGE

The outside air temperature gauge, illustrated in figure 3-4, is used to

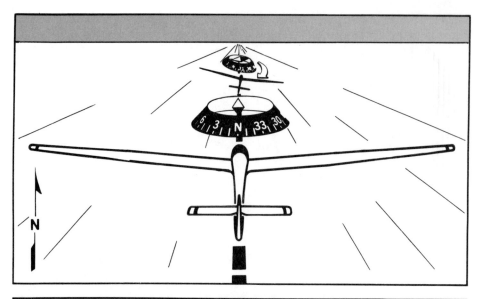

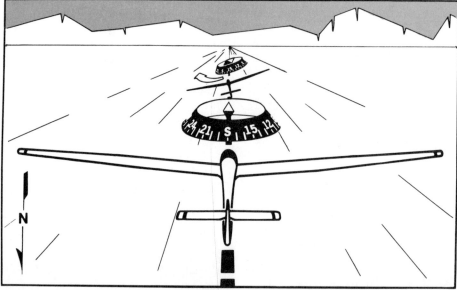

Fig. 3-3. Northerly Turning Error

determine the freezing level when carrying water ballast and to calculate true airspeed in flight. It is mounted in the aircraft in a position where the temperature sensing element can be exposed to the outside air. Normally, a bright metal shield is used to protect the sensitive element of the gauge from direct sunlight and from damage. The dial on most gauges is calibrated in both degrees Celsius and degrees Fahrenheit.

YAW STRING

One of the least expensive and most efficient slip/skid indicators is the yaw string, a piece of yarn mounted in the

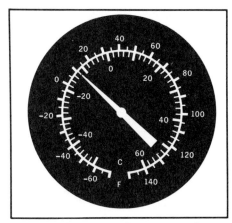

Fig. 3-4. Outside Air Temperature Gauge

free airstream in front of the pilot, as shown in figure 3-5. The yarn remains aligned with the sailplane when the controls are properly coordinated, but indicates a slip by moving toward the outside of a turn, or a skid by moving toward the inside.

INCLINOMETER

The internally mounted slip indicator, or inclinometer, illustrated in figure 3-6, usually is mounted at the bottom of the turn-and-bank instrument; or it may be mounted as a separate instrument. It consists of a metal ball suspended in a damping oil-filled curved glass tube. When the sailplane is in coordinated flight, the ball remains centered at the bottom of the glass tube. The ball moves to the inside of the turn to indicate a slip, or to the outside to indicate a skid.

PITOT-STATIC SYSTEM

The basis for determining a sailplane's airspeed, altitude, and rate of climb or descent is the measurement of difference in air pressure. The device which makes this measurement possible is usually a metal diaphragm, or bellows, called an *aneroid*. The aneroid expands or contracts in response to changing air pressure, and

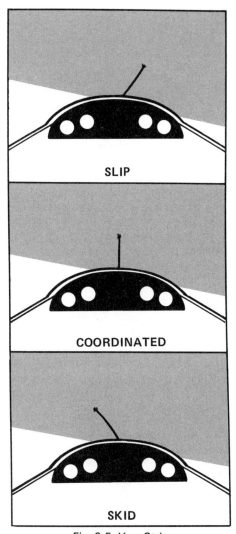

Fig. 3-5. Yaw String

mechanically converts the changes to instrument readings. This system includes a pitot tube for measuring impact (ram) air pressure and one or more static ports for measuring barometric static pressure (air pressure at flight altitude).

The pitot tube usually is located on the front of the sailplane facing the craft's line of flight. Venting is accomplished by connecting the instrument cases to a

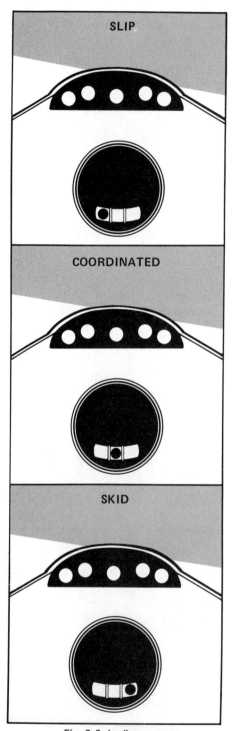

Fig. 3-6. Inclinometer

static vent opening (static port) which is located in such a position that it will not pick up ram or turbulent air pressures.

AIRSPEED INDICATOR

The airspeed indicator measures the *difference* between impact and static pressure. When the sailplane is parked on the ground, these two pressures are equal. When it is moving through the air, however, the pressure in the pitot line becomes greater than the pressure in the static line, as shown in figure 3-7.

This difference in pressure expands a small diaphragm inside the instrument and, through a mechanical linkage, moves a pointer to register indicated airspeed on the instrument face. A typical airspeed indicator is pictured in figure 3-8. The airspeed indicator displays the speed at which the sailplane is moving through the air, *not* the speed at which it is moving over the ground.

AIRSPEED DEFINITIONS

Three airspeed definitions — indicated, calibrated, and true — are of particular importance to soaring pilots. These airspeeds are discussed in the following paragraphs.

Indicated airspeed (IAS) is the direct instrument reading obtained from the airspeed indicator. It is uncorrected for variation in atmospheric density or any installation and instrument errors.

Calibrated airspeed (CAS) is the indicated airspeed corrected for instrument and installation (or position) errors. Within the speed range of most sailplanes, these errors are negligible, and indicated airspeed may be considered the same as calibrated airspeed.

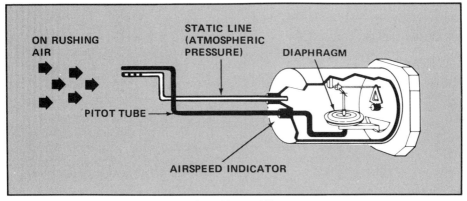

Fig. 3-7. Airspeed System

If a significant error is present, an airspeed indicator calibration table is provided by the manufacturer, either on a cockpit placard or in the flight manual.

True airspeed (TAS) is the actual speed of the sailplane through the airmass. True airspeed is calibrated airspeed corrected for existing temperature and pressure.

ALTIMETER

The altimeter is connected to the static system through an outlet in the back of the case. This outlet serves as a vent to allow the static atmospheric pressure to move into and out of the case as the sailplane climbs and descends.

Figure 3-9 shows how changes in atmospheric pressure surrounding the aneroid cause it to expand or contract. As the sailplane climbs to altitude, the air moves out of the case because of the decrease in outside atmospheric pressure. The sealed aneroid expands, resulting in an upscale pointer movement. As the sailplane descends, air moves into the case due to the increase in outside atmospheric pressure. The aneroid contracts, resulting in a downscale pointer movement.

Actual barometric pressure decreases approximately one inch of mercury for every 1,000 feet of altitude. Therefore a change of one inch in the pressure setting will result in a change of 1,000 feet in the altimeter reading.

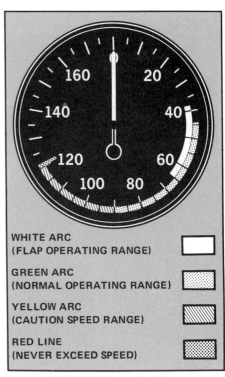

WHITE ARC
(FLAP OPERATING RANGE)

GREEN ARC
(NORMAL OPERATING RANGE)

YELLOW ARC
(CAUTION SPEED RANGE)

RED LINE
(NEVER EXCEED SPEED)

Fig. 3-8. Airspeed Indicator

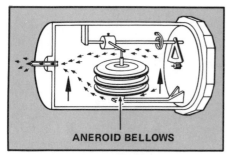

ANEROID BELLOWS

Fig. 3-9. Aneroid Expansion

READING THE ALTIMETER

A typical altimeter face is illustrated in figure 3-10. The large hand indicates hundreds of feet, with 20-foot increments marked on the dial face. The middle sized hand indicates thousands of feet, and the small hand shows tens of thousands. In the illustration, the altimeter indicates 3,080 feet above sea level. The cross-hatched area at the bottom of the face is masked as the sailplane climbs above 10,000 feet. On a

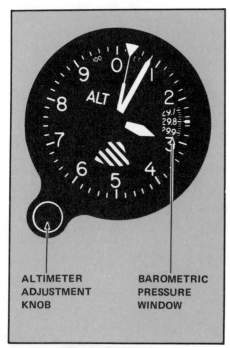

ALTIMETER ADJUSTMENT KNOB   **BAROMETRIC PRESSURE WINDOW**

Fig. 3-10. Altimeter

rapid descent out of a mountain wave, appearance of the cross-hatched area would serve as a warning that the sailplane was below 10,000 feet.

SETTING THE ALTIMETER

Altimeters are equipped with a barometric pressure setting window for adjusting the altimeter to compensate for variations in atmospheric pressure. A knob is located at the bottom of the instrument for this adjustment.

ALTITUDE DEFINITIONS

Altitude is the vertical distance above a specific reference level. Pilots should be familiar with the following definitions of altitude:

Indicated Altitude — the altitude read directly from the altimeter when it is set to the current altimeter setting, or to field elevation if an altimeter setting is not available.

True Altitude — the actual height above sea level, or indicated altitude corrected for pressure and temperature deviations from standard. Elevations plotted on aeronautical charts are true altitudes.

Absolute Altitude — the actual height above the terrain. It may be abbreviated AGL, for above ground level.

Pressure Altitude — the altitude indicated on an altimeter set to a barometric pressure of 29.92. It is used in computer solutions for true airspeed, density altitude, and true altitude.

Density Altitude — pressure altitude corrected for temperature deviations from the standard atmosphere. It is used in predicting aircraft performance.

ALTIMETER ERRORS

Altimeters are calibrated on the basis of both a standard pressure (29.92 in. Hg.) and a standard temperature (59°F) at sea level with a standard rate of decrease in temperature and pressure as altitude is increased. If either of these factors is significantly different from standard, an erroneous altitude will be indicated. *Colder* than standard temperatures cause the altimeter to indicate an altitude *higher* than the sailplane's actual altitude.

The same situation exists when flying from a high pressure area to a lower pressure area without resetting the barometric pressure window. The sailplane in figure 3-11, maintaining the same indicated altitude while flying from high pressure to an area of lower pressure, actually will be descending. A good rule of thumb used by many pilots is "from high to low or hot to cold, look out below."

VARIOMETER

Another important aspect of soaring is the speed and direction of altitude change. The rate-of-climb indicator used in powered aircraft can provide this information, but not quickly or accurately enough for soaring. To meet the needs of the sailplane pilot, the *variometer* was developed.

The variometer operates on the same principle as the altimeter — the higher the altitude, the less static air pressure. Figure 3-12 illustrates the operation of the vane-type variometer used in many sailplanes. The insulated reference chamber is a tank of air connected to the static port through the variometer. As the sailplane climbs, reduced pressure at the static port causes air to flow out of the reference chamber, past the vane, to the static port. This deflects the vane upward, and the attached needle on the face of the indicator shows a rate of climb. In a descent, the higher pressure is at the static port. The air flows toward the reference chamber, resulting in a rate-of-descent indication.

Sensitivity of the vane is controlled by the tension of the hairspring which returns it to the neutral position. Competition sailplanes may be equipped with two or more variometers, one of which may be extremely sensitive, for locating weak lift. A less sensitive one may be used to determine average lift in turbulent air.

The electric variometer operates by the cooling effect of airflow on a thermistor, an element designed to change in electrical resistance as its temperature changes. As the air flows into or out of the reference chamber, it flows

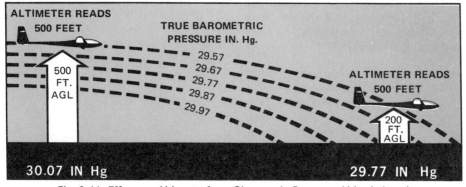

Fig. 3-11. Effect on Altimeter from Changes in Pressure Altitude Levels

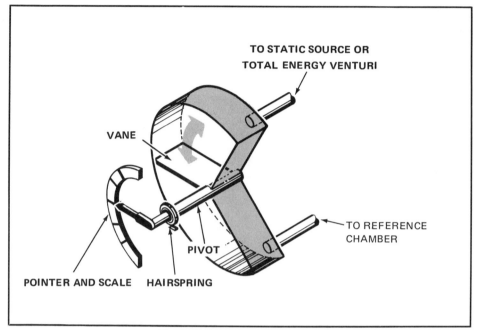

TO STATIC SOURCE OR
TOTAL ENERGY VENTURI

VANE

TO REFERENCE
CHAMBER

PIVOT

POINTER AND SCALE   HAIRSPRING

Fig. 3-12. Vane-type Variometer

across one of two thermistors in a bridge circuit. An electric meter measures the imbalance across the bridge and indicates a rate of climb or descent.

An advantage of the electric variometer is that its sensitivity can be adjusted in flight to suit existing air conditions. An audible signal can be added to indicate lift, rising in pitch as the lift increases. This makes it possible to concentrate attention outside the sailplane while circling in a thermal. Audible signal devices also can be attached to non-electric variometers.

Some vertical speed instruments also are equipped with a movable rim speed scale, as illustrated in figure 3-13. This scale indicates proper interthermal speeds to fly for maximum cross-country performance. During the glide between thermals, the index arrow is set at the rate of climb already made or expected in the next thermal. The

variometer needle then points to the speed to fly between thermals.

TOTAL ENERGY COMPENSATORS

Variometer indications are very sensitive to changes in pressure altitude caused by airspeed. If a sailplane is

Fig. 3-13. Variometer with Speed Ring

dived in still air and then abruptly pulled up, the variometer indicates a rate of descent during the dive and a rate of climb during the pull-up. This is sometimes referred to as a "stick thermal." Therefore, when flying a sailplane without some type of compensation, a constant airspeed must be maintained for an accurate variometer indication.

A total energy system senses these airspeed changes and tends to cancel out the resulting variometer climb or dive indications. One type of total energy system consists of a small venturi mounted in the air stream and connected to the static outlet of the variometer. If the sailplane is nosed down, it picks up speed, and the increased air flow through the venturi decreases the pressure at the static outlet. Since the sailplane is losing altitude, the normal static pressure increases somewhat. If the venturi is properly designed and placed, the net effect is to reduce climb and dive errors caused by airspeed changes of the sailplane.

Another total energy system in common use employs a diaphragm-type compensator placed in the line from the pitot to the line coming from the reference chamber, as illustrated in figure 3-14. The deflection of this diaphragm is proportional to the speed change effects on the pitot pressure; it pulses just enough flow into the indicator line to cancel out the undesirable indications. If properly adjusted, the indicator shows only when the sailplane is climbing in rising air, without being affected by airspeed changes. Restrictors are installed in both systems to adjust the sensitivity, or response speed, of the variometer.

NETTO

A variometer may be additionally compensated so that it indicates the vertical movement of the airmass, regardless of the sailplane's climb or descent rate. Rather than using a diaphragm, as in figure 3-14, a calibrated capillary is installed which allows a constant pressure on the capacity side of the variometer, and only the change in the static pressure is reflected on the variometer. This is called the NETTO system.

GYRO INSTRUMENTS

Gyroscopic instruments, while considered almost a necessity in powered aircraft, are infrequently found in sailplanes. One reason is that gyro instruments are not allowed in SSA sanctioned contests. Another is that a pilot must be instrument rated, maintain instrument flight proficiency, and (when in controlled airspace) have clearance from air traffic control to fly in clouds. It is not only unlawful, but very dangerous for a pilot who is not trained for instrument flight to enter a cloud or any other weather condition which prevents visual reference to the ground. These instruments are discussed here only to establish a basic knowledge of the information they provide and how they operate.

GYROSCOPIC PRINCIPLES

The primary trait of a rotating gyro rotor is its *rigidity in space*. This means that it tends to maintain its plane of

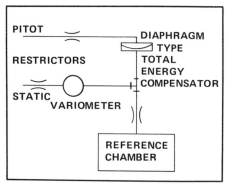

Fig. 3-14. Total Energy Compensator

rotation unless disturbed by an outside force. The second useful characteristic is that when an outside force is applied, the reaction occurs 90° in the direction of rotation from the point where the force is applied. The desired results are obtained by mounting the gyro in the aircraft with its plane of rotation parallel to a specific axis.

TURN COORDINATOR

The turn coordinator illustrated in figure 3-15 is the gyro instrument most frequently found in sailplanes. With this instrument and the pitot-static instruments, safe flight attitudes can be maintained without outside visual references.

The gyro in the turn coordinator is mounted in the aircraft to take advantage of its precession. When the aircraft turns, the symbolic aircraft tilts in the direction of the turn. The amount the symbol tilts is proportional to the rate of turn. The inclinometer at the bottom of the turn coordinator was discussed earlier.

An older instrument operating on the same principle is the turn-and-bank indicator, in which a vertical needle tips to the left or right to indicate a turn. Marks on either side of neutral indicate a specific rate of turn.

The most common power source for rate-of-turn indicators is either 12 volt or 24 volt D.C., which is compatible with batteries commonly carried in sailplanes. Some older turn-and-bank indicators operate by vacuum power, which requires either a motor-driven pump or a venturi mounted in the airstream. Neither is generally deemed satisfactory for sailplanes.

ATTITUDE INDICATOR

A typical attitude indicator is illustrated in figure 3-16. Its gyro is mounted in a horizontal plane with freedom of motion about all three axes. This allows it to remain in the horizontal position so that the aircraft literally moves around it. For this reason it is frequently referred to as an artificial horizon.

The presentation allows the aircraft symbol to indicate motion about the pitch and roll axes, thus showing the attitude as it would appear using outside visual references. It is the only instrument which provides both pitch and roll information.

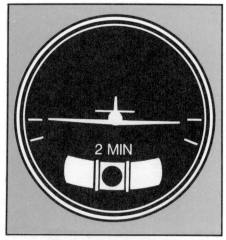

Fig. 3-15. Turn Coordinator

Fig. 3-16. Attitude Indicator

Attitude indicators are not widely used in sailplanes because they are expensive and their power supply is complicated. The instrument used in light aircraft is usually vacuum-driven, which is impractical for sailplanes. Electrically powered attitude indicators now available usually use either 26 or 110 volts A.C., which requires a strong battery and an inverter. As a result, most sailplane owners choose to avoid the expense, weight, and complexity of an attitude indicator installation.

Fig. 3-17. Barograph

BAROGRAPHS

When attempting to qualify for records or badges, it is necessary to make a permanent record of pressure altitude. This is accomplished by use of a *barograph*, an instrument designed to record pressure over a period of time. Recorded pressures can be calibrated to representative altitudes, a procedure which should be accomplished by an appropriately equipped shop at least once a year.

The most common type of barograph is illustrated in figure 3-17. It has been removed from its case so the components can be seen. It consists of a drum driven by a clock mechanism, which rotates once during a selected period, from one to as much as several hours. The drum is usually covered with aluminum foil which is then smoked over a piece of burning camphor. When the barograph is turned on, the aneroid-driven stylus contacts the smoked foil, scratching a record of pressure and elapsed time.

At the end of the flight, the smoked foil is sprayed with plastic to fix the trace. The resulting record, called a *barogram*, is submitted along with the application for a badge or record to prove an altitude claim or that no intermediate landing was made on a distance flight.

Another type of barograph uses an ink trace on graph paper. While this type requires much less preflight effort, many pilots feel that the ink system is unsuitable because of clogging, blotting, or freezing at high altitude.

RADIO EQUIPMENT

Depending on weight and usage considerations, transmitter/receiver equipment, or transceivers, may be installed in the sailplane. The advantages of two-way radio capability include air-to-air contact with other sailplanes or the tow plane, communication with ground based facilities, including the retrieve crew, and emergency broadcasts. Most sailplanes use VHF, or very high frequency, radios with one to 720 communication channels. Frequency allocations are published in the *Airman's Information Manual* and on aeronautical charts.

The range at which broadcasts may be received depends on the output strength of the transmitter and the height of the sailplane above the ground. VHF radio waves travel in a straight line, or line-of-sight. Consequently, with no intervening obstructions, the maximum distance for VHF communication is about 40 miles from an altitude of 1,000 feet, increasing to about 90 miles at 5,000 feet.

Most transceivers operate on a 12-volt battery. Choice of a battery should be based on weight and operational limitations, as well as temperature ranges of normal usage. Additional considerations are discharge rate, ease of recharging, and size.

USING THE MICROPHONE

The first and most basic factor in good communication is proper use of the microphone. The hand microphone is the most common. To obtain clear, readable transmissions, most hand microphones should be held so the lips lightly touch the face of the mike. Using the mike in this position allows the pilot to transmit in a normal conversational volume level, and also prevents the transmission of most background noise. Also, it is very important to speak *directly* into the mike. The transmission will sound fuzzy and indistinct if the words are spoken across the face of the mike.

Radio microphones have keys or buttons which must be depressed during transmissions and released when the message is complete. The key triggers a switch in the radio transmitter which enables the radio to transmit voice signals on the selected frequency as long as the mike key is depressed. The pilot should be careful *never* to depress the transmitter key when someone else is transmitting on the same frequency, or the transmission will cause interference. All that is heard on a frequency when two stations are transmitting at the same time is a loud squeal.

Proper radio usage and an understanding of the various flight instruments available are essential to the efficient operation of the sailplane. The pilot who can effectively utilize all the aircraft's capabilities will derive maximum performance, safety, and enjoyment from the soaring experience.

SOARING

Chapter
Four

Weather
for Soaring

INTRODUCTION Soaring performance depends largely on the weather. A sailplane flies "within the weather" and remains aloft only when in a rising parcel of air. Sailplane pilots must be cognizant of weather factors which affect their ability to remain aloft. They must consider not only whether they can go up, but also whether they can stay up and how good the soaring will be.

In this chapter, weather items will be examined for their effects on soaring performance and safety. The discussions of temperature, pressure, wind, and clouds are the keys to an understanding of each successive weather element.

THE ATMOSPHERE

The earth's atmosphere is a mixture of gases having physical properties of weight, temperature, and moisture. Each of these properties, or characteristics, exerts an influence on global weather patterns and the realm of aviation. Without the aid of atmospheric forces, soaring flight would be impossible.

ATMOSPHERIC PRESSURE

Atmospheric pressure is the force exerted by the weight of the atmosphere due to the gravitational pull of the earth. The pressure at the earth's surface is the result of the total weight of all the air above. Thus, the air near the earth's surface is more compressed or dense than the air at higher altitudes. For example, the air at an altitude of 18,000 feet is approximately half as dense as at sea level, and the pressure or weight is approximately one-half, as illustrated in figure 4-1.

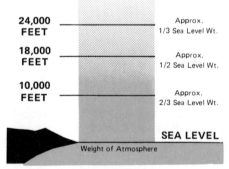

ALTITUDE Vs. WEIGHT OF THE ATMOSPHERE

24,000 FEET	Approx. 1/3 Sea Level Wt.
18,000 FEET	Approx. 1/2 Sea Level Wt.
10,000 FEET	Approx. 2/3 Sea Level Wt.
	SEA LEVEL

Weight of Atmosphere

Fig. 4-1. Pressure vs. Altitude

Pressure is measured by a barometer and is expressed in inches of mercury (in. Hg.) and in millibars. At sea level on a standard, or average day, atmospheric pressure is 29.92 in. Hg. or 1013.2 millibars. Actual measurements made at observation stations are

converted to comparable sea level values. This provides a standard reference point to compensate for varying station elevations.

Air density, or pressure, is also affected by temperature. Cold air is more dense, and therefore, heavier than warm air. In an attempt to attain equilibrium, air tends to flow from high pressure to low pressure. This atmospheric characteristic causes the three-cell circulation pattern, illustrated in figure 4-2, which in turn, causes the prevailing westerly winds and the general west-to-east weather movement in the United States.

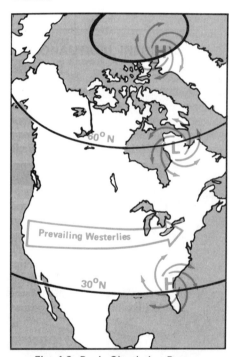

Fig. 4-2. Basic Circulation Pattern

THE STANDARD ATMOSPHERE

Continual temperature and pressure fluctuations in the atmosphere create various problems for those who require a fixed standard of reference. To arrive at a standard, conditions throughout the atmosphere were averaged for all latitudes, seasons, and altitudes. The result is a *standard atmosphere* with a temperature of 59 °F (15 °C), atmospheric pressure of 29.92 in. Hg., and standard rates of temperature and pressure change with height. This standard is used to calibrate the pressure altimeter and develop aircraft performance data.

PRESSURE LAPSE RATE

As altitude increases through the atmosphere, the weight of the air above becomes less and less. Pressure decreases roughly one inch for each 1,000-foot increase in altitude, within the lower few thousand feet of the atmosphere. This rate-of-decrease slows as more altitude is gained. The rate at which atmospheric pressure decreases with altitude in the standard atmosphere is called the *pressure lapse rate.*

TEMPERATURE LAPSE RATE

Temperature also decreases with altitude. In the standard atmosphere, the *temperature lapse rate* is 2 °C (3.5 °F) per 1,000 of altitude within the troposphere. Since this is an average, the exact value seldom exists. In fact, it is not uncommon to encounter a temperature *increase* with an increase in altitude. This is called a *temperature inversion.*

An inversion often develops near the ground on clear, cool nights when wind is light. The ground cools much faster than the overlying air. Air in contact with the ground cools, while the temperature a few hundred feet above changes very little. Thus, temperature increases with altitude until the inversion layer is passed.

WIND

Local wind conditions are determined primarily by two factors — pressure gradient and topography. Pressure gradient is the rate of transition from high pressure to low pressure. *Isobars* are drawn on weather charts to connect points of equal atmospheric pressure. They provide a clear picture of the current pressure system and the steepness of the pressure gradient, as shown in figure 4-3. Closely spaced isobars indicate a steep pressure gradient and strong winds. If the isobars are widely spaced, the slope is gentle and winds are generally light.

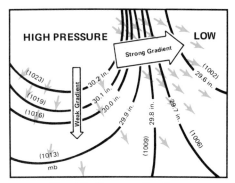

Fig. 4-3. Pressure Gradient

Topographic, or terrain features disrupt the natural wind flow at and near the earth's surface, causing the wind to change direction and sometimes, speed. The greatest amount of deflection takes place over rough terrain, such as hills and mountains. Steep hills and mountain slopes deflect the wind upward and create an excellent source of lift. This type of lift, called orographic lift, is discussed later in this chapter.

THERMAL PRODUCTION

It has been estimated that about 80 percent of all soaring depends on thermal lift — lift created by *convective updrafts.* Solar heat that has been

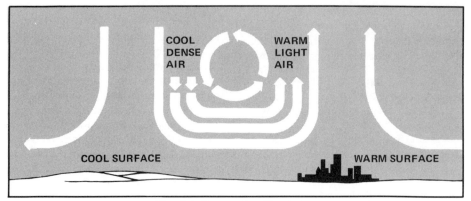

Fig. 4-4. Convective Circulation

absorbed by the earth's surface warms the air near the surface. As the air is heated, it expands and becomes less dense than the cooler air aloft. The cool air sinks and displaces the warm air, forcing it to rise, as illustrated in figure 4-4. As the replacement air is heated, it also expands and is forced to rise. The resulting pattern of updrafts and downdrafts is called *convective circulation.*

Convective circulation and, therefore, thermal production, depends on uneven heating at the surface. Ground areas that absorb the most heat are the best sources of thermals, especially when those areas are surrounded by terrain with low heat absorption rates. Thermals also are produced by such cultural heat sources as chimneys, factories, and cities.

Cool air must sink to force the warm air upward. Therefore, updrafts and downdrafts, or areas of lift and sink, coexist side by side. However, fast rising thermals generally cover a small percentage of a convective area. An equal amount of sinking air is spread over a larger area. This causes the downdrafts to be slower than the updrafts, allowing sailplanes to gain altitude in thermals and hold altitude loss in downdrafts to a minimum, as shown in figure 4-5.

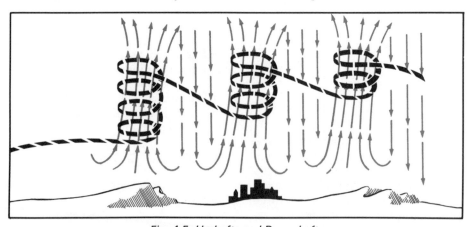

Fig. 4-5. Updrafts and Downdrafts

INSTABILITY

Unstable air is another prerequisite to thermal activity. Air tends to stabilize at night as the earth's surface loses heat by radiation. Until the surface is sufficiently reheated by solar radiation, convection is impossible. Extensive cloud cover can obstruct the sun's rays and prolong the stable condition.

Temperature inversions also cause the air to become stable. When an inverted layer of warm air overlies cooler air at or near the surface, it resists any vertical movement by the lower air. Convection is suppressed and thermals do not form until the inversion "burns off" or lifts enough to allow soaring beneath the inversion.

LAND AND SEA BREEZES

The convective circulation patterns associated with land and sea breezes provide another source of thermal lift that can be used by sailplanes. Land absorbs and radiates heat faster than water. This creates a temperature and pressure difference over the two kinds of surfaces.

On sunny days, the cool, dense air over the ocean moves inward and forces the warmer coastal air to rise. The air

rising from over the land then moves seaward at a higher altitude. As the cycle is repeated, the circulation pattern shown on the left side of figure 4-6 develops.

At night, the direction of air movement is reversed. The land cools rapidly after sundown, while the water releases heat more slowly. Cool air from over land then moves seaward and sets up the land breeze circulation pattern on the right side of figure 4-6.

Sometimes the wedge of cool air from a sea breeze is called a *sea breeze front*, illustrated in figure 4-7. If sufficient moisture is present, a line of cumuliform clouds just inland may mark the front. The properties of a sea breeze front and the extent of its penetration inland depend on such factors as the difference in land and sea temperatures, general wind flow, moisture, and terrain.

The sea breeze front moving from the Los Angeles coastal plain into the Mojave Desert has been dubbed the "smoke front" or "smog front." It has intense thermal activity and offers excellent lift along the leading edge of the front. As shown in figure 4-8, this "smoke front" converges with two other sea breezes of different origins to

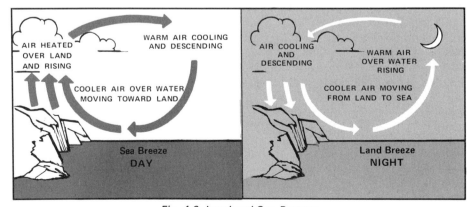

Fig. 4-6. Land and Sea Breezes

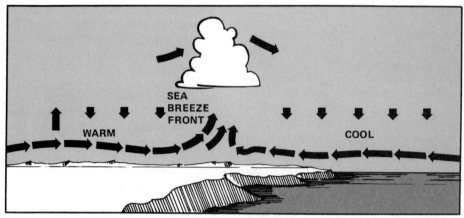

Fig. 4-7. Sea Breeze Front

form the San Fernando convergence zone and the Elsinore Convergence Zone.

VALLEY BREEZES

Valley breezes occur in the daytime when the side of a mountain is warmed by the sun. As the air close to the mountain side is heated, it expands and is forced to rise by cooler air flowing up from the valleys, as shown in figure 4-9. At night, the hillside and adjacent air cools and sinks into the valleys, creating a mountain breeze.

THERMAL INDEX

Thermals are a product of instability — their height depends on the depth of

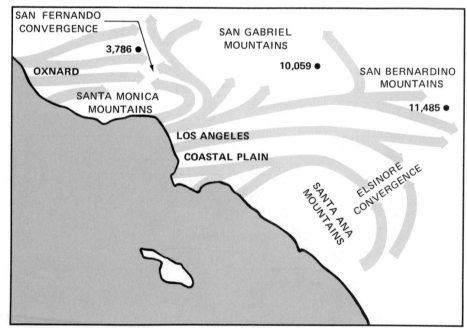

Fig. 4-8. The "Smoke Front"

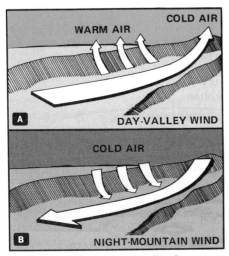

Fig. 4-9. Mountain and Valley Breezes

the unstable layer and their strength depends on the degree of instability. To arrive at an estimate of thermal height and strength, a thermal index (TI) is computed using the pseudo-adiabatic chart illustrated in figure 4-10.

A thermal index may be computed for any level but, ordinarily, indices are computed for the 850- and 700-milibar levels, or about 5,000 and 10,000 feet respectively. These levels are selected because they are in the altitude domain of routine soaring and because temperatures are routinely available for these two levels.

Three temperature values are needed — the observed 850-millibar and 700-millibar temperatures and forecast maximum temperature. In the following example, plotted on figure 4-10, the temperatures and field elevation are assumed.

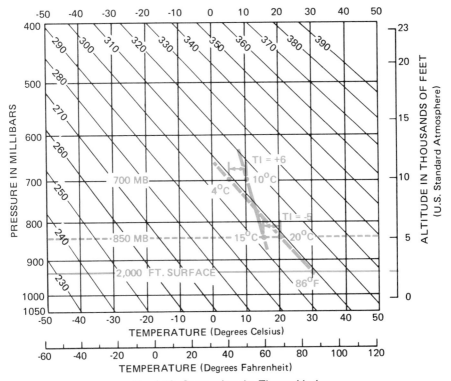

Fig. 4-10. Computing the Thermal Index

850-millibar temperature . . . . 15°C
700-millibar temperature . . . . 10°C
Forecast maximum
temperature. . . . . 86°F(30°C)
Field elevation . . . . 2,000 feet

1. Plot the three temperatures, placing the maximum temperature at field elevation.

2. Draw a line through the 850-millibar and 700-millibar temperature plots (the heavy solid line on the illustration).

3. Draw another line (the heavy dashed line) through the maximum temperature point, parallel to the diagonal lines (dry adiabats).

4. Note that the dashed line intersects the 850-millibar level at 20°C and the 700-millibar level at 4°C.

5. Algebraically subtract the temperatures noted in Step 4 from actual observed temperatures at corresponding levels. Note the difference is -5°C at 850-millibars (15-20 = -5) and +6 at 700-millibars (10-4 = +6). These values are the thermal indexes at the two levels.

Strength of thermals is proportional to the magnitude of the negative value of the TI. A TI of -8 or -10 predicts very good lift and a long soaring day. Thermals with this high a negative value will be strong enough to hold together, even on a windy day. A TI of -3 indicates a very good chance of sailplanes reaching the altitude of this temperature difference. A TI of -2 to 0 leaves much doubt; and a positive TI offers even less hope of thermals reaching the altitude.

The TI is a forecast value. A miss in the forecast maximum or a change in temperature aloft can alter the picture considerably. The example in figure 4-10 should promise fairly strong thermals to above 5,000 feet but no thermals to 10,000.

Often the National Weather Service will have no upper air sounding taken near a soaring base. Sailplane pilots may need to do their own forecasting of the thermal index using the "do-it-yourself" method.

The first step is to obtain a local sounding. A tow aircraft can be sent aloft about sunrise to read outside air temperatures from the aircraft thermometer and altitudes from the altimeter. The temperatures should be recorded at 500-foot intervals after leveling off briefly to allow the thermometer to stabilize. The information may be radioed back to the ground, or it may be recorded in flight and analyzed after landing. When using the latter method, the temperatures should be read on both ascent and descent and averaged for each level. This type of sounding is an airplane observation. The sounding is plotted on the pseudo-adiabatic chart using the altitude scale rather than the pressure scale.

Next, a forecast of the maximum temperature is needed. Usually, this forecast temperature can be obtained from the local forecast. If not, today's weather can be compared with yesterday's. This information can then be plotted in the same manner used previously to compute the thermal index.

OROGRAPHIC LIFT

Orographic, or *hill* lift is produced when wind strikes the side of a hill and is deflected upward. The amount of lift generated depends on the speed and direction of the wind and the steepness and height of the hill.

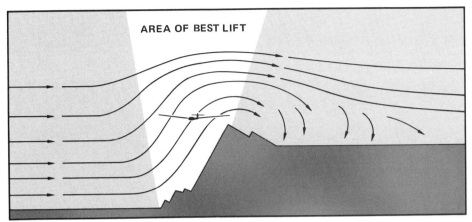

Fig. 4-11. Ridge Lift

Winds of 15 knots or more must be present to produce good ridge soaring, and it must be within 30° to 40° of a direction perpendicular to the ridge. Hill lift may provide soaring to about two to three times the height of the hill. An *unstable* air condition produces the most satisfactory hill soaring performance.

When hills are steep, induced eddies are created which destroy the potential lift. Therefore, a gradual slope is most favorable for soaring updrafts since the air flows in a more streamlined fashion. Figure 4-11 illustrates the area of best lift in the airflow over a ridge.

MOUNTAIN WAVES

As air flows over a mountain range, it is forced aloft on the windward side and descends on the leeward side, as shown in figure 4-12. This vertical oscillation is known as a *mountain wave*, and may continue for several hundred miles downwind from the mountain range. The actual intensity and duration of the wave depends on the wind velocities involved, the temperature lapse rate, and the height and steepness of the range.

Mountain waves occur most often in the fall, winter and spring. The ideal terrain for wave formation is a high, extended barrier, such as a mountain range, with a steep drop to the leeward side. At the top of the ridge, the wind speed should be at least 25 knots from a direction no more than 30° away from the perpendicular. The probability of wave formation is increased by greater wind speeds at higher altitudes. Smaller mountains, such as the Appalachians, require only about 15 knots of wind speed.

The amplitude of mountain waves is affected primarily by the stability of the layer being displaced by the mountain. Wave flow is usually strongest between one and three hours after sunrise and before sunset.

CLOUDS

Clouds are *signposts* that can show a weather-wise soaring pilot the locations of turbulence, storm systems, icing, and possible thermal activity. With experience, it is possible to read the existing weather situation and recognize changing conditions by watching the clouds.

Fig. 4-12. Mountain Wave

CLOUD FORMATION

Moisture enters the atmosphere as water vapor produced by evaporation. The amount of moisture a mass of air is capable of holding depends on temperature — warm air has a higher moisture capacity than cold air. *Relative humidity* is a measure of the moisture content of the air and is expressed as a percentage of the maximum moisture the air can hold.

When water vapor is added to the air, or the air temperature decreases, relative humidity approaches 100 percent, or saturation. The temperature to which the air must be cooled to exceed saturation is called the *dewpoint*. At the dewpoint, condensation takes place and visible moisture appears in the form of clouds.

A good indication of how close the air is to saturation is the temperature spread taken from weather reports. This is the numerical difference between the temperature and the dewpoint. As the "spread" approaches zero, because of the addition of moisture (rising dewpoint) or because of cooling of the air (lowering temperature), the relative humidity approaches 100 percent; low clouds or fog are likely to form.

READING THE CLOUDS

Cumulus clouds are formed by rising air currents and have the greatest significance for finding lift. Generally, they mark the tops of lift or at least indicate there was thermal uplift recently. It is important to recognize the subtle hints of a growing cumulus cloud. It begins as a mere hazy wisp in the air. If an area along the flight path has such wisps, uplift may be present. Since the average life of a summer cumulus is fairly short, many of these small clouds will actually be decaying, and mark sinking air. Keen observation is needed to determine whether a cumulus cloud is still growing or has begun to dissipate.

Cumulus clouds grow only with active thermals, as shown on the left and in the center of figure 4-13. On the right, the thermal has subsided and the cloud is decaying. Look for a thermal only under a cumulus with a concave base and sharp upper outlines. A cumulus with a convex base or fragmentary outline is dissipating; the thermal under it has subsided. Most often, a cloud just beginning to grow, as on the left side of the illustration, is the better choice because of its longer life expectancy.

Stratocumulus clouds are irregular masses of clouds spread out in a rolling or puffy layer. They are whitish in color, normally with darker spots, and usually are composed of rounded

Fig. 4-13. Life Cycle of Cumulus Cloud

masses which fuse together and become indistinct when rain appears.

The fair weather cumulus clouds, shown in figure 4-14, often are formed over land by rising air currents and, therefore, disappear at night when the lifting action recedes. These are referred to as fair weather cumulus until they begin to over-develop to form cumulonimbus.

Cumulonimbus clouds form the familiar thunderhead, shown in figure 4-15, and produce thunderstorm activity, including heavy rain, hail, and icing. These clouds grow from cumulus when the air is highly unstable. Violent thermals just beneath and within highly-developed cumulus and cumulonimbus clouds often are so strong that they will continue to carry a sailplane upward, in spite of the pilot's efforts to descend. Cumulonimbus clouds can be extremely hazardous and should be avoided.

Stratus clouds, illustrated in figure 4-16, are quite uniform and resemble fog. They have a fairly uniform base and a dull gray appearance. Stratus clouds make the sky appear heavy and, oc-

casionally, produce fine drizzle or very light snow with fog.

Stratus or layer clouds are formed by the cooling or lifting of a layer of air over a wide area. These clouds indicate the steady ascent of an entire mass of air with relatively uniform characteristics throughout. If a situation such as this persists, it may lead to deeper and denser nimbostratus clouds, widespread rain or snow, and prolonged poor soaring weather.

Nimbostratus clouds are the true rain or snow clouds. They appear wet and have a darker appearance than ordinary stratus clouds. Precipitation usually reaches the ground in the form of

Fig. 4-14. Fair Weather Cumulus

Fig. 4-15. Cumulonimbus Clouds

Fig. 4-16. Stratus Clouds

continuous rain, snow, or sleet. Nimbostratus clouds often are accompanied by fractostratus, commonly known as *low scud*, when the wind is blowing strongly.

Cirrus clouds, shown in figure 4-17, are composed almost entirely of ice crystals due to the extremely cold temperatures at higher altitudes. These clouds include cirrocumulus and cirrostratus.

Cirrus cloud bands, or shields, may signal a coming change in the weather with lowering ceilings, cloud cover, and precipitation within 12 to 24 hours. They may be encountered at very high flight altitudes and, in themselves, present very little hazard.

Lenticular clouds mark the crests of mountain waves. They are easily recognizable by their lens-shaped appearance. Lenticular clouds in successive bands downwind from the mountain mark a series of wave crests, and their spacing marks the wave length. Below the wave crests, *rotor* clouds may form to mark the area of extreme turbulence.

FRONTAL WEATHER

Airmasses which have different properties of temperature and/or moisture content do not mix to any appreciable degree. When different airmasses collide, they form a *front* or frontal zone which may be hundreds of miles long and many miles wide.

COLD FRONTS

A cold front is a wedge of advancing dense, cold air replacing warm air at the surface. It is called a cold front because the cold air is forcing its way under the warm air. Intense cold fronts normally are oriented in a line from the northeast to the southwest and their movement is toward the east or southeast in the Northern Hemisphere. Cold fronts are classified as either fast or slow-moving.

Fast-moving cold fronts may move across the surface at speeds above 30 m.p.h. and may contain winds as high as 60 m.p.h. Generally, their speed is faster in the winter than in the summer, causing the slope to steepen. The result is a narrow band of weather called a

Fig. 4-17. Cirrus Clouds

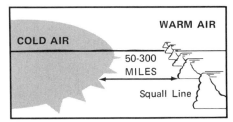

Fig. 4-18. Cold Front Profile

squall line. Squall lines may develop as much as 50 to 300 miles ahead of and parallel to the front, as shown in figure 4-18. The cloud tops in the squall line average 40,000 feet or higher. Gusty and turbulent winds usually are present upon passage of a fast-moving cold front, with rapidly clearing weather after frontal passage.

The frontal slope of a *slow-moving cold front* is less steep and the warm air is not lifted as quickly or violently as with the fast-moving cold front. This results in a broad cloud cover extending well over the front. If the warm air is stable as it is being lifted, stratiform clouds develop. If the warm air is moist and unstable, however, cumulus-type clouds normally are present.

WARM FRONTS

A *warm front* is created when a warm airmass overtakes and replaces a cold airmass. The speed of a warm front is approximately half that of a cold front. The less dense, warm air gradually moves up the slope and does not produce the typical bulge associated with a cold front. This occurs because ground friction drags the bottom edge of the retreating cold air. This, in turn, creates a broad cloud system which extends typically from the surface portion of the front to about 500 to 700 miles in advance of the surface front.

The types of clouds that form depend on the moisture content and the stability of the air as it rises up the slope, and are similar to those depicted in figure 4-19. When the air is stable, the sequence of clouds encountered with the approach of a warm front is as follows: cirrus, cirrostratus, altostratus, and nimbostratus. Precipitation increases gradually with the approach of a warm front and usually continues until after frontal passage.

If the air is unstable, the sequence of the clouds is: cirrus, cirrocumulus, altocumulus, and cumulonimbus. Cumulonimbus clouds frequently are embedded in the cloud masses as a warm front approaches.

Showery precipitation usually occurs with the advance of an unstable warm front. Low clouds in the form of stratus and fog sometimes form, creating areas of poor visibility and low ceilings over a great area. If the retreating cold air has temperatures below freezing, the precipitation may be in the form of freezing rain or ice pellets.

STATIONARY FRONTS

When a front has little or no movement, it is called a *stationary front*. This condition exists when opposing airmasses are of equal pressure. In the case of a stationary front, the surface wind tends to blow parallel to the front, instead of against or away from it. The weather phenomena associated with stationary fronts are

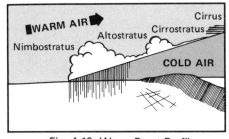

Fig. 4-19. Warm Front Profile

comparable to those found in a warm front, but usually are less intense in nature and cover wider areas.

OCCLUDED FRONTS

Occluded fronts develop when a cold front overtakes a warm front and lifts the warm air above the surface, as shown in figure 4-20. Many times the rain remains in the center of a low pressure system. Occluded fronts are of two types, cold and warm, designated by the front that develops at the surface.

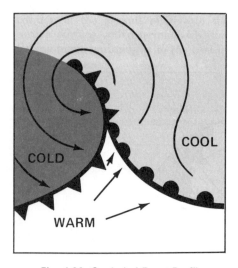

Fig. 4-20. Occluded Front Profile

The occlusion starts at the center of the low and progresses outward as the faster-moving cold front overtakes the warm front. The weather associated with occluded fronts usually consists of widespread rains and cloud cover with poor visibility and possible icing.

WEATHER HAZARDS

Many types of weather phenomena are needed to produce lift and to help soaring pilots find lift. Other types, however, produce hazardous conditions that must be recognized and avoided.

Obstructions to vision, severe turbulence, and thunderstorms all create situations that are especially dangerous to sailplanes.

OBSTRUCTIONS TO VISION

Obscured sky conditions are caused by various forms of visibility restrictions, such as drizzle, snow, smog, or fog. *Total obscuration* means the sky is totally hidden from the ground observer.

Fog is a stratiform cloud near the surface. It consists of small water droplets or ice crystals suspended in the atmosphere. Although they may be too small to see with the naked eye, they are so numerous that visibility is reduced.

Haze consists of very fine dust or salt particles suspended in the atmosphere. Flight visibility on hazy days depends on several things: the height of the haze layer, its intensity, the position of the sun, and the direction the pilot is looking. When the sun is low and unobscured by clouds above the haze, flying or landing into the sun can be hazardous. Although it is usually only found at low altitudes, the top of a haze layer can reach as high as 15,000 feet AGL.

Smoke usually is found near large industrial areas and restricts the forward visibility in much the same way as haze. When smoke is produced by forest fires, it is normally in concentrated layers with generally good visibility above and below.

Smog is technically a mixture of smoke and fog and can produce very poor visibility. Today, however, the term "smog" has been applied to any heavy concentration of atmospheric pollution. It is normally present in large industrial areas and is similar to haze or smoke. When the top layer of smog is well defined, visibility above it is usually very good.

Cloud droplets combine to form *precipitation.* The type of precipitation depends on the temperature and the stability or instability of the air.

Rain is liquid water drops falling from a cloud. Intermittent or continuous rain is an indication of stable clouds. The drops usually are moderate in size, and the rain is most likely the result of widespread uplifting of air, which is characteristic of a large area of clouds and precipitation.

Rain showers are associated with unstable air. The drops are large, due to the strong vertical currents associated with unstable air. These vertical currents tend to hold the drops in the cloud for a longer period of time and allow them to collect more moisture. Rain showers are usually of rather short duration.

Drizzle is found only with stable clouds. It occurs when there is little or no upward motion and the small droplets that normally would remain suspended in the air fall as precipitation.

Snow is a result of the moisture in the air forming as ice crystals. Snow can fall either as showers from convective clouds or continuously from stratiform clouds.

Ice pellets form when rain falls through a layer of subfreezing air. Ice pellets are almost always associated with stable conditions where a wedge of cold air forces warm moist air aloft.

Hail is a product of a thunderstorm. Supercooled water droplets collide with a growing hailstone and freeze on impact to give it a layered structure

similar to an onion. Hail, like other forms of precipitation, normally falls from the base of the cloud. In some cases, however, the updrafts are so strong the hailstones are thrown out of the cloud and may be encountered in clear air.

Freezing rain, often referred to as glaze, is a result of supercooled rain striking subfreezing surfaces and immediately freezing. This type of precipitation occurs when rain from a warmer layer aloft falls into freezing temperatures at lower levels.

THUNDERSTORMS

Thunderstorms produce the most severe type of weather known to mankind. They create a hazard for all types of flight activity, since the tops of cumulonimbus clouds may reach elevations in excess of 65,000 feet. These hazards are not confined just to the storm area itself. Pilots flying outside the thunderstorm cell, but near the storm area, can encounter hail and extreme turbulence.

There are three stages in the development of a thunderstorm. The first stage is known as the *cumulus* stage. The main feature of this stage is the cumulus cloud and the updraft which may extend from near the earth's surface to the cloud tops. Water droplets are very small, but grow into raindrops as the clouds build upward. Many times the raindrops remain in the liquid state, even above the freezing level.

The second, or *mature* stage, occurs as rain begins to fall. By this time, raindrops and ice particles have grown to such a size they can no longer be supported by updrafts. The mature stage occurs approximately 10 to 15 minutes after the cloud has built beyond the freezing level in the atmosphere. Occasionally, during the mature stage, a cloud may build as high as 50,000 to 65,000 feet; but, 25,000 to 30,000 feet is the norm.

Severe updrafts and downdrafts occur in the mature stage. As the raindrops fall, they pull air with them and create downdrafts that may exceed 2,500 feet per minute. This causes gusty winds at the surface as the downdrafts strike the earth and spread outward.

The third and final stage is the *dissipation* stage. This stage is characterized by the collapse of the cumulonimbus cloud. Downdrafts continue to develop and spread vertically and horizontally while updrafts weaken and finally dissipate completely. Soon the entire thunderstorm becomes an area of downdrafts. Rain decreases, then ceases, and the thunderstorm begins to dissipate. The top of the thunderstorm, at this point, begins to develop an anvil appearance with the point of the anvil in the direction of the prevailing winds. The three stages are illustrated in figure 4-21.

Airmass thunderstorms most often result from surface heating and are short-lived. When the storm reaches maturity, rain falls through or beside the updraft. Friction from the falling rain retards the updraft and reverses it to a downdraft. As the surface is cooled by the precipitation and downdraft, thermal activity ceases and the storm dies. These storms occur most frequently in the late afternoon and have a life span of 20 minutes to one and one-half hours.

Steady-state thunderstorms usually are associated with weather systems. Fronts, converging winds, and pressure troughs aloft force upward motion, spawning these storms which often form into squall lines. Afternoon heating intensifies them.

In a steady-state storm, precipitation falls outside the updraft, allowing the updraft to continue unabated. The updrafts become stronger and last much longer than in airmass storms, and may persist for several hours.

TORNADO HAZARDS

A tornado is an exceedingly violent whirling storm with a small diameter, usually a quarter of a mile or less, which extends from the base of a

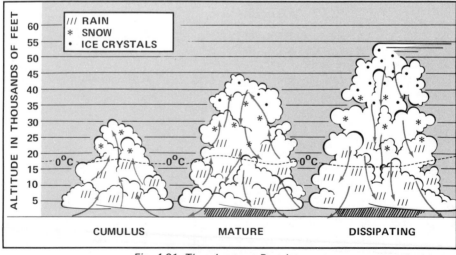

Fig. 4-21. Thunderstorm Development

cumulonimbus or thunderstorm cloud. The track length of a tornado on the ground may be from a few hundred feet to 300 miles; the average is less than 25 miles. Data from recent tornado studies indicate that the velocities of tornadic winds are in the general range of 150 to 300 miles per hour. A large reduction of pressure in the center, due to spiraling of the air, seems to cause buildings in the path of the storm to explode. The speed of the storm over the earth's surface is comparatively slow, usually 25 to 40 m.p.h.

Most tornadoes in the United States occur during late spring and early summer, and are associated with thunderstorm activity. Statistics show that the majority of tornadoes appear about 75 to 180 miles ahead of a cold front along a prefrontal squall line.

TURBULENCE

Movement of the air, or turbulence, is caused by thermal, mechanical, frontal, and large scale wind shear lifting. *Thermal turbulence* is caused largely by thermal or convective uplift. This type of turbulence can reach severe limits in the interiors of towering cumulus and cumulonimbus clouds.

Mechanical turbulence has the same origin as wind shear. When the air near the surface of the earth flows over obstructions, the normal horizontal flow is disturbed and transformed into a complicated pattern of eddies and other irregular air movements. The strength of mechanical turbulence depends on the speed of the wind, the roughness of the terrain, and the stability of the air.

Mountain waves may be accompanied by turbulence. Many pilots have reported the flow in these waves is often remarkably smooth, while others have reported severe turbulence.

The first wave has more intense action because of its proximity to the mountain terrain. Some of the most dangerous features of the mountain wave are the turbulent areas in and below roll clouds.

Frontal turbulence is caused by the lifting of warm air by a frontal surface. The most severe cases of frontal turbulence are generally associated with fast-moving cold fronts. The mixing between the two airmasses and the wind shear add to the intensity of the turbulence.

AVIATION WEATHER SERVICES

Aviation weather for preflight planning is available in all major metropolitan areas and many smaller cities. The telephone numbers or radio frequencies of these outlets can be found in the *Airport/Facility Directory* or the local telephone directory under the United States Government listing. One or more of the following should be accessed when a weather briefing for a flight is desired.

1. National Weather Service (NWS) offices
2. Flight Service Station (FSS) or Automated Flight Service Station (AFSS)
3. Transcribed Weather Broadcast (TWEB)
4. Telephone Information Briefing Service (TIBS)

WEATHER BRIEFINGS

Where possible, a pilot should go to the flight service station or National Weather Forecast Office for a weather briefing. Current and forecast weather information is available at these offices, and briefers are able to provide assistance necessary for preflight planning. Because of FSS consolidation, it is often necessary to obtain a telephone weather briefing. Depending on the local area, a number of sources are available for weather information.

Transcribed Weather Broadcasts (TWEBs) are transmitted continuously over selected low frequency NDBs (190-535 kHz) and/or VORs. Frequencies are published on aeronautical charts. The broadcasts are made from a series of individual tape recordings, and changes are transcribed into the tapes as they occur. At some locations, telephone access to the recording is provided (TEL-TWEB). The information in a TWEB varies with the type of recording equipment that is available. Generally, the broadcast includes route-oriented data with specially prepared National Weather Service forecasts, in-flight advisories, winds aloft, and preselected information such as weather reports, NOTAMs, and special notices.

At some locations, the information is broadcast over the local VOR only and is limited to items such as the hourly weather for the parent station and up to five adjacent stations, local NOTAM information, terminal forecast for the parent station, adverse weather conditions, and other potentially hazardous conditions. TWEBs are designed primarily for preflight and inflight planning. A TWEB should not be considered as a substitute for a formal weather briefing. The phone number for TWEB is listed in the *Airport/Facility Directory*.

An *Automated Flight Service Station (AFSS)* also permits users to access a complete menu of recorded weather information from a touch-tone phone. After reaching the AFSS, pilots will hear an informational recording telling how to access further information or how to go directly to a weather briefer. For example, *Telephone Information Briefing Service (TIBS)* provides a continuous recording of meteorological and/or aeronautical information. These automated systems are easy to use and they provide local and route-oriented information. After selecting the recordings needed,

pilots can transfer directly to a briefer if more detailed information is required.

Because of FAA consolidation, many airports are beyond local calling distance. To counter this problem, many FSSs have toll-free telephone numbers. To use these numbers, dial "1+800-WX-BRIEF" (992-7433). You also can check the *Airport/Facility Directory* under "FAA and NWS Telephone Numbers" or the U.S. Government section of your local telephone directory for further details. Another method of calling an FSS is through a "direct line," which may be available at a local airport or FBO.

Enroute Flight Advisory Service (EFAS) is an FSS service specifically designed to provide timely enroute weather information upon pilot request. Pilots usually can contact an EFAS specialist from 6 A.M. to 10 P.M. local time anywhere in the conterminous U.S. The discrete EFAS frequency, 122.0 MHz, is established for pilots of aircraft flying between 5,000 feet AGL and 17,500 feet MSL. Different frequencies are allocated for each ARTCC area for operations above 18,000 feet MSL.

The weather advisories received are tailored to the type of flight conducted and are appropriate to the route and cruising altitude. In addition, EFAS is a central collection and distribution point for pilot reports (PIREPs), so pilots normally receive very current or real-time weather information. This includes any thunderstorm activity along the route.

WEATHER REPORTS AND FORECASTS

Weather observations are taken at most larger airports and transmitted at periodic intervals to the National Meteoro-

```
TAF KPIT 091730Z 091818 15005KT 5SM HZ FEW020 WS010/31022KT
    FM1930 30015G25KT 3SM SHRA OVC015 TEMPO 2022 1/2SM +TSRA
    OVC008CB
    FM0100 27008KT 5SM SHRA BKN020 OVC040 PROB40 0407 1SM -RA BR
    FM1015 18005KT 6SM -SHRA OVC020 BECMG 1315 P6SM NSW SKC


METAR KPIT 091955Z COR 22015G25KT 3/4SM R28L/2600FT TSRA OVC010CB
18/16 A2992 RMK SLP045 T01820159
```

Forecast	Explanation	Report
TAF	Message type: TAF-routine or TAF AMD-amended forecast, METAR-hourly, SPECI-special or TESTM-non-commissioned ASOS report	METAR
KPIT	ICAO location indicator	KPIT
091730Z	Issuance time: ALL times in UTC "Z", 2-digit date, 4-digit time	091955Z
091818	Valid period: 2-digit date, 2-digit beginning, 2-digit ending times	
	In U.S. METAR: CORrected ob; or AUTOmated ob for automated report with no human intervention; omitted when observer logs on	COR
15005KT	Wind: 3 digit true-north direction, nearest 10 degrees (or VaRiaBle); next 2-3 digits for speed and unit, KT (KMH or MPS); as needed, Gust and maximum speed; 00000KT for calm; for METAR, if direction varies 60 degrees or more, Variability appended, e.g. 180V260	22015G25KT
5SM	Prevailing visibility: in U.S., Statute Miles & fractions; above 6 miles in TAF Plus6SM. (Or, 4-digit minimum visibility in meters and as required, lowest value with direction)	3/4SM
	Runway Visual Range: R; 2-digit runway designator Left, Center, or Right as needed; "/"; Minus or Plus in U.S., 4-digit value, FeeT in U.S., (usually meters elsewhere); 4-digit value Variability 4-digit value (and tendency Down, Up or No change)	R28L/2600FT
HZ	Significant present, forecast and recent weather: see table (on back)	TSRA
FEW020	Cloud amount, height and type: SKy Clear 0/8, FEW >0/8-2/8, SCaTtered 3/8-4/8, BroKeN 5/8-7/8, OVerCast 8/8; 3-digit height in hundreds of ft; Towering CUmulus or CumulonimBus in METAR; in TAF, only CB. Vertical Visibility for obscured sky and height "VV004". More than 1 layer may be reported or forecast. In automated METAR reports only, CLeaR for "clear below 12,000 feet"	OVC010CB
	Temperature: degrees Celsius; first 2 digits, temperature "/" last 2 digits, dew-point temperature; Minus for below zero, e.g., M06	18/16
	Altimeter setting: indicator and 4 digits; in U.S., A-inches and hundredths; (Q-hectoPascals, e.g., Q1013)	A2992

Forecast	Explanation	Report
WS010/31022KT	In U.S. TAF, non-convective low-level (≤2,000 ft) Wind Shear; 3-digit height (hundreds of ft); "/"; 3-digit wind direction and 2-3 digit wind speed above the indicated height, and unit, KT	
	In METAR, ReMarK indicator & remarks. For example: Sea-Level Pressure in hectoPascals & tenths, as shown: 1004.5 hPa; Temp/dew-point in tenths °C, as shown: temp. 18.2°C, dew-point 15.9°C	RMK SLP045 T01820159
FM1930	FroM and 2-digit hour and 2-digit minute beginning time: indicates significant change. Each FM starts on new line, indented 5 spaces.	
TEMPO 2022	TEMPOrary: changes expected for < 1 hour and in total, < half of 2-digit hour beginning and 2-digit hour ending time period	
PROB40 0407	PROBability and 2-digit percent (30 or 40): probable condition during 2-digit hour beginning and 2-digit hour ending time period	
BECMG 1315	BECoMinG: change expected during 2-digit hour beginning and 2-digit hour ending time period	

Fig. 4-22. Key to Aviation Weather Observations and Forecasts

Table of Significant Present, Forecast and Recent Weather - Grouped in categories and used in
the order listed below; or as needed in TAF, No Significant Weather.

QUALIFIER

Intensity or Proximity
- Light   "no sign" Moderate   + Heavy
VC Vicinity: but not at aerodrome; in U.S. **METAR**, between 5 and 10SM of the point(s) of
    observation; in U.S. **TAF**, 5 to 10SM from center of runway complex (elsewhere within 8000m)

Descriptor

MI Shallow	BC Patches	PR Partial	TS Thunderstorm
BL Blowing	SH Showers	DR Drifting	FZ Freezing

WEATHER PHENOMENA

Precipitation

DZ Drizzle	RA Rain	SN Snow	SG Snow grains
IC Ice crystals	PE Ice pellets	GR Hail	GS Small hail/snow pellets
UP Unknown precipitation in automated observations			

Obscuration

BR Mist (≥5/8SM)	FG Fog (<5/8SM)	FU Smoke	VA Volcanic ash
SA Sand	HZ Haze	PY Spray	DU Widespread dust

Other

SQ Squall	SS Sandstorm	DS Duststorm	PO Well developed
FC Funnel cloud	+FC tornado/waterspout		dust/sand whirls

Fig. 4-23. Key to Aviation Weather Observations and Forecasts

logical Center (NMC) in Washington, D.C. The NMC is the central data processing center for the collection and distribution of basic weather observations.

Aviation routine weather reports (METAR), are used to compile information concerning existing surface weather from the various observation stations. These reports are transmitted every hour. Figure 4-22 is a key to aviation routine weather reports. The top portion of the key includes a sample report.

NOTAMs (Notices to Airmen) are included at the end of some aviation report sequences to indicate information of interest regarding the airport. NOTAM information usually is written in code to save space on the report. An explanation of this code normally can be found on the display boards where aviation weather reports are posted.

Several types of weather forecasts also are available to aviators. A key to their interpretation is included as figure 4-23.

Terminal Aerodrome forecasts (TAF), predict weather conditions for large air terminals throughout the country and are issued four times daily. Airport weather is forecast for a 24-hour period.

Certain National Weather Forecast Offices are designated as forecast centers to predict aviation weather within their *areas*. These reports, called *area forecasts*, are issued three times a day (four in Hawaii) and cover a period of 12 hours, plus a general outlook for an additional six hours. Area forecasts include a statement concerning expected icing conditions, plus the height of the freezing level.

Winds and temperatures aloft forecasts predict wind speed and direction plus temperatures for nine altitude levels. The forecast temperatures aloft can be used to compute an expected thermal index, if actual observed temperatures are not available.

SIGMETs and AIRMETs are advisories of potentially hazardous aviation weather. They may be obtained through FSS telephone, in-person, or radio briefings, as well as through TWEBs. SIGMETs, *Significant Meteorological Information*, involve weather significant to the safety of *all* aircraft. They concern severe or extreme turbulence or icing, or widespread dust or sandstorms or volcanic ash lowering visibilities to less than three miles or volcanic eruptions. *Convective SIGMETs* concern large areas of thunderstorms above a certain radar-measured intensity, lines of thunderstorms, embedded thunderstorms, and tornadoes. Convective SIGMETs also are issued for hail of 3/4-inch or greater diameter. Low-level wind shear, severe or greater turbulence, and severe icing are always implied by convective SIGMETs, though not specified. Alphabetic designators NOVEMBER through YANKEE, except SIERRA and TANGO, are used only for SIGMETs, while designators SIERRA, TANGO, and ZULU are used for AIRMETs.

AIRMETs, *Airman's Meteorological Information*, may be of significance to any pilot or aircraft operator. They are of particular concern to operators and pilots of aircraft sensitive to the phenomena described below and to pilots without instrument ratings. AIRMETs cover moderate icing, moderate turbulence, large areas where visibility is less than three miles and/or ceilings are less than 1,000 feet, extensive mountain obscurement, and sustained winds of 30 knots or more at the surface. SIGMETs of both types, as well as AIRMETs, are transmitted by FSS computers. AIRMETs are issued on a scheduled basis every six hours, with unscheduled amendments issued as required. AIRMETs have fixed alphanumeric designators with ZULU for icing and freezing level data, TANGO for turbulence, strong surface winds, and windshear, and SIERRA for instrument flight rules and mountain obscuration.

Pilot Reports (PIREPs) contain significant weather information reported by pilots in flight. This information can be very valuable since pilots can supply first-hand information on existing conditions. These reports are compiled by FSS personnel and passed on to pilots in weather briefings and broadcast aviation weather reports. Pilots are urged to cooperate and volunteer reports of significant weather information.

Although they vary considerably in quality, *televised weather briefings and forecasts* have much to offer the pilot. Network-level coverage tends to be very general in nature. Another weather information source is the direct user access terminal (DUAT) system which permits pilots to receive weather briefings electronically. Pilots can access DUAT through toll-free numbers and a personal computer equipped with a modem. Since weather briefing procedures are subject to new technology, make sure you check the *Aeronautical Information Manual* or the *Airport/Facility Directory* for the latest systems descriptions.

WEATHER CHARTS

In addition to reports and forecasts, the National Weather Service also has a variety of weather charts that provide valuable meteorological information. A pilot is provided a pictorial representation of the weather by referring to these charts. *The surface analysis chart, the weather depiction chart,* and the *low-level significant weather prognostic chart* are the most important types.

The *surface analysis chart* gives the velocity and direction of the wind, the temperature, humidity, dewpoint, and some other weather data. In addition, this chart provides a general picture of the atmospheric pressure pattern at the surface of the earth by showing the position of highs, lows, and fronts. A

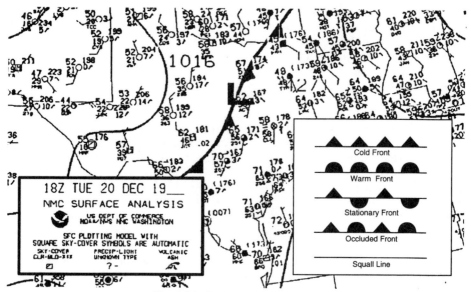

Fig. 4-24. Surface Analysis Chart

sample surface analysis chart is shown in figure 4-24.

The *weather depiction chart*, shown in figure 4-25, is issued every three hours. An abbreviated station model is used on a weather depiction chart to show visibility, type of weather, amount of sky cover, and the height of the cloud base.

The *radar summary chart*, shown in figure 4-26, normally is reproduced every hour. Since radar echoes change in

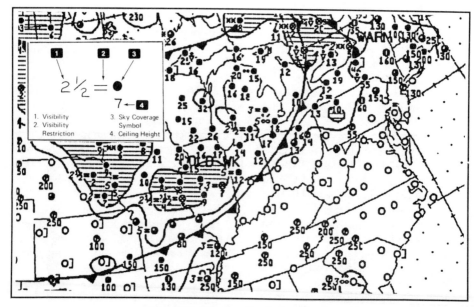

Fig. 4-25. Weather Depiction Chart

shape and intensity in a matter of minutes, the data shown on this map is not current. However, it does show general storm areas and movements over the nation.

The *low-level significant weather prognostic chart*, shown in figure 4-27, is divided into *two* forecast periods. The two panels on the left show the weather prognosis for a 12-hour period and those on the right for a 24-hour period. The valid times and titles for each panel are shown. Low-level prognostic charts are issued every six hours.

The two upper panels portray cloud cover, altitudes of the freezing level, and areas where turbulence can be expected. The panels on the bottom are the forecaster's *best estimate* of the location of frontal and pressure systems, as well as the areas and types of precipitation.

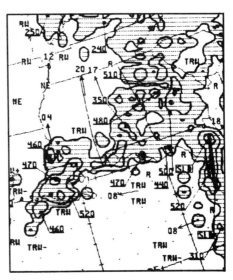

Fig. 4-26. Radar Summary Chart Excerpt

While the accuracy of these charts has improved greatly over the past decade, it should be remembered that they are *still* forecasts. If the pilot compares an

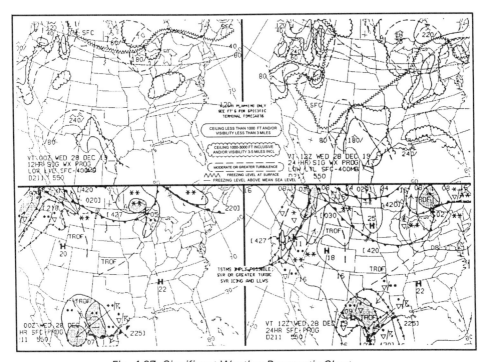

Fig. 4-27. Significant Weather Prognostic Chart

actual observed chart for a particular time period with the *prognostic* chart for the same time period, they may look quite different.

This chapter has presented the most important weather considerations and the sources of information available. With this knowledge as a base, and the additional knowledge gained from personal observation and experience, it will be easier to locate and use those all-important areas of rising air.

While most recreational soaring is accomplished in the vicinity of the gliderport, when it comes time to try for badges, a working knowledge of the weather is essential. The pilots who get the most out of their sailplanes are those who combine flying skill with the ability to read the weather signs.

SOARING

Chapter Five

Medical Factors

INTRODUCTION Soaring pilots should know
enough about aviation medical factors to safely
handle any situation. The high altitude environment where a sailplane may operate has different
effects on the human body than those experienced
on the ground. The major factors all pilots should
be aware of include the effect of decreasing pressure of the atmosphere with increasing altitude,
the role of temperature and turbulence, effects of
drugs, smoking, and alcohol on a pilot's ability
to perform, and visual and positional sensations
during flight.

THE ATMOSPHERE

The atmosphere provides oxygen and filters out harmful radiation from the sun. The presence of the atmosphere prevents excessive heat loss in both plants and animals, and maintains the surface temperature range required for survival. This large volume of air has tremendous weight. At sea level, it exerts a pressure of about 15 pounds per square inch on the body — or a total of about 20 tons on the average person, as shown in figure 5-1. This weight sounds formidable, but at sea level it is quite compatible with man's existence because the body's inner pressure equalizes the surrounding pressure.

Close to the earth, the air is most compressed and, therefore, most dense.

As a body rises into the atmosphere, however, a decrease in pressure is experienced. At 18,000 feet it is only one-half as much as at sea level. Besides adapting to the rarified air at altitude, the pilot's body must adjust to dropping temperatures. Even in summer, the temperature of the air at 18,000 feet is near the freezing point. On some days, it is much lower. In this abnormal habitat, survival depends on the ability of the body to adapt.

Oxygen is transported throughout the body in the bloodstream. The red blood cells contain a complex substance called hemoglobin which picks up oxygen at the lungs, carries it to the tissues for use, picks up carbon dioxide at the tissues, and transports it to the lungs for exhalation. The amount of oxygen that can be carried in the blood

ALTITUDE	PRESSURE	TEMP ($^\circ$C)
55,000	1.32	-57°
50,000	1.68	-57°
45,000	2.14	-57°
40,000	2.72	-57°
35,000	3.46	-55°
25,000	5.45	-35°
18,000	7.34	-21°
10,000	10.1	-5°
5,000	12.2	5°
S.L.	14.7 psi	15°

Fig. 5-1. Pressure and Temperature Decrease with Altitude

depends, to a large extent, on the *pressure* that the oxygen gas from the air exerts on the blood as it passes through the lungs.

At 10,000 feet, the blood of a person who is exposed to outside air can still carry oxygen at 90 percent of its capacity. At this altitude, the flight performance of *healthy* pilots is impaired only after some time, when they may find themselves a little less dexterous than usual at tuning radios,

slower at making decisions, and less able to sustain close concentration.

Although an individual who is suffering from a lack of oxygen may remain conscious for a longer period, only a limited amount of time is available to perform *useful* acts. The "time of useful consciousness" at any altitude is the maximum length of time the exposed individual has to perform the necessary tasks for survival. The times and altitudes for "time of useful consciousness" are illustrated in figure 5-2.

ALTITUDE	TIME OF EXPOSURE	SYMPTOMS	TIME OF USEFUL CONSCIOUSNESS
40,000'			5-15 sec.
35,000'	15 to 45 seconds	Immediate unconsciousness (with little or no warning!)	30-45 sec.
30,000'			45-80 sec.
25,000'			2-3 min.
	5 minutes	Same symptoms as "15,000 to 18,000 feet" only more pronounced with eventual unconsciousness.	
20,000'			5-12 min.
18,000'	30 minutes	Impairment of judgment and vision, high self-confidence, euphoria, disregard for sensory perceptions, poor coordination, sleepiness, dizziness, personality changes as if intoxicated, cyanosis (bluing).	
15,000'			
14,000'	several hours	Headache, fatigue, listlessness, non-specific deterioration of physical and mental performance.	
10,000'			

Fig. 5-2. Altitude Effects and Time of Useful Consciousness

HYPOXIA

Lack of oxygen is the greatest single danger to man at high altitudes, despite the importance of pressure and temperature. The shortage of oxygen in the human body results in a condition called hypoxia, which simply means oxygen starvation. When a pilot inhales air at high altitude, there isn't enough oxygen pressure to force adequate amounts of this vital gas through the membranes of the lungs into the bloodstream so it can be carried to the tissues of the body. The function of various organs, including the brain, is then impaired.

Unfortunately, the nature of hypoxia makes the pilot the poorest judge of its symptoms. The first symptoms of oxygen deficiency are misleadingly pleasant, resembling mild intoxication from alcohol. Because oxygen star-

vation strikes first at the brain, the higher faculties are dulled. The ability to correct mistakes diminishes and the mind no longer functions properly. Hands and feet become clumsy and the victim begins to feel drowsy, languid, and nonchalant with a false sense of security. The last thing in the world a pilot suffering from hypoxia feels a need for is oxygen, as illustrated in figure 5-3.

As hypoxia gets worse, the victim becomes dizzy or feels a tingling of the skin. Some pilots get a dull headache. Oxygen starvation gets worse the longer a person remains at an altitude, or climbs higher. The heart races, lips and skin under the fingernails begin to turn blue, the field of vision narrows, and the instruments start to look fuzzy. But hypoxia, by its nature, makes the victims feel confident they are doing a better job of flying than ever before.

Fig. 5-3. Hypoxia Symptoms

Smoking reduces the ability of the blood to carry oxygen and lowers the altitude where these symptoms are experienced. Regardless of acclimatization, endurance, or other attributes, every pilot suffers the consequences of hypoxia when exposed to inadequate oxygen pressure.

It is essential that pilots carry oxygen and use it before the onset of hypoxia. The only accurate indicator of when oxygen is needed is the altimeter.

Here are some general suggestions which apply to young, healthy flyers. Pilots who are older, overweight, out of condition, or smoke heavily should limit themselves to a ceiling of 8,000 to 10,000 feet unless oxygen is available.

1. Carry oxygen in the sailplane or don't fly above 12,500 feet.
2. Use oxygen on every flight above 12,500 feet. You'll probably need it.
3. Use oxygen on flights *near* 12,500 feet. It won't hurt you and you'll be a much sharper pilot.
4. Breathe normally when using oxygen. Rapid or extra-deep breathing also can cause loss of consciousness.

Flying above 12,500 feet without using oxygen is like playing Russian roulette — the odds are the pilot *may* not get hurt, but it's a deadly game! At 20,000 feet, vision deteriorates to the point that seeing is almost impossible, breathing is labored, and the heart beats rapidly. The victim hasn't the vaguest idea what is wrong, or whether anything is wrong. At 25,000 feet a person will collapse and death is imminent unless oxygen is restored.

No one is exempt from the effects of hypoxia. Everyone needs an adequate supply of oxygen. Some pilots may be able to tolerate a few thousand feet more of altitude than some others, but no one is really very far from average. Serious trouble is waiting for pilots who try to test themselves to prove how much higher they can fly or how much longer they can function without supplemental oxygen.

HYPERVENTILATION

Some people believe breathing faster and deeper at high altitudes can compensate for oxygen lack. This is only partially true. Such abnormal breathing, known as hyperventilation, also causes a person to flush from the lungs and blood much of the carbon dioxide the system needs to maintain the proper degree of blood acidity. The chemical imbalance in the body then produces dizziness, tingling of the fingers and toes, sensation of body heat, rapid heart rate, blurring of vision, muscle spasms and, finally, unconsciousness. The symptoms resemble the effects of hypoxia and the brain becomes equally impaired.

Pilots are most likely to hyperventilate while flying under stress or at high altitude. For example, the stressful feeling of unexpectedly encountering extreme turbulence in the rotor area of a mountain wave, or finding an area of high sink over water or mountainous terrain may make them unconsciously breathe more rapidly or deeply than necessary.

Pilots who suffer an unexpected attack of hyperventilation with no knowledge of what it is or what causes it, may become terrified — thinking that they are experiencing a heart attack or something equally ominous. In the resulting panic and confusion, it is possible to actually lose consciousness and control of the sailplane.

A little knowledge is all that is needed to avoid hyperventilation problems. Since the word itself means excessive ventilation of the lungs, the solution lies in restoring respiration to normal using the following procedures.

1. Ensure that hyperventilation, and not hypoxia, is at the root of the symptoms.
2. If oxygen is in use, check the equipment and the flow rate.
3. If everything appears normal, make a conscious effort to slow down the rate and decrease the depth of breathing. Talking, singing, or counting aloud often helps.
4. Normally paced conversation tends to slow down a rapid respiratory rate. If you have no one with you, talk to yourself. Nobody will ever know.

Normal breathing is the cure for hyperventilation. Once the proper carbon dioxide level is restored, recovery is rapid.

BODY GASES AND PRESSURE EFFECTS

In an unpressurized sailplane climbing to higher and higher altitudes, the body is exposed to decreasing pressure on its outer surfaces. Because the pressure inside the body is still the same as it was on the ground, strange things begin to happen. Gases trapped in the cavities start expanding in an effort to equalize the pressure with that of the environmental gas. This phenomenon can cause some discomfort. The expanding gas trapped in such places as the sinuses, behind the eardrum, and in the stomach may lead to a headache, ear pain, or a feeling of abdominal fullness.

At 8,000 feet, the gases in the body expand to a volume of about 20 percent greater than that at ground level. If the rate of climb is gradual and the pilot's physical condition is good, adjustments to this change are easy and comfortable. At 18,000 feet, the gas bubbles more than double their normal size; the expansion continues as the sailplane gains altitude. A very rapid change of altitude is naturally more hazardous and uncomfortable than a slow change.

The discomforts resulting from the expansion of trapped gases usually can be reduced by slowing the rate of ascent. If they persist, however, the pilot should descend to a lower altitude where the atmosphere is denser. Most of the gas in the intestines is swallowed air, but some is formed by the digestive process. The amount of gas varies with the individual and with the type of food eaten. The following "diet don'ts" may help to minimize abdominal gas.

1. Don't eat too quickly before a flight.
2. Don't eat too much (swallowed air increases with each bite).
3. Avoid large quantities of fluid, especially carbonated beverages.
4. Don't eat gas-forming foods (beans, cabbage, onions, raw apples, cucumbers, melons, or any greasy foods).
5. Avoid chewing gum on the way up — it may result in your swallowing a great deal of air.

In addition to gases trapped in the body cavities, a considerable volume of gas (primarily nitrogen) exists in solution within the body. That is, it is dissolved in the blood and other body tissues, especially fat. When the outside pressure falls, these gases tend to come out of solution and form gas bubbles, just as carbonated beverages release bubbles when the cap is removed and the pressure escapes. These bubbles can produce a severe pain around the joints or muscles, called "bends." The same bubble formation in the lung tissue is called the "chokes" and is recognized by a burning sensation or stabbing pain in the chest area, a cough, and difficulty in breathing. Needless to say, the pilot's ability to fly could be severely affected.

These physical difficulties are seldom experienced below 25,000 feet so the low-altitude pilots need not be too concerned. If a pilot is operating a high-performance sailplane at higher flight levels and suspects the bends or chokes, the quickest relief can be obtained by descending to a lower altitude.

SCUBA DIVING

Any type of flying after scuba diving can be dangerous, particularly if the person has been diving to depths for any length of time. The increased pressure of the water causes excess nitrogen to be absorbed into the body. Plenty of time should be allowed to rid the body of this excess gas, or it is possible to experience the bends below an altitude of 10,000 feet. The minimum recommended time between diving and flying is 24 hours.

THE EARS

Pilots flying in unpressurized sailplanes usually encounter a problem of ear discomfort during ascent or descent. To understand why this happens and how to counteract it, a simple grasp of the structure of the ear is helpful.

The external ear canal (the small tube leading down to the eardrum) is always

at the same pressure as the atmosphere surrounding the body. The middle ear, where pressure problems arise, is a small air-filled cavity situated within the bone of the skull. It is separated from the external ear canal by the eardrum. The other side of the middle ear is connected to the nasal cavity by the eustachian tube, as depicted in figure 5-4.

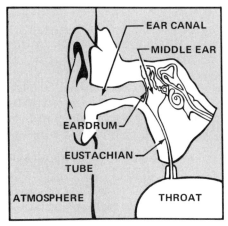

Fig. 5-4. Structure of the Ear

As the sailplane ascends, the atmospheric pressure decreases as does the pressure in the external ear canal. The middle ear, being an enclosed cavity, stays at ground-level pressure. When the pressure in the middle ear exceeds that of the external ear canal, the eardrum starts to bulge outward somewhat. The middle ear is sensitive to this change and requires only a slight excess of pressure to open the eustachian tube so that gas may pass by this route through the nose or mouth. In this way, pressure is equalized on both sides of the eardrum. The pilot may be aware of this pressure change by alternating sensations of ear "fullness" and "clearing."

Conditions within the ear are reversed during descent. As the surrounding air pressure increases, the middle ear, which has accommodated itself to the reduced pressure at altitude by the process just described, is at a *lower* pressure than the external ear canal. Consequently, the outside air forces the eardrum to bulge *inward*. This condition is much more difficult to relieve since air must be introduced back up the eustachian tube to equalize the pressure. The partial vacuum in the middle ear also tends to collapse rather than inflate the walls of the eustachian tube. This can best be remedied by closing the mouth, pinching the nostrils shut, and blowing slowly and gently to build up pressure in the mouth and nose. At some point in the procedure, it will be possible to feel air entering the middle ear, and an immediate improvement in the ability to hear.

If a pilot has a cold, the tissue around the nasal end of the eustachian tube probably is swollen, and ear problems can be expected in flight. To prevent a perforated eardrum, flights should be postponed or conducted at lower altitudes. Although a perforated eardrum generally heals rapidly, in some cases hearing is permanently impaired or the middle ear becomes infected and causes prolonged disability.

VISION

Vision is perhaps the most vital faculty in flying. Even on the ground, reduced or impaired vision can be dangerous in certain circumstances. In flight it is always dangerous.

A number of factors such as hypoxia, carbon monoxide, alcohol, drugs, fatigue, heavy smoking, and even bright sunlight can affect vision. Optical illusions such as misjudging the horizon because of slanted banks of clouds may occur as a result of the brain's interpretation of the images received from the eye. Some specific rules for protecting vision are:

1. Get plenty of sleep before a long flight or a high altitude flight.
2. Use oxygen as previously recommended.
3. Wear sunglasses on bright days.
4. Remember that drugs, alcohol, and heavy smoking have adverse effects on vision.

VERTIGO

An archaic definition of disorientation literally meant "difficulty in facing the east." To the pilot, it more often means "which way is up?" Disorientation, or vertigo, is actually a state of temporary spatial confusion resulting from misleading information sent to the brain by various sensory organs. The body's elaborate navigational system was superbly designed for locomotion on the ground at a normal gait, but it can be tricked during sudden acceleration or turning flight.

When seated on an unstable moving platform at altitude, and exposed to certain angular accelerations or centrifugal forces, pilots are susceptible to innumerable confusing, disorienting, experiences when the horizon is not visible. Pilots may think they are climbing or in a straight glide during gliding turns, and as though they are diving during recoveries from level turns. These alarming sensations are due primarily to misinterpretation of messages sent to the brain by the two primary sensory organs — the semicircular canals of the inner ear and groups of pressure-sensitive nerve endings located mainly in the muscles and tendons. In a sailplane, these organs may send the brain inaccurate reports.

The semicircular canals in each inner ear consist of tiny hollow tubes bent to form a half-circle, as shown in figure 5-5. Each canal is positioned approximately at a right angle to the other two and each is filled with a fluid. At the outer end of each, there is an expanded portion containing a mass of fine hairs. Acceleration of the inner ear assembly in any direction sets the fluid in motion within the appropriate canal causing the hairs to deflect, as illustrated in figure 5-6. This, in turn, stimulates nerve endings and sends directional messages to the brain. Operating as a unit, this detection system forms a device by which pilots can readily identify "yaw," "pitch," and "roll."

With this perfect arrangement, a person should have no difficulty ascertaining direction and attitude. As in all complex systems, however, there is a certain amount of built-in error. If the rate of directional change is quite small, and not confirmed by the eyes, the change will be virtually undetectable.

In straight-and-level flight, the fluid in the semicircular canals is at rest and the little hair detectors are alert and ready for action. Any directional change of the sailplane causes a reaction in the proper canal and signals to the brain which direction the sailplane has moved.

As a pilot enters a constant-rate turn, the system goes to work; the hairs bend over and the proper signal travels to the brain indicating the direction of turn. Continuing the same turn for about 30 to 45 seconds allows the fluid in the canal to catch up and the hairs to return to their upright position.

Here's where trouble begins. If unable to see the ground and establish a visual reference, the pilot is just seconds away from the famous "graveyard" spiral shown in figure 5-7. In a turn, the inner ear machinery indicates straight-and-level flight. As the airspeed builds up in

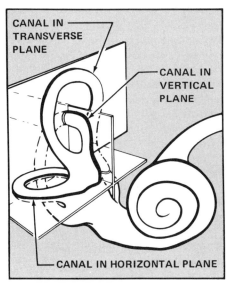

Fig. 5-5. Semi-Circular Canals

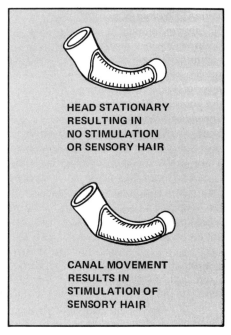

HEAD STATIONARY
RESULTING IN
NO STIMULATION
OR SENSORY HAIR

CANAL MOVEMENT
RESULTS IN
STIMULATION OF
SENSORY HAIR

Fig. 5-6. Stimulation of Sensory Hairs

the turn, the pilot may have the sensation of a level dive, and pull back on the stick. Increased back pressure on the controls only tightens the turn and causes structural failure or a curving flight path into the ground. A glimpse of the horizon usually allows the pilot to get the sailplane squared away again to straight flight.

Fig. 5-7. "Graveyard" Spiral

The fluid, which continues to move while returning to level flight, begins to creep back to neutral after the sailplane is leveled. The fluid continues to flow after the canal has come to rest, bending the hairs along with it because of its momentum. The pilot has the sensation of turning in the *opposite* direction from which recovery has just been made. Unless the horizon is still visible, the pilot instinctively banks *away* from the imaginary turn, and the cycle starts again.

Without instrument training and proper attitude indicating instruments,

the chances of maintaining a normal sailplane attitude in limited visibility are extremely rare. Repeated small control movements may eventually create a sensation of gradual turning. The pilot may misinterpret the bank angle and have a false impression of banking when in a skid or a slip.

Spatial disorientation occurs most often in instrument conditions created by rain, fog, clouds, smoke, or dark nights. It is aggravated by other factors such as unfamiliarity with the sailplane or flight situation, fear or worry, and excessive head movements.

Vertigo can occur anytime the outside visual reference is temporarily lost; for example, during map reading, changing a radio frequency, computing a navigational problem, or whatever else a pilot might need to do inside the cockpit. Nearly all experienced pilots have had a brush with vertigo, usually minor and of short duration; however, it can be disastrous. Pilot error resulting from vertigo has been identified as the contributing cause of many accidents.

The danger of vertigo may be reduced by understanding its nature and causes, avoiding the flight conditions which tend to cause vertigo, and remembering vertigo can happen to anyone.

FATIGUE

Fatigue is a general term which is difficult to define medically. Fatigue may be described as a depletion of body energy reserves, leading to below-par performance. A pilot should understand the causes and prevention of the two broad categories of fatigue — acute and chronic — because they lower efficiency.

Chronic fatigue extends over a long period of time and usually has psychological roots. Continuous strain on the job, for example, can produce chronic fatigue. A person may experience this condition in the form of weakness, tiredness, palpitations of the heart, breathlessness, headaches, or irritability. Sometimes chronic fatigue even creates stomach or intestinal problems and generalized aches and pains throughout the body. When the condition becomes serious enough, it can lead to emotional illness.

Acute fatigue, on the other hand, is short-lived and is a normal occurrence in everyday living. It is the kind of tiredness felt after a period of strenuous effort, excitement, or lack of sleep. Rest after exertion and eight hours of sound sleep ordinarily cure this condition.

A special type of acute fatigue, called "skill fatigue," is mentioned here because pilots are especially susceptible to it. Skill fatigue has two main effects on performance.

1. *Timing disruption* — The pilot appears to perform a task as usual, but the timing of each component is slightly off. This makes the pattern of the operation less smooth; each component is performed as though it were separate, instead of part of an integrated activity.
2. *Disruption of the perceptual field—* Attention is concentrated on movements or objects in the center of the field of vision and neglects those in the periphery. This may be accompanied by loss of accuracy and smoothness in control movements.

Acute fatigue has many causes, but the following are among the most important for the pilot.

1. *Mild hypoxia* (oxygen deficiency)
2. *Physical stresses* produced by the sailplane, such as fighting severe turbulence, icing conditions, or malfunctioning of the equipment.
3. *Psychological stress*, some of it emotional and some resulting from the demanding intellectual activity required for successful flight operations or fear resulting from a tight situation.
4. *Depletion of physical energy* resulting from psychological stress. Sustained psychological stress accelerates the glandular secretions which prepare the body for quick reactions during an emergency. These secretions make the circulatory and respiratory systems work harder, and the liver releases energy to provide the extra fuel needed for brain and muscle work. When this reserve energy supply is depleted, the body lapses into generalized and severe fatigue.

Acute fatigue can be prevented by a proper diet and by adequate rest and sleep. A well-balanced diet prevents the body from having to consume its own tissues as an energy source. Adequate rest maintains the body's store of vital energy. A person can sleep best in quiet, comfortable surroundings; excitement and worry diminish the benefits of sleep. A pilot should get approximately eight hours of sleep before a flying activity, and more if especially tired, tense, or ill.

Keeping the body in top physical condition makes a person less susceptible to fatigue. In addition to getting regular exercise, pilots should avoid obesity which lowers flight performance, taxes the body, and shortens life. Pilots suffering from either chronic fatigue or acute fatigue should *stay on the ground* until alertness and energy are restored.

MOTION SICKNESS

Although motion sickness is un-commmon among experienced pilots, it does occur occasionally, and jeopardizes flying efficiency, particularly in turbulent weather when peak skill is required. Student pilots are frequently surprised by an uneasiness usually described as motion sickness that is probably a result of anxiety, un-familiarity, turbulence, or steep spirals.

Motion sickness is caused by continued stimulation of the tiny portion of the inner ear which controls your sense of balance. The symptoms are progressive. First, desire for food is lost. Then saliva collects in the mouth and perspiration begins. Eventually, nausea, disorientation, and headaches occur. If air sickness becomes severe enough, it is possible to become completely incapacitated.

The preventive drugs for airsickness which are available over the counter or by prescription should not be taken. These medications may make a pilot drowsy or depress the brain functions in other ways. Research has shown that most motion sickness drugs cause a temporary deterioration of navigational skills or other tasks demanding keen judgment.

Motion sickness can be relieved during flight by opening the air vents, loosening clothing, using oxygen, and focusing on a point outside the sailplane. Unnecessary head movements also should be avoided and a landing made as soon as possible. Increased skills and self-confidence usually eliminate airsickness.

DRUGS

The word "drug" evokes an image in the minds of many people far different from its actual medical meaning. The term "drug" is often interpreted to mean marijuana, heroin, LSD, bar-biturates, or amphetamines. Actually, a drug is any chemical compound administered to produce a specific effect on the body.

The illicit use of the "psychoactive drugs" which distort the mental process, hardly needs to be discussed here. Certainly no responsible pilot would consider mixing any of these drugs with flying.

However, legitimate medications taken for minor ailments can also jeopardize safe flight by their subtle or unpredictable effects on the pilot. This includes both prescribed and over-the-counter medications. Even the simplest of home remedies should be suspect, including aspirin, cold tablets, cough mixtures, and laxatives.

Recent studies of aircraft accidents suggest certain categories of drugs may have side effects which contribute to pilot error and, hence, to accidents. These are:

1. *Antihistamines* — a group of drugs widely prescribed and readily available for sufferers from hay fever and other allergies. Drowsiness is a commmon side effect.

2. *Tranquilizers* — a variety of agents usually prescribed for nervousness and hypertension. These, too, may reduce alertness.

3. *Reducing agents and "pep" pills* — a class of drugs generally containing amphetamines. They can produce a feeling of high spirits and false confidence, while actually crippling one's judgment and leading to reckless errors.

4. *Barbiturates, nerve tonics, and pain killers* — a broad category of

medications intended primarily to relieve anxiety or reduce pain. These drugs generally suppress mental alertness.

Some other dangers which may accompany pill taking are:

1. *Drug allergies* — An allergic response to a drug can arise unexpectedly and dramatically, disabling a pilot in flight.
2. *Unexpected side reactions* — Different people may react in different ways to the same medication. For example, a drug which has no significant side effects in most individuals may, in a few, produce nausea or vertigo.
3. *Change of effect* — High-altitude flying or "G" forces have been observed to change the effect of some medications.
4. *Effect of drug combinations* — Two drugs taken at the same time can produce an unexpected result. They may cancel each other out, render each other more potent, or cause a side reaction not experienced with either medicine alone. For example, dangerously high blood pressure has resulted from the use of nose sprays by persons taking antidepressants at the same time. Even eating some foods in combination with certain medicines has produced dangerous physical effects.

A pilot should be just as cautious with over-the-counter remedies as with prescription medications. The need for medicine implies the presence of an illness and sick people have no business in the air. The safest rule is to take *no* medicine before or during flight.

ALCOHOL

Everyone knows that alcohol impairs the efficiency of the human mechanism.

This fact has been emphasized again and again. Studies have positively proved that drinking and performance deterioration are closely linked. Estimates indicate that alcohol is a major factor in nearly 50 percent of all automobile accidents. Analyses of aircraft accidents over the past several years implicated alcohol as a contributing factor in almost 40 percent of the crashes in the early 1960's. Discovery of the problem, education, and regulation had decreased this factor to around 20 percent in the late 1960's and early 1970's.

In "hangar sessions" among experienced pilots, there is almost 100 percent agreement that drinking and flying don't mix. Yet, the accident record shows that far too many pilots have ignored their own better judgment and paid with their lives. An automobile moves in only two dimensions. An airplane moves in three, making its safe operation infinitely more complex. Therefore, any pilot who is not in top condition is severely handicapped. Even straight-and-level flight from one point to another requires a high degree of judgment, attention, coordination, and skill. Hundreds of decisions must be made, some on the basis of incomplete information. Obviously, then, anything which detracts from the ability to make successive correct decisions increases the chances of an accident.

The alcohol consumed in beer and mixed drinks is simply *ethyl alcohol*, a central nervous system depressant. From a medical point of view, it acts on the body much like a general anesthetic. The "dose" is generally much lower and more slowly consumed in the case of alcohol, but the basic effects on the system are similar.

Alcohol is easily and quickly absorbed by the digestive tract. The bloodstream absorbs about 80 to 90 percent of the alcohol in a highball within 30 minutes on an empty stomach, as shown in figure 5-8. Beer works a little slower, but not much. Food slows down the absorption rate.

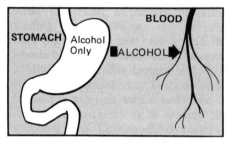

Fig. 5-8. Alcohol Absorption

The effect of alcohol is greatly multiplied when a person is exposed to altitude. Two drinks on the ground are equivalent to three or four at altitude. The reason for this is that, chemically, alcohol interferes with the ability of the brain to utilize oxygen. The effects are rapid because alcohol passes so quickly into the bloodstream. In addition, the brain is a highly vascular organ which is immediately sensitive to changes in the blood's composition. For the pilot, then, the lower oxygen availability at altitude, along with the lower capability of the brain to use what oxygen *is* there, adds up to a deadly combination.

The body requires about three hours to rid itself of all the alcohol contained in *one* mixed drink or *one* beer. The Federal Aviation Regulations make it illegal to fly for at least eight hours after taking a single drink. Most wise pilots allow a minimum of 12 hours.

DEHYDRATION AND HEATSTROKE

Dehydration is the term given to a critical loss of water from the body. The first noticeable effect of dehydration is

fatigue, which in turn makes top physical and mental performance difficult, if not impossible. A sailplane pilot flying for a long period of time in hot summer temperatures or at high altitude is particularly susceptible to dehydration for two reasons: the clear canopy offers no protection from the sun and, at high altitude, there are fewer air pollutants to diffuse the sun's rays. The result is that the pilot is continually exposed to heat which the body attempts to regulate by perspiration. If this fluid is not replaced, fatigue progresses to dizziness, weakness, nausea, tingling of hands and feet, abdominal cramps, and extreme thirst.

Heatstroke is a condition caused by any inability of the body to control its temperature. Onset of this condition may be recognized by the symptoms of dehydration, but also has been known to be recognized only by complete collapse.

To prevent these symptoms, it is recommended that an ample supply of water be carried and used at frequent intervals on any long flight whether thirsty or not. Wearing light colored, porous clothing and a hat provides protection from the sun, and keeping the cockpit well ventilated aids in dispelling excess heat.

PSYCHOLOGICAL ASPECTS

A pilot's attitude and general mental state are just as important to safe flight as the condition of the sailplane. Any disturbing feelings which affect a person's ability to concentrate are a potential threat. These include anger, fear, frustration, depression, worry, and anxiety.

The "compulsive flyers" have a special psychological quirk. They can't stand to turn back. They have a tendency to stretch their skills beyond safe limits. Whether pride or simply an inflexible personality is at fault, they continue ahead in marginal situations — sometimes at the cost of life.

A certain amount of anxiety is inevitable in flying. In small amounts, anxiety is even desirable. It is nature's way of keeping a pilot slightly keyed up for routine tasks and alert to danger. But excessive anxiety, like other troubling emotions, can detract from the ability to concentrate in the cockpit — and perhaps lead to disaster.

If a pilot brings problems from the ground into the air, it is easy to become distracted from the job at hand and the body becomes less able to adjust to various stresses. Memory, judgment, and presence of mind are crucial during flight and, surprisingly, muscular skills are closely linked with mental capacity. When one becomes defective, the other usually does, too.

Occasionally, a pilot who has family or job problems starts to carry these worries over into flying, as illustrated in figure 5-9. In other words, one becomes preoccupied with fears about flying or possible physical reactions at altitude. Although anxiety of this sort is usually temporary, it can dangerously affect flight performance and cause further emotional problems if it is ignored.

Fig. 5-9. A Preoccupied Mind

PHYSIOLOGICAL TRAINING

The FAA's Office of Aviation Medicine coordinates and conducts a highly comprehensive physiological training program designed to advance the pilot's knowledge of aeronautics and improve general aviation flight safety. This program is available to all interested pilots. The only prerequisite is a valid Airman Medical Certificate, Class III, or better. Parental or guardian consent is required for student pilots under the age of 21.

Training is presented at the Civil Aeromedical Institute in Oklahoma City, Oklahoma, and at many U.S. Air Force, U.S. Navy, and NASA installations throughout the United States. There is no charge for the program in Oklahoma City. The other facilities require a nominal administrative fee. The training is identical at all facilities.

Anyone wishing to participate in the program should contact the Civil Aeromedical Institute for application forms and the directory of military locations. Applicants are notified by return mail as to where and when to report, and preference of location and time will be considered when scheduling the instruction.

The course includes a full day of activity. Experts in the field of aviation physiology present classroom lectures on disorientation, hyperventilation, vision, hypoxia, medications, illness, stress, smoking, and other physiological problems which might threaten safe flight. Indoctrination in the operation of oxygen equipment is followed by an altitude chamber flight. The chamber flight enables each trainee to actually experience the symptoms of mild hypoxia climaxed by simulated rapid decompression. The training is invaluable, and every pilot, whether flying professionally or for pleasure, should take advantage of the opportunity to participate in the program.

Inquiries should be directed to:

Department of Transportation
Federal Aviation Administration
Aeronautical Center
The Civil Aeromedical Institute
Physiological Operations & Training
Section, AAC-143
P. O. Box 25082
Oklahoma City, Oklahoma 73125

Regulations for Sailplane Pilots

INTRODUCTION Just as a driver must learn the laws concerning the operation of an automobile, the pilot must know the Federal Aviation Regulations that pertain to aircraft operations. Every U.S. citizen is protected by federal regulations in many different ways. Aircraft, like automobiles, guns, and drugs, must be used in a manner that will not endanger the safety or rights of others. To protect the interests of the public, including those who fly as well as those who do not, the Federal Aviation Administration has been charged by Congress with regulating the activities of civil aviation in the United States. The FARs have been written and published to carry out this task, and are revised and brought up-to-date periodically to meet the constantly changing needs of aviation.

There are many organizations which represent various kinds of pilots, operators, and other segments of the industry, and they work closely with the FAA to try to make the FARs fair and beneficial to everyone in aviation. The organizations fill a definite need for someone to speak for both the pilot's and the aviation industry's interests.

This chapter contains excerpts selected for the glider pilot from Federal Aviation Regulations Part 1. It also includes a description of Parts 43, 61, 71, and 91, as well as NTSB Part 830. The sections listed for each Part contain pertinent data and should be studied carefully.

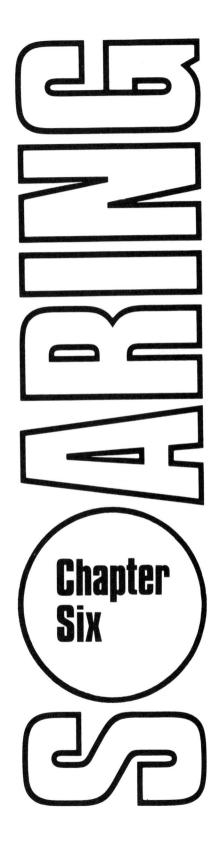

SOARING

Chapter Six

PART 1 - DEFINITIONS
AND ABBREVIATIONS

Part 1 of the FAR(s) alphabetically lists the definitions of terms used in the subsequent regulations. In addition, any abbreviations or symbols used in the FARs are defined and explained in Part 1. Only those definitions of significant importance or of general interest to the sailplane pilot have been included.

1.1 General definitions.

As used in subchapters A through K of this chapter unless the context requires otherwise:

"Administrator" means the Federal Aviation Administrator or any person to whom he has delegated his authority in the matter concerned.

"Aircraft" means a device that is used or intended to be used for flight in the air.

"Airframe" means the fuselage, booms, nacelles, cowlings, fairings, airfoil surfaces (including rotors but excluding propellers and rotating airfoils or engines), and landing gear of an aircraft and their accessories and controls.

"Airport" means an area of land or water that is used or intended to be used for the landing and takeoff of aircraft, and includes its buildings and facilities, if any.

"Airship" means an engine-driven lighter-than-air aircraft that can be steered.

"Air traffic" means aircraft operating in the air or on an airport surface, exclusive of loading ramps and parking areas.

"Air traffic clearance" means an authorization by air traffic control, for the purpose of preventing collision between known aircraft, for an aircraft to proceed under specified traffic conditions within controlled airspace.

"Air traffic control" means a service operated by appropriate authority to promote the safe, orderly, and expeditious flow of air traffic.

"Appliance" means any instrument, mechanism, equipment, part, apparatus, appurtenance, or accessory, including communications equipment, that is used or intended to be used in operating or controlling an aircraft in flight, is installed in or attached to the aircraft, and is not part of an airframe, engine, or propeller.

"Approved," unless used with reference to another person, means approved by the Administrator.

"Armed Forces" means the Army, Navy, Air Force, Marine Corps, and Coast Guard, including their regular and reserve components and members serving without component status.

"Balloon" means a lighter-than-air aircraft that is not engine driven, and that sustains flight through the use of either gas buoyancy or an airborne heater.

"Calibrated airspeed" means indicated airspeed of an aircraft, corrected for position and instrument error. Calibrated airspeed is equal to true airspeed in standard atmosphere at sea level.

"Category" —
(1) As used with respect to the certification, ratings, privileges, and limitations of airmen, means a broad classification of aircraft. Examples include: airplane; rotorcraft; glider; and lighter-than-air; and
(2) As used with respect to the certification of aircraft, means a grouping

of aircraft based upon intended use or operating limitations. Examples include: transport; normal; utility; acrobatic; limited; restricted; and provisional.

"Ceiling" means the height above the earth's surface of the lowest layer of clouds or obscuring phenomena that is reported as "broken," "overcast," or "obscuration," and not classified as "thin" or "partial."

"Civil aircraft" means aircraft other than public aircraft.

"Class" —
(1) As used with respect to the certification, ratings, privileges, and limitations of airmen, means a classification of aircraft within a category having similar operating characteristics. Examples include: single engine; multiengine; land; water; gyroplane; helicopter; airship; and free balloon; and
(2) As used with respect to the certification of aircraft, means a broad grouping of aircraft having similar characteristics of propulsion, flight, or landing. Examples include: airplane; rotorcraft; glider; balloon; landplane; and seaplane.

"Commercial operator" means a person who, for compensation or hire, engages in the carriage by aircraft in air commerce of persons or property, other than as an air carrier or foreign air carrier or under the authority of Part 375 of this Title. Where it is doubtful that an operation is for "compensation or hire," the test applied is whether the carriage by air is merely incidental to the person's other business or is, in itself, a major enterprise for profit.

"Controlled airspace" means an airspace of defined dimensions within which air traffic control service is provided to IFR flights and to VFR flights in accordance with the airspace classification.

NOTE — Controlled airspace is a generic term that covers Class A, Class B, Class C, Class D, and Class E airspace.

"Crewmember" means a person assigned to perform duty in an aircraft during flight time.

"Equivalent airspeed" means the calibrated airspeed of an aircraft corrected for adiabatic compressible flow for the particular altitude. Equivalent airspeed is equal to calibrated airspeed in standard atmosphere at sea level.

"Flap extended speed" means the highest speed permissible with wing flaps in a prescribed extended position.

"Flight crewmember" means a pilot, flight engineer, or flight navigator assigned to duty in an aircraft during flight time.

"Flight level" means a level of constant atmospheric pressure related to a reference datum of 29.92 inches of mercury. Each is stated in three digits that represent hundreds of feet. For example, flight level 250 represents a barometric altimeter indication of 25,000 feet; flight level 255, an indication of 25,500 feet.

"Flight plan" means specified information, relating to the intended flight of an aircraft, that is filed orally or in writing with air traffic control.

"Flight time" means the time from the moment the aircraft first moves under its own power, or on-tow, for the purpose of flight until the moment it comes to rest at the next point of landing. ("Block-to-Block" time.)

"Flight visibility" means the average forward horizontal distance, from the cockpit of an aircraft in flight, at which prominent unlighted objects may be seen and identified by day and prominent lighted objects may be seen and identified by night.

"Glider" means a heavier-than-air aircraft, that is supported in flight by the dynamic reaction of the air against its lifting surfaces and whose free flight does not depend principally on an engine.

"Ground visibility" means prevailing horizontal visibility near the earth's surface as reported by the United States National Weather Service or an accredited observer.

"Indicated airspeed" means the speed of an aircraft as shown on its pitot static airspeed indicator calibrated to reflect standard atmosphere adiabatic compressible flow at sea level uncorrected for airspeed system errors.

"Instrument" means a device using an internal mechanism to show visually or aurally the attitude, altitude, or operation of an aircraft or aircraft part. It includes electronic devices for automatically controlling an aircraft in flight.

"Kite" means a framework, covered with paper, cloth, metal, or other material, intended to be flown at the end of a rope or cable, and having as its only support the force of the wind moving past its surfaces.

"Landing gear extended speed" means the maximum speed at which an aircraft can be safely flown with the landing gear extended.

"Landing gear operating speed" means the maximum speed at which the landing gear can be safely extended or retracted.

"Lighter-than-air aircraft" means aircraft that can rise and remain suspended by using contained gas weighing less than the air that is displaced by the gas.

"Load factor" means the ratio of a specified load to the total weight of the aircraft. The specified load is expressed in terms of any of the following: aerodynamic forces, inertia forces, or ground or water reactions.

"Maintenance" means inspection, overhaul, repair, preservation, and the replacement of parts, but excludes preventive maintenance.

"Major alteration" means an alteration not listed in the aircraft, aircraft engine, or propeller specifications —
(1) That might appreciably affect weight, balance, structural strength, performance, powerplant operation, flight characteristics, or other qualities affecting airworthiness; or

(2) That is not done according to accepted practices or cannot be done by elementary operations.

"Major repair" means a repair —
(1) That, if improperly done, might appreciably affect weight, balance structural strength, performance, powerplant operation, flight characteristics, or other qualities affecting airworthiness; or
(2) That is not done according to accepted practices or cannot be done by elementary operations.

"Medical certificate" means acceptable evidence of physical fitness on a form prescribed by the Administrator.

"Minor alteration" means an alteration other than a major alternation.

"Minor repair" means a repair other than a major repair.

"Navigable airspace" means airspace at and above the minimum flight altitudes prescribed by or under this chapter, including airspace needed for safe takeoff and landing.

"Night" means the time between the end of evening civil twilight and the beginning of morning civil twilight, as published in the American Air Almanac, converted to local time.

"Operate," with respect to aircraft, means use, cause to use or authorize to use aircraft, for the purpose (except as provided in 91.10 of this chapter) of air navigation including the piloting of aircraft, with or without the right of legal control (as owner, lessee, or otherwise).

"Operational control," with respect to a flight, means the exercise of authority over initiating, conducting, or terminating a flight.

"Over-the-top" means above the layer of clouds or other obscuring phenomena forming the ceiling.

"Parachute" means a device used or intended to be used to retard the fall of a body or object through the air.

"Person" means an individual, firm, partnership, corporation, company, association, joint-stock association, or governmental entity. It includes a trustee, receiver, assignee, or similar representative of any of them.

"Pilotage" means navigation by visual reference to landmarks.

"Pilot in Command" means the pilot responsible for the operation and safety of the aircraft during flight who has been designated as pilot-in-command before or during flight and holds the appropriate category, class, and type rating.

"Positive control" means control of all air traffic, within designated airspace, by air traffic control.

"Preventive maintenance" means simple or minor preservation operations and the replacement of small standard parts not involving complex assembly operations.

"Prohibited area" means designated aispace within which the flight of aircraft is prohibited.

"Rating" means a statement that, as a part of a certificate, sets forth special conditions, privileges, or limitations.

"Restricted area" means airspace designated under Part 73 of this chapter within which the flight of aircraft, while not wholly prohibited, is subject to restriction.

"Show," unless the context otherwise requires, means to show to the satisfaction of the Administrator.

"Small aircraft" means aircraft of 12,500 pounds or less, maximum certificated takeoff weight.

"Special VFR conditions" mean meteorological conditions that are less than those required for basic VFR flight in controlled airspace in which some aircraft are permitted flight under visual flight rules.

"Special VFR operations" means aircraft operating in accordance with clearances within controlled airspace in meteorological conditions less than the basic VFR weather minima. Such operations must be requested by the pilot and approved by ATC.

"Standard atmosphere" means the atmosphere defined in *U. S. Standard Atmosphere, 1962* (Geopotential altitude tables).

"Time in service," with respect to maintenance time records, means the time from the moment an aircraft leaves the surface of the earth until it touches it at the next point of landing.

"Traffic pattern" means the traffic flow that is prescribed for aircraft landing at, taxiing on, or taking off from, an airport.

"True airspeed" means the airspeed of an aircraft relative to undisturbed air. True airspeed is equal to equivalent airspeed multiplied by $(po/p)^{1/2}$.

"Type"

    (1)   As used with respect to the certification, ratings, privileges, and limitations of airmen, means a specific make and basic model of aircraft, including modifications thereto that do not change its handling or flight characteristics. . .

    (2)   As used with respect to the certification of aircraft, means those aircraft which are similar in design. . .

"United States," in a geographical sense, means (1) the States, the District of Columbia, Puerto Rico, and the possessions, including the territorial waters, and (2) the airspace of those areas.

"VFR over-the-top," with respect to the operation of aircraft, means the operation of an aircraft over-the-top under VFR when it is not being operated on an IFR flight plan.

1.2 Abbreviations and symbols.

In Subchapters A through K of this chapter:

"ATC" means air traffic control.

"CAS" means calibrated airspeed.

"EAS" means equivalent airspeed.

"FAA" means Federal Aviation Administration.

"IAS" means indicated airspeed.

"IFR" means instrument flight rules.

"MSL" means mean sea level.

"TAS" means true airspeed.

"V_A" means design maneuvering speed.

"V_B" means design speed for maximum gust intensity.

"V_D" means design diving speed.

"V_F" means design flap speed.

"V_{FE}" means maximum flap extended speed.

"VFR" means visual flight rules.

"VHF" means very high frequency.

"V_{LE}" means maximum landing gear extended speed.

"V_{LO}" means maximum landing gear operating speed.

"V_{NE}" means never-exceed speed.

"VOR" means very high frequency omnirange station.

"VORTAC" means collocated VOR and TACAN.

"V_S" means the stalling speed or the minimum steady flight speed at which the airplane is controllable.

"V_{SO}" means the stalling speed or the minimum steady flight speed in the landing configuration.

1.3 Rules of construction.

(a) In Subchapters A through K of this chapter, unless the context requires otherwise:
  (1) Words importing the singular include the plural;
  (2) Words importing the plural include the singular; and
  (3) Words importing the masculine gender include the feminine.

(b) In subchapters A through K of this chapter, the word:
  (1) "Shall" is used in an imperative sense;
  (2) "May" is used in a permissive sense to state authority or permission to do the act prescribed, and the words "no person may. . ." or "a person may not. . ." mean that no person is required, authorized, or permitted to do the act prescribed; and
  (3) "Includes" means "includes but is not limited to."

(Authority: 1.1 to 1.3 issued under sec. 313(a) of the Federal Aviation Act of 1958 (49 U.S.C. 1354(a)).

SELECTED REGULATION REFERENCES

FAR PARTS 43, 61, 71, AND 91

It is recommended that pilots review up-to-date copies of FAR Parts 43, 61, 71, and 91. After becoming generally familiar with pertinent parts of the regulations, it will be easy to look up any rule when necessary.

Part 43, *Maintenance, Preventive Maintenance, Rebuilding and Alteration*, is an important regulation. It describes the qualifications needed to perform various types of maintenance, the intervals at which it is required, and the maintenance records which are necessary. The items which may be done by the holder of a pilot's certificate on an aircraft which that person owns or operates are listed. The pilot should also know how to insure that the required maintenance done by others is up-to-date.

Part 61 is titled *Certification: Pilots and Flight Instructors*. It deals with the requirements for obtaining pilot certificates or ratings, and medical certificates. Also included are the rules pilots must follow in keeping logbooks correctly and in maintaining themselves legally current for the type of flying they are doing. The sections of FAR Part 61 which are most applicable are as follows:

1, 2, 3, 5, 11, 13, 14, 15, 16, 17, 19, 23, 25, 27, 29, 31, 33, 35, 37, 39, 41, 43, 45, 47, 49, 51, 53, 56, 57, 59, 60, 61, 63, 69, 71, 73, 75, 81, 83, 85, 87, 89, 93, 95, 102, 103, 105, 107, 109, 113, 121, 123, 125, 127, 129, 133, 181, 183, 185, 187, 189, 191, 193, 195, 197, 199.

Part 71 deals with controlled airspace, and the following sections should be studied:

1, 9, 31, 33, 41, 51, 61, 71, 75.

Part 91 contains the operating, flight, and maintenance rules and is extremely important. The most applicable sections are:

1, 3, 7, 9, 13, 15, 17, 101, 103, 107, 109(a), 111, 113, 119, 121, 123, 125, 127, 129, 130, 131, 133, 135, 137, 138, 139, 141, 143, 155, 157, 159, 173, 203, 209, 211, 213, 215, 303, 305, 307, 309, 311, 313, 319, 401, 403, 405, 407, 409, 413, 417, 419, 715, 903.

NATIONAL TRANSPORTATION SAFETY BOARD PART 830

In addition to the FARs, pilots must be familiar with NTSB Part 830, *Rules Pertaining to the Notification and Reporting of Aircraft Accidents or Incidents and Overdue Aircraft, and Preservation of Aircraft Wreckage, Mail, Cargo, and Records*. Subpart A deals with the applicability of this part and appropriate definitions. Subpart B outlines the types of accidents and incidents for which notification is required and the items of information which should be included in the notification. Subpart C contains the regulations for the preservation of aircraft wreckage, mail, cargo, and records, and Subpart D details the written reports which must be submitted.

Copies of FARs and NTSB regulations may be obtained from the U.S. Government Printing Office, either issued current to the date of purchase, or with a continuing subscription, which assures that revisions to the rules will be sent as they are made. Private companies, such as Jeppesen Sanderson, Inc., also publish many of these regulations.

Other government publications of use in studying for sailplane ratings are contained in advisory circulars. They are available from the U.S. Government Printing Office.

Flight Publications and Airspace

INTRODUCTION The national airspace system has expanded steadily to keep pace with the rapidly developing aviation community. Pilot procedures and knowledge requirements are continually changing. New airports are opening, old ones are closing, new regulations replace old ones, new factors affecting safety of flight are uncovered, while new flight techniques are established. These are just a few reasons why it is important that a pilot become familiar with the national airspace system and aeronautical information publications, including the *Aeronautical Information Manual*.

SOURCES OF AVIATION INFORMATION

Sailplane pilots planning cross-country flights need information about various safety factors. Several sources are available; they complement and supplement each other. Aeronautical charts are the primary source of information for navigation within the national airspace system. Figure 7-1 illustrates additional sources of aeronautical information, including *Notices to Airman, the Aeronautical Information Manual,* and the *Airport/Facility Directory.*

AERONAUTICAL CHARTS

The aeronautical chart is the primary tool for planning and conducting a cross-country flight. From the information on an aeronautical chart, it is possible to determine the course and distance between points on the ground, facilities available at airports, checkpoints for navigation purposes, radio aids to navigation, and intervening obstacles such as terrain, man-made obstructions, and airspace restrictions. A complete discussion of aeronautical charts is contained in a later chapter.

NATIONAL NOTICES TO AIRMEN SYSTEM

Information that may affect the safety of a flight is provided in *Notices to Airmen* (NOTAMs). These notices contain information on such items as maintenance being performed at an airport, changes to aeronautical charts, or changes to the Federal Aviation Regulations. Notices concerning short duration items, such as an inoperative radio aid, are carried at the end of surface aviation weather reports.

AERONAUTICAL INFORMATION MANUAL

The *Aeronautical Information Manual* (AIM) contains basic flight information and ATC procedures. It is designed to present the basic information required to fly in the U.S. National Airspace system,

Fig. 7-1. Aeronautical Information Publications

factors affecting safety of flight, health and medical facts of interest to pilots, and emergency procedures. In addition, a standardized glossary of aeronautical terms is provided.

AIRPORT/FACILITY DIRECTORY

The Airport/Facility Directory is designed for use with aeronautical charts and covers the conterminous United States, Puerto Rico, and the Virgin Islands. All of these directories contain information on airports and their facilities, communications, navigation aids, FSS/Weather Service telephone numbers, ATC frequencies, part-time control zones, and pertinent special notices essential to air navigation.

The Airport/Facility Directory also lists changes to aeronautical charts which occur between editions, as well as areas and times of parachute jumping activity. Checkpoints and test facilities for VOR receivers also are listed. Locations where Enroute Flight Advisory Service weather information may be obtained by radio are listed, as well as navaids which transmit Transcribed Weather Broadcasts (TWEBs). The volumes of the Airport/ Facility Directory for different sections of the U. S. are available by subscription.

AIRSPACE UTILIZATION

Aviation was not as popular in its infancy as it is today. In the beginning, the airspace was open to virtually anyone who had enough adventurous spirit to attempt the thrill of flight. Today, however, the airspace is used by every conceivable type of aircraft. To accommodate the many types of aircraft with vast differences in performance, the airspace has been divided

into various segments. This is called airspace utilization. The three segments of airspace to be discussed are uncontrolled, controlled, and special use.

UNCONTROLLED AIRSPACE

Uncontrolled, or Class G, airspace is that area which has not been designated as Class A, B, C, D, or E airspace and is essentially uncontrolled by ATC. Although air traffic control does not have the responsibility or authority to exercise control over aircraft in Class G airspace, several regulations apply to flight operations conducted in this important airspace segment.

VFR weather minimums in uncontrolled airspace are shown in figure 7-2. Normally, all uncontrolled, or Class G, airspace terminates at the base of Class E airspace at 700 or 1,200 feet AGL, or at 14,500 feet MSL.

CONTROLLED AIRSPACE

Controlled airspace means an airspace of defined dimensions within which air traffic control service is provided to IFR flights and to VFR flights in accordance with the airspace classification. Controlled airspace is a generic term that covers Class A, Class B, Class C, Class D, and Class E airspace. Class F airspace is not designated in the United States. VFR flight is permitted in all controlled airspace except Class A. Basic VFR flight visibilities and cloud clearance minimums are increased in controlled airspace, as shown in figure 7-2. You may want to refer back to this illustration during the following discussion of airspace reclassification.

All aircraft conducting flights within the United States must meet special equipment requirements. At altitudes above 10,000 feet MSL (excluding 2,500 feet AGL and below), the aircraft must be equipped with a 4096-code transponder

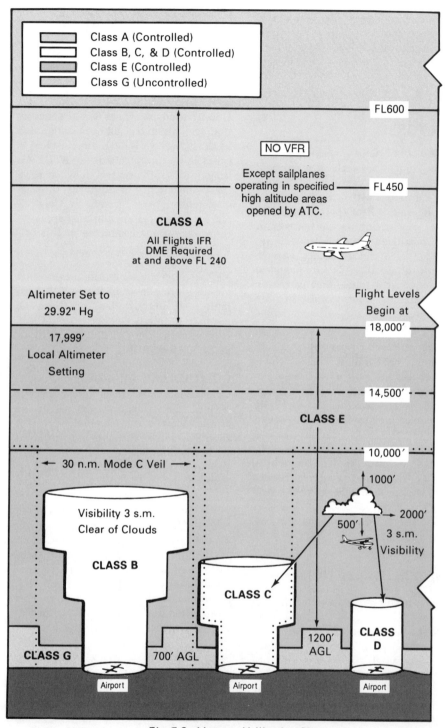

Fig. 7-2. Airspace Utilization Plan

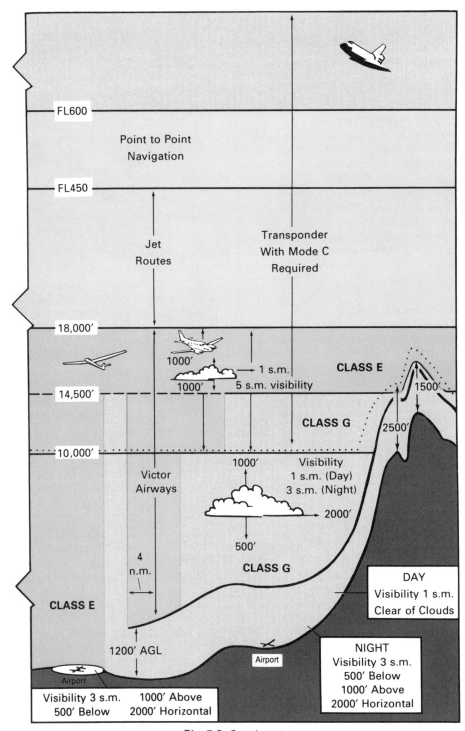

Fig. 7-2. Continued

with automatic pressure altitude reporting equipment. Exceptions to this rule are described in FAR 91.215. One of the exceptions is that sailplanes operating up to 18,000 feet are not required to have a transponder.

CLASS A AIRSPACE

Within the conterminous United States, Class A airspace extends from 18,000 feet MSL to flight level 600 (approximately 60,000 feet MSL). High altitude "windows" are commonly used to permit VFR sail-plane flights in Class A airspace without the requirement for transponders, flight plans, and assigned altitudes. ATC permission to use the windows must be obtained before entering the airspace.

CLASS B AIRSPACE

Class B airspace has been designated at some of the country's major airports to provide ATC separation for all arriving and departing traffic at the primary airport, as well as other airports in the terminal area. Pilot participation is mandatory, and an ATC clearance must be received before entering Class B airspace. The pilot and equipment requirements for conducting operations in Class B airspace are specified in FAR Part 91. The typical shape of Class B airspace is shown in figure 7-3.

CLASS C AIRSPACE

Class C airspace has been designated at many other airports where ATC provides radar vectoring and sequencing on a full time basis for all IFR and VFR aircraft. Participation in Class C service is mandatory and all aircraft must establish and maintain radio contact with ATC. Unless otherwise authorized by ATC, communications must be established prior to entering Class C airspace and maintained while operating within the area. Aircraft departing the primary airport must contact ATC before departure, while those departing a satellite

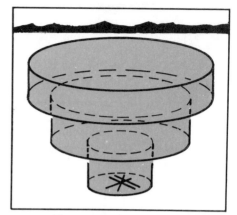

Fig. 7-3. Class B Airspace

airport must contact ATC as soon as practicable after takeoff. Operating rules for Class C airspace are contained in FAR Part 91. Typical dimensions for Class C airspace are shown in figure 7-4.

CLASS D AIRSPACE

Class D airspace has been designated at airports with operating control towers which are not associated with Class B or C airspace. Generally, the airspace from the surface to 2,500 feet above the airport elevation (charted in MSL) is included as shown in figure 7-5.

The "87" in brackets means the ceiling of Class D airspace is at 8,700 feet MSL. This is based on the field elevation of 6,156 feet (rounded to 6,200) and added to 2,500 feet for a ceiling of 8,700 feet MSL. The lateral dimensions of the surface area of Class D airspace are indicated by the blue segmented line on sectional charts.

Unless otherwise authorized, each person must establish two-way radio communications with the ATC facility providing air traffic services prior to entering Class D airspace and, thereafter, maintain those communications while in the airspace. No separation services are provided to VFR aircraft. The configuration of each Class D airspace area is

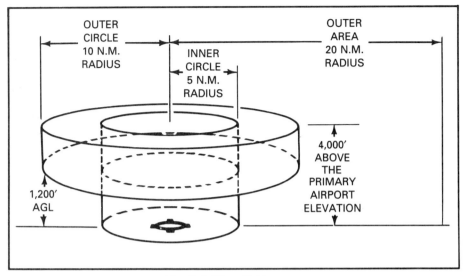

Fig. 7-4. Class C Airspace

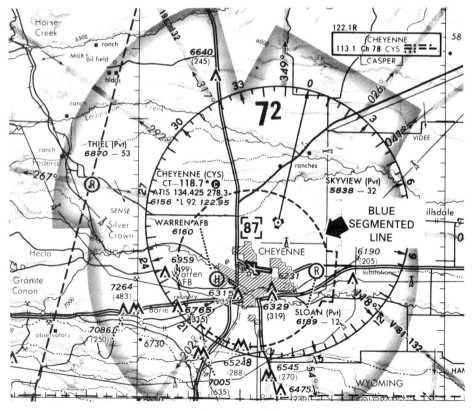

Fig. 7-5. Class D Airspace

individually tailored and when instrument procedures are published, the airspace will normally be designed to contain the procedures. Arrival extensions for instrument approach procedures may be Class D or Class E airspace.

CLASS E AIRSPACE

Several types of airspace may be designated as Class E. Generally, if the airspace is not Class A, Class B, Class C, or Class D, and it is controlled airspace, it is Class E airspace. Class E airspace extends upward from either the surface or a designated altitude to the overlying or adjacent controlled airspace. When designated as a surface area, the airspace will be configured to contain all instrument procedures. Also in this class are Federal airways, airspace beginning at either 700 or 1,200 feet AGL used to transition to or from the terminal or enroute environment, and enroute domestic, and offshore airspace areas

designated below 18,000 feet MSL. Unless designated at a lower altitude, Class E airspace begins at 14,500 feet MSL over the United States, including that airspace overlying the waters within 12 nautical miles of the coast of the 48 contiguous States and Alaska. Class E airspace does not include the airspace 18,000 MSL or above.

The lateral dimensions of the surface area of Class E airspace designated for airports which have approved instrument approaches are shown on sectional charts with a magenta segmented line. The example in figure 7-6 shows Class E airspace extending upward from the surface around Perry Stokes Airport near Trinidad. Notice that a Federal airway, V389, passes directly over the airport. This is an example of one type of Class E airspace overlying another. To the east, notice the distinctive boundary which identifies additional Class E airspace beginning at 8,500 feet MSL.

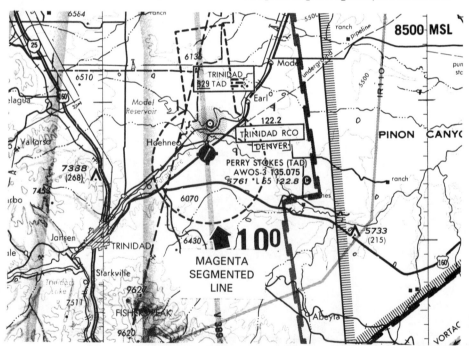

Fig. 7-6. Class E Airspace

TRSA

Terminal Radar Service Areas (TRSAs) are designated at several terminal locations. At these locations, TRSA service provides separation between all participating VFR aircraft and all IFR aircraft operating within the designated airspace. Pilot participation is urged but not mandatory. If a pilot does not want TRSA service, the phase "Negative TRSA Service" or a similar comment should be made on initial contact with approach control or ground control. The lateral dimensions of TRSA airspace are depicted on sectional charts by a solid black boundary with the effective altitudes printed as shown in figure 7-7. The primary airport(s) within the TRSA become Class D airspace. The remaining portion of the TRSA overlies other controlled airspace which is normally Class E airspace beginning at 700 or 1,200 feet and established to transition between the enroute and terminal environment.

SPECIAL USE AIRSPACE

Some activities conducted within the airspace or on the surface require limita-tions on aircraft operations. These special airspace segments, which are shown on sectional charts, include prohibited, restricted, warning, military operations, and alert areas.

Except for MOAs, the numerical designation of a special use airspace area is preceded by a letter designating its type. For example, "P" indicates prohibited; "R," restricted; "W," warning, and "A" alert. A list of the prohibited, restricted, warning, and alert areas depicted on a given sectional chart is printed in the chart margin. The appropriate authority to contact if transition through a restricted or warning area is desired also is provided.

PROHIBITED AREAS

Prohibited areas are portions of the airspace within which the flight of aircraft is not permitted. Such areas are generally established for reasons of national security or national welfare. An example of a prohibited area is the area surrounding the White House and the Congress in Washington, D.C., as seen in figure 7-8.

RESTRICTED AREAS

Restricted areas include the airspace within which the flight of aircraft, while not wholly prohibited, is subject to certain limitations. These areas denote the existence of unusual, often invisible, hazards to aircraft, such as artillery firing, aerial gunnery, or the flight of guided missiles. Penetration of restricted areas without authorization

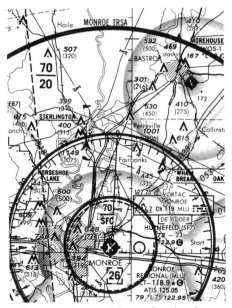

Fig. 7-7. Terminal Radar Service Area

Fig. 7-8. Prohibited Area

from the controlling agency may be extremely hazardous, as well as a violation of FARs. An example of a restricted area as it appears on a sectional chart is shown in figure 7-9.

MILITARY OPERATIONS AREAS

The sailplane pilot should be aware of *military operations areas,* such as those depicted in figure 7-10, and the potential hazards created by numerous high speed jet aircraft. These areas are shown on sectional charts and current information concerning altitudes and hours of operation may be obtained from any flight service station within 100 miles.

MOAs are identified by names such as "Tarheel' and "Reese 4." Flight within an MOA is not restricted for VFR aircraft, but pilots are urged to exercise extreme caution. Both the pilots of aircraft participating in activities within the area and pilots transiting the MOA are fully responsible for collision avoidance.

ALERT AREAS

Alert area airspace may contain a high volume of pilot training or an unusual type of aerial activity. Flight within alert areas is not restricted, but pilots are urged to exercise extreme caution.

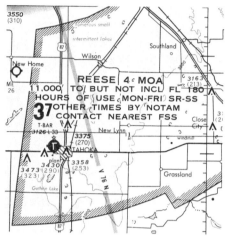

Fig. 7-10. Military Operations Area

MILITARY TRAINING ROUTES

MTRs, *Military Training Routes,* are marked VR (VFR) or IR (IFR) on sectional charts. They normally occur below 10,000 feet. Information about altitudes and hours of operation can be obtained from any FSS within 100 miles.

This chapter has presented a summary of information from various flight publications, and a discussion of the national airspace system. Further study of this information will help build your knowledge and confidence level.

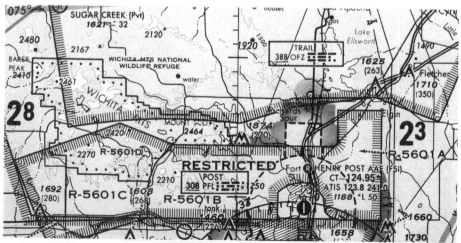

Fig. 7-9. Restricted Area

SOARING

Aeronautical Charts and Navigation

INTRODUCTION For convenience, the linear representations of the earth's spherical surface have been flattened and depicted on charts. Familiarity with charts and the ability to interpret and use the information they provide are skills essential to navigation.

Aerial navigation consists of safely flying an aircraft along a predetermined course. Accuracy is extremely important since inaccurate navigation can make completion of a cross-country flight difficult, if not impossible.

This chapter will cover the charts used for navigation and the types of navigation used today. Primary emphasis will be placed on two types of navigation — pilotage and dead reckoning.

Chapter Eight

PROJECTIONS

The techniques used in converting a portion of the earth's spherical surface to a flat, small-scale representation are known as *projections*. In the process of flattening, however, there is a certain amount of distortion of the surface represented. Figure 8-1 illustrates that an orange peel, like the earth, cannot be flattened without distortion.

Fig. 8-1. Flattening Produces Distortion

LATITUDE AND LONGITUDE

Each projection technique attempts to minimize distortion; however, each has its limitations. The principal map projection used in air navigation and discussed in this chapter is the *Lambert Conformal Conic* shown in figure 8-2.

To locate positions on the earth's surface, or on any representation of the earth's surface, some method of referencing an exact point must be used. The method accepted worldwide

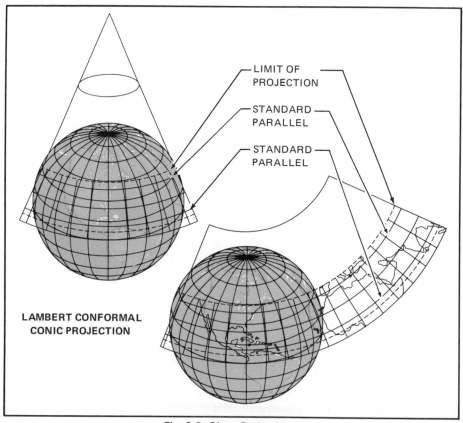

LIMIT OF
PROJECTION

STANDARD
PARALLEL

STANDARD
PARALLEL

LAMBERT CONFORMAL
CONIC PROJECTION

Fig. 8-2. Chart Projections

uses a system based on lines of *latitude* and *longitude*. The *Equator* is a line running east and west around the earth midway between the poles. Other lines around the earth parallel to the Equator are called *parallels*, or *lines of latitude*, as illustrated in figure 8-3. The Equator is labeled 0° latitude and the other lines of latitude are numbered in degrees from 0 to 90 north and south from the Equator.

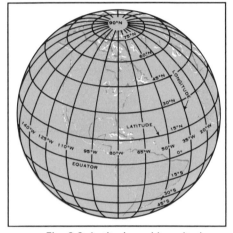

Fig. 8-3. Latitude and Longitude

Meridians, or *lines of longitude*, are drawn from pole to pole. The direction of these lines is always true north or south, as seen in figure 8-3. These lines are numbered starting at the *Prime Meridian*, which is the line of longitude passing through the observatory at Greenwich, England. The Prime Meridian is labeled 0° of longitude and the other meridians are numbered in degrees east and west of the Prime Meridian. There are 360° of longitude; 180° are labeled east longitude and the remaining 180° are labeled west longitude. The line of longitude labeled 180° is called the *International Date Line* and is on the opposite side of the world from the Prime Meridian.

The lines of longitude and latitude are printed and labeled on the chart. Each degree interval is divided into 60 equal segments called *minutes*. Minutes are indicated by the symbol, ('), and are marked along the lines of longitude and latitude in 30 minute, 5 minute, and 1 minute segments, as illustrated in figure 8-4.

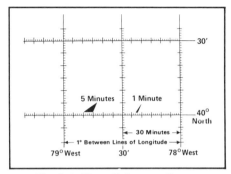

Fig. 8-4. Chart Reference System

With the system of lines just discussed, any location may be designated by *geographical coordinates* or, in other words, the intersection of the lines of longitude and latitude on the chart. In figure 8-5, the coordinates of a gliderport are given as 40°15'N, 78°18'W. In this example, the gliderport is located 40° and 15' north of the zero line of latitude, or Equator, and 78° and 18' west of the Prime Meridian.

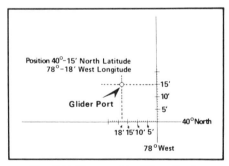

Fig. 8-5. Geographical Coordinates

THE EARTH'S TRUE NORTH POLE AND MAGNETIC NORTH POLE

The position of the earth's True North Pole, or point about which it would appear to rotate if viewed from space, and the position of the earth's Magnetic North Pole are not the same. In fact, the Magnetic North Pole is located on Prince of Wales Island, Canada, approximately 1,000 miles south of the geographic, or True North Pole. The problem introduced into navigational planning and piloting technique is simply this: navigational charts are oriented toward *true north* and the compass needle in the sailplane points to the *Magnetic North Pole*. This angular difference between the direction of true north and the direction of magnetic north is called *magnetic variation*. Figure 8-6 shows that the position of the aircraft relative to the earth's surface will determine whether the magnetic variation is to the east or

to the west of true north. When the aircraft's position on the earth is in alignment with true north and magnetic north, no variation exists.

Most charts show variation with *isogonic lines*, which are lines connecting points of equal magnetic variation. When flying on a true north heading, the aircraft compass, as seen in figure 8-7, would read 348° rather than 360° because the magnetic variation is 12° east (of true north). To fly south at the same point, the aircraft compass would read 168° rather than 180° because the variation at any point is always constant, regardless of the sailplane's heading.

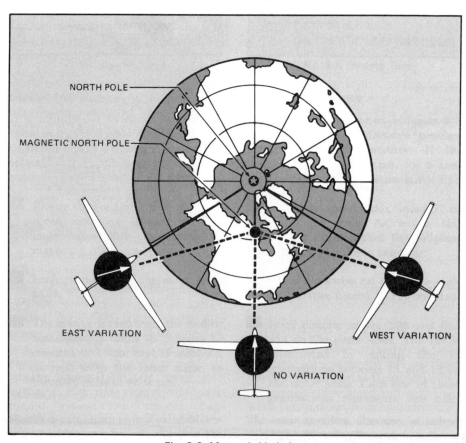

Fig. 8-6. Magnetic Variation

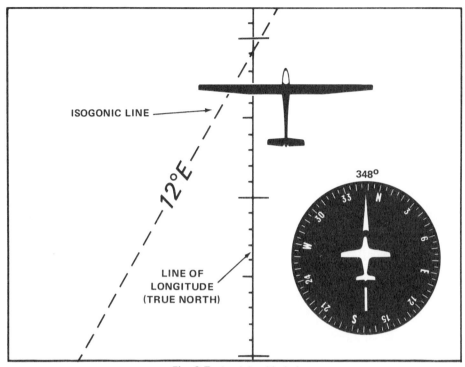

Fig. 8-7. Applying Variation

MEASURING DIRECTION IN DEGREES OF THE COMPASS

Direction is measured in degrees clockwise from north. The *compass rose* in figure 8-8 shows the relationship for the basic points of the compass and direction in degrees. For example, north is 360° (0°), east is 090°, south is 180°, northwest 315°, and so on. If 0°, or north, is oriented with the True North Pole, then *true* direction results. If 0° is oriented with magnetic north, then *magnetic* direction results.

CHARTS

Aeronautical charts are a necessary part of a pilot's equipment for any flight away from the local area. The type of chart used for flight by visual references shows all significant topography (terrain, natural and man-made features) and most aeronautical

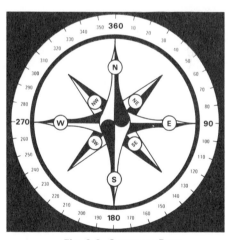

Fig. 8-8. Compass Rose

information. Pilots should be familiar with the charts described here in their relative order of importance.

Sectional charts are the charts most commonly used by soaring pilots. Each

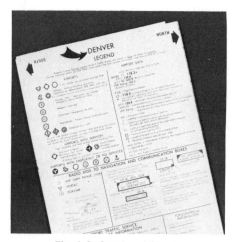

Fig. 8-9. Sectional Chart

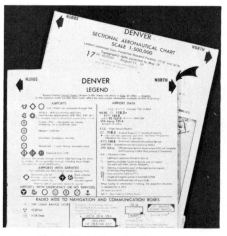

Fig. 8-10. Using the Sectional

sectional chart shows a portion of the United States and is identified by the name of a principal city such as the Denver Sectional shown in figure 8-9. The scale on the sectional chart is 1:500,000, or about eight statute miles to one inch.

The convenient size of the folded sectional chart provides for easy handling, storage, and identification, especially while in flight. The sectionals are printed back to back, making it possible to cover the 48 contiguous states with 37 charts. The "NORTH" side of the chart is visible when the chart is extended to the right from the legend margin in the direction of the arrow, as depicted in figure 8-10. The chart must be turned upside down to use the "SOUTH" side. It also should be extended in the direction of the arrow.

Some sectional charts include plotting instructions, as shown in figure 8-11, for using the overlap feature to plot to a point on the other side of the chart. A direct course is easily plotted between points on the north and south panels using this method.

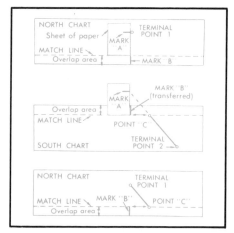

Fig. 8-11. Plotting Instructions

The name of each sectional chart is displayed prominently at the top of the chart legend panel, illustrated by item 1 in figure 8-12. The date when the chart becomes effective, as well as the date the chart is considered obsolete for use in navigation are found on the same panel, as shown in figure 8-12, item 2. It is important to check the dates on the charts so the most current publication is used.

World Aeronautical Charts (WAC) are similar to sectional charts except that

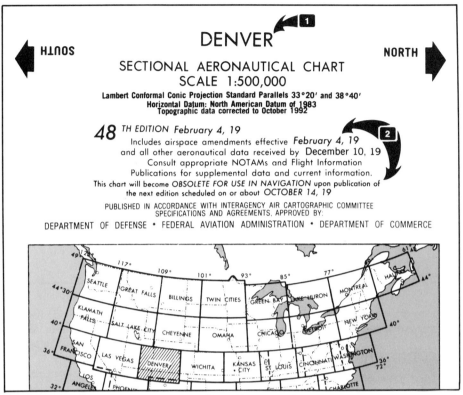

Fig. 8-12. Chart Name and Date

WAC charts are drawn to a scale which is one-half that of a sectional chart. WAC charts use a 1:1,000,000 scale, which is about 16 statute miles to 1 inch and, therefore, omit some detail. WAC charts normally are used for navigation of higher performance airplanes or for long trips where frequent change of charts enroute is bothersome. Some soaring pilots like to use these charts for long cross-country flights that would cross two or more sectionals. They are also excellent charts for back-up purposes. Each WAC chart is identified by a number, as seen in figure 8-13. These charts are revised and issued once a year.

VFR terminal area charts are large-scale charts (1:250,000) for VFR navigation in the vicinity of Class B air-

space. These charts provide a great amount of detail within a limited area and are used by sailplane

Fig. 8-13. World Aeronautical Chart

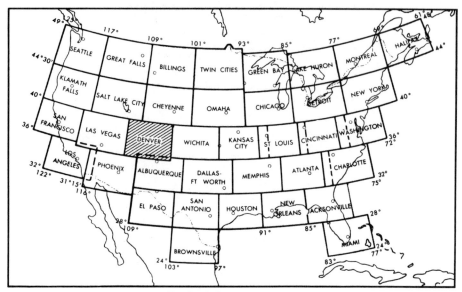

Fig. 8-14. Legend of Charts

pilots to stay out of Class B airspace. They are revised every six months.

SELECTING CHARTS

The front panel of each chart has a map of the United States showing the city names and areas of coverage, as illustrated in figure 8-14. This is the Denver Sectional. It is wise to carry additional charts of the surrounding area during flight, particularly if the course is near the edge of the chart. Otherwise, in the event of an unplanned course change, deteriorating weather, or adverse winds, a flight may have to be continued over unfamiliar terrain without the necessary charts.

CHART INTERPRETATION AND USE OF SYMBOLS

Sectional charts are printed in several colors, depending on the range of elevations encompassed by the chart. Terrain elevations below 1,000 feet are shown by light green; 1,000 to 2,000 feet by darker green; 2,000 to 3,000 feet by yellow; and elevations above 3,000 feet are shown by various shades of

brown, as shown in figure 8-15, item 1. The highest terrain elevation on a particular chart is shown at the top of the color band legend (item 2). The legend for certain elevations also is specified (item 3), and contour intervals are shown (item 4).

Water (lakes, rivers, etc) is shown in blue. Roads are depicted by magenta lines; heavy magenta lines indicate principal highways, and narrower lines indicate less heavily traveled roads. The relative size and shape of cities is indicated by a yellow area outlined in black. Yellow squares represent towns; small towns, villages, and hamlets are represented by small circles.

SYMBOLS USED ON THE SECTIONAL CHART

It is recommended that the chart excerpt in figure 8-16 be referred to each time a new number is encountered to obtain the greatest benefit from the following explanation of sectional chart symbols. This should help reinforce the meaning of each symbol represented.

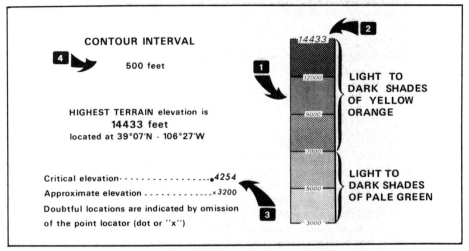

Fig. 8-15. Elevation Legend

1 The information enclosed within the magenta box describes the name, frequency, two-letter identifier, and Morse code for the Idder nondirectional radio beacon (NDB). The magenta color is used *for all* low-frequency radio information.

2 The magenta dot pattern represents the location of the Idder nondirectional radio beacon.

3 Maximum elevation figures are centered in the areas completely bounded by *ticked* lines of latitude and longitude and are represented in thousands and hundreds of feet, including elevations of vertical obstructions. The numbers "08" are used to represent the elevation of 800 feet.

4 A power transmission line and its supporting towers are represented by this symbol.

5 A shaded light blue color represents a body of water. The black line on the southeast end of the Bundick Lake represents a man-made dam.

6 The terrain elevation at the location of the dot is 175 feet mean sea level (MSL). This is the highest elevation in the immediate area.

7 The inverted "V" represents an obstruction whose height at the top is less than 1,000 feet above ground level (AGL). The number 374 represents the elevation of this obstruction above mean sea level, and the number 243 in parentheses represents the height above ground level.

8 Shaded blue lines represent rivers or streams.

9 The number "100" represents the MSL altitude of the adjacent contour line, or line connecting points of equal elevation.

10 A lookout tower, which is air marked for identification, is shown here. The site number is 90 and the base of the tower is 89 feet MSL.

11 The open-air theater symbol is on the southeast side of the city of Lake Charles.

12 This is a restricted-use, or private airport, not open to the general public. It may be used as a landmark or an emergency landing site.

13 The HOTROCK 2 MOA is shown by a solid magenta line with cross-hatched lines extending into the MOA. A table in the chart margin lists the name, altitude and time of use, and the controlling agency for all MOAs shown on the chart.

14 This line of longitude is 93° west of the Prime Meridian in Greenwich, England.

15 This symbol represents an isogonic line (line of equal magnetic variation) which is 4°30' east on this chart.

16 The location of small towns or villages, such as Reeves, is shown with a circle.

17 Shaft mines or quarries are represented by two cross pick axes. Just below this symbol is a group of obstructions 1,000 feet AGL or higher.

18 The Lake Charles TRSA is shown by concentric black circles. The numbers in the segment between the two outer circles indicate that TRSA service is available between 2,000 and 7,000 feet.

19 Interstate freeways are depicted with a double magenta line.

20 The shape and relative size of the town of Sulpher is represented by the area outlined in yellow.

21 The black dots represent storage tanks.

22 The line with single crossbars represents a single-track railroad. Abandoned railroads are shown by a broken line.

23 The letters "FSS" indicate that a flight service station is available on the field at the Beauregard Parish Airport.

24 The Lake Charles Control Tower frequency is 120.7 MHz. When an FAA control tower is available, the airport name will be printed in *blue*.

25 The dashed blue line surrounding the Lake Charles Airport defines the boundaries of Class D airspace.

26 This symbol represents a VORTAC station.

27 The blue box contains information on the Lake Charles VORTAC; frequency 113.4. The flight service station transmits and receives on 122.3.

28 The solid black square is used to represent a variety of landmarks. In this case it is a pumping station.

29 Oil wells are indicated here by a small, open circle.

30 The Welsh Airport is 18 feet above sea level, has lighting for night operations, and a runway that is 2,700 feet long. The Common Traffic Advisory Frequency (CTAF) of 122.8 MHz is followed by a circle containing a "C." At nontower airports the CTAF circle is magenta while blue is used at airports with parttime control towers.

31 The airport information and symbol are printed in magenta indicating that a control tower is *not* available. An airport with a pictorial runway representation has at least one paved runway which is 1,500 feet or

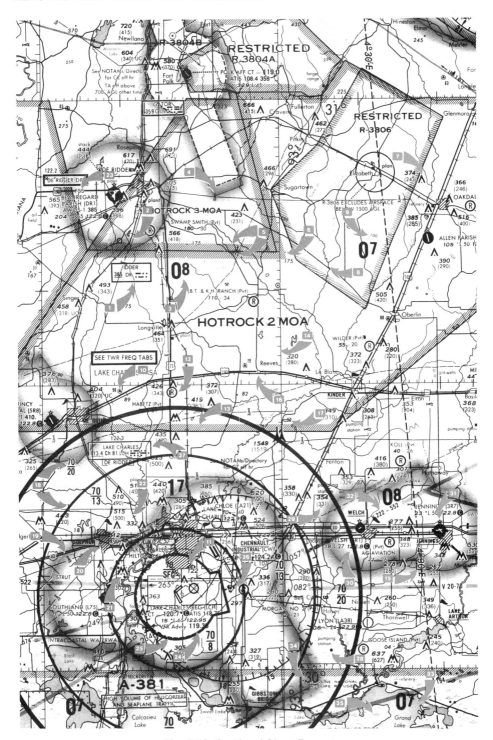

Fig. 8-16. Sectional Chart Excerpt

more in length. The star above the airport symbol indicates the presence of a rotating beacon.

32 The airway extending northeast from the Lake Charles VORTAC on the 57° radial is V-222-552. This VHF airway connects two navigational facilities.

33 Large bodies of water provide excellent VFR checkpoints.

34 The numerals indicate that this east-west line of latitude is 30° north of the Equator.

35 Swamps and marshes are depicted by horizontal blue lines interspersed with short vertical dashes suggesting clumps of marsh grass common in such areas.

NAVIGATION

Several factors come into play when the normal ground references surrounding home base disappear from sight on a cross-country flight. The first is to find and use the rising columns of air that enable the flight to be continued. The second is knowing where the flight is going. This section will discuss the means of navigation available to the sailplane pilot. The methods used to navigate a sailplane on a cross-country are demanding, but certainly not impossible, as proven by the many pilots who succeed daily.

The basic types of navigation used by soaring pilots are pilotage and dead reckoning. Pilotage is the means of navigating by visual reference to landmarks, and is the type most commonly used on cross-country flights. Dead reckoning is the determination of position from the record of courses flown, the distance covered, and the known or estimated drift. A third type, radio navigation, while not

commonly used in soaring, should be understood by commercial glider pilot applicants. Radio navigation uses fixed transmitting stations to determine flight position.

PILOTAGE

Pilotage adds precision to dead reckoning navigation. Pilotage is the art of fixing an aircraft's position with the aid of a map or chart; dead reckoning computations can then be used to predict some future position along the line of flight by computed time and distance. There is a chance of becoming lost if too much time is allowed to pass without fixing the aircraft's position on a chart while navigating by pilotage in a powered aircraft.

The sailplane pilot must be even more attentive than the power pilot to prevent loss of orientation while searching for lift, spiraling in a thermal, watching the variometer, and all the other attention-demanding tasks required to keep the sailplane airborne. It is easy to become so engrossed in gaining altitude that the landmarks on the ground lose any resemblance to those on the chart.

CHECKPOINTS

To perform accurate pilotage procedures with dead reckoning navigation, visible checkpoints or landmarks are necessary in establishing the aircraft's position. A checkpoint is good only if it provides usable information. It is important that the checkpoint have one or more distinctive, easily recognizable features. A peculiar bend in a road or river, an odd-shaped town or lake, the highest hill or mountain top in the area, or an airport with a specific runway layout may be good choices. Checkpoints should be

GOOD CHECKPOINTS	POOR CHECKPOINTS
MOUNTAINOUS AREAS	
The pilot should look for prominent peaks, passes, gorges and ridge lines. Transmission lines, railroads, bridges, highways and lookout stations are excellent checkpoints.	Smaller ridges and peaks are sometimes hard to see and will be similar in size and shape.
COASTAL AREAS	
Look for unusual features of the coast line. Note positions of towns, cities and lighthouses and make use of whatever radio aids are available.	Coast lines without prominent features.
SEASONAL CHANGES	
Use unusually shaped wooded areas in the winter. Dry lakes and dry riverbeds if they contrast with the surrounding terrain.	Frozen lakes and open country in the winter usually are poor. In desert sections of the country, small lakes and rivers may be dried up in the summer, and in wet seasons may be larger and will possibly change shape.
HEAVILY POPULATED AREAS	
Large and small cities with definite shapes and with outstanding checkpoints such as rivers, lakes, speedways, railroad yards, underpasses, race tracks, grain elevators and stadiums.	Small cities and towns that are close together and with no definite shape are sometimes hard to locate.
OPEN AREAS — FARM COUNTRY	
Look for any city, town or village with easily identified structures or prominent terrain features. Prominent paved highways, large railroads, race tracks, fairgrounds, factories, bridges and underpasses make excellent checkpoints.	Farms, private airstrips, small villages rather close together are sometimes hard to identify from the air.
FORESTED AREAS	
The most prominent checkpoints will be transmission lines and railroad right-of-ways, roads, highways, cities and towns. In some instances, forest lookout towers and marked terrain features make excellent checkpoints.	Extended forest areas with few breaks or outstanding characteristics of terrain. Trails and small roads without cleared right-of-ways are difficult to identify.

Fig. 8-17. Checkpoints

within several miles of the intended course at convenient intervals — 5 to 10 miles apart.

Checkpoints should be selected prior to flight. The chart and its legend should be studied to find which ones are most suitable. Time over the next checkpoint can be estimated by dead reckoning navigation, or the computation of time and distance in flight while cruising between thermals. Comparison of time and visual observation of checkpoints make it easy to locate the exact position of the aircraft along the true course line and also to compute groundspeed. In some parts of the country, section lines can be used very effectively for maintaining alignment with the projected flight path by comparing the angle of interception between the sailplane and section line to determine drift or track across the ground. Figure 8-17 describes both good and poor checkpoints to be used for pilotage.

RADIO NAVIGATION — VOR

In the late 1940's, a system of navigation was developed called the *very high frequency omnidirectional range* (VOR). Today, there are approximately 900 VOR stations in the United States operated by the Federal Aviation Administration, state agencies, and private operators.

VOR RADIALS

A VOR station transmits beams called *radials* outward in every direction, as shown in figure 8-18. An airborne VOR receiver is used to detect these radiated signals and indicate the aircraft's exact position, enabling a pilot to follow a radial to or from a VOR.

Each radial is numbered according to its *bearing from* the station. A compass

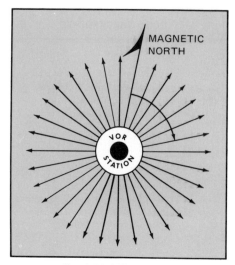

Fig. 8-18. VOR Radials

rose is drawn around each VOR on a chart, with the 0° radial pointed toward magnetic north. Thus, the 090° radial of a VOR represents a magnetic course of 090° away from the station. It is located 90° clockwise from the 0° radial. The radials are all magnetic courses and many are used to form the *Victor airways* connecting most VOR's.

VOR NAVIGATION

The VOR is the most popular and easiest to use of the various radio navigational aids. Figure 8-19 shows a close-up view of a modern navigation/communication (nav/com) radio and VOR indicator. The radio is crystal-tuned and has separate volume controls and positive-action squelch.

The communications transceiver is located in the left half of this radio and the navigation receiver, which occupies the right half of the radio, has 200 channels with a frequency range of 108.00 to 117.95 MHz and 50 kHz spacing.

The VOR indicator has three basic components which are used to interpret

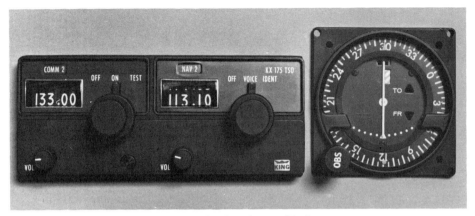

Fig. 8-19. VOR Receiver and Indicator

radio signals, as depicted in figure 8-20. The three basic components are:

1. *Course Deviation Indicator (CDI)* — The vertical needle, which swings to the left or right, indicates whether the aircraft is to the left of course, the right of course, or exactly on course.

2. *TO-FROM Indicator* — This component indicates whether the course selected will take the aircraft TO the station or FROM the station. It also provides positive indications of station passage.

3. *Course Selector* — The course selector (OBS) has an azimuth graduated in 360° which can be rotated to select the desired radial, or to find the aircraft's position. The course is shown at the top of the dial, while the reciprocal, or opposite course, is on the bottom index.

VOR ORIENTATION

The use of VOR equipment can best be explained using two VOR stations to plot a sailplane's position. Assume a cross-country flight in a sailplane appropriately equipped with VOR equipment, and two VOR stations (Broom and Crate) are available.

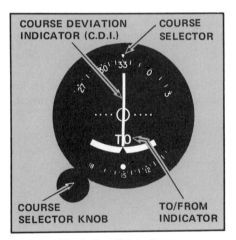

Fig. 8-20. VOR Indicator

To determine the sailplane's position, either station is tuned on the VOR receiver; for example, Broom. Once the station is properly identified, the course selector knob is turned in either direction until the CDI is centered and a FROM indication is displayed on the TO/FROM indicator. The next step is to read the bearing off the course selector and plot this as a radial from the Broom VOR, as illustrated in figure 8-21. In this example, the 075° radial is used. The second station, Crate, is then tuned and the same procedures are performed. As illustrated in figure 8-21, the 335° radial from the Crate VOR is

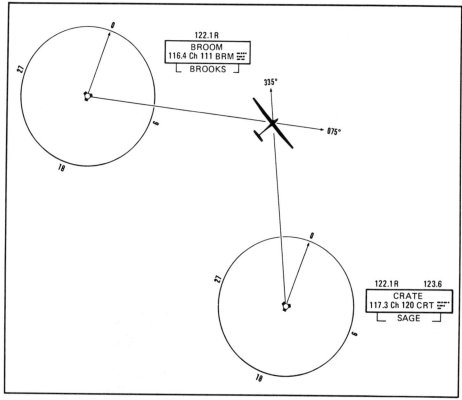

Fig. 8-21. Using the VOR

plotted. With both radials plotted, the position of the sailplane is at the intersection of the two lines. The same procedure can be followed with one VOR station and a prominent landmark such as a highway, railroad, or river. Position can be determined by radial intersection along such features.

Navigational errors can cause serious problems for the unprepared pilot, but they can be avoided through sound planning. The aeronautical charts for the soaring area should be carefully studied and used in conjunction with the navigational techniques of pilotage, dead reckoning, and radio navigation.

SOARING

Computations for Soaring

Chapter Nine

INTRODUCTION Pretrip planning and inflight problems usually involve computations that are awkward and time-consuming to solve by hand. The flight computer, however, makes solving these problems, easy, fast, and accurate.

This chapter covers the basic operations of the flight computer and computations applicable to the soaring training program. A good understanding of the computer permits pilots to fly with greater confidence through more efficient flight planning and navigation.

CALCULATOR SIDE

The calculator side of the flight computer is basically a circular slide rule with special indices for solving flight problems. Additional scales provide solutions for true airspeed, true altitude, and density altitude.

THE SCALES

The slide rule function on the calculator side of the computer consists of three scales, as shown in figure 9-1, items 1, 2, and 3. The outer scale (item 1), is fixed to the computer. The middle and inner scales (items 2 and 3), are printed together on the rotating disc attached to the center of the computer. With the three scales on this side of the computer, it is simple to establish the mathematical ratios which are the basis of problem solving.

The outer scale is used to represent *miles*, or *true airspeed*. When used to represent miles, this scale provides the distance traveled or speed of the sailplane. TAS on the outer scale is the abbreviation for *true airspeed*.

The graduations on the middle scale are used for *time* in *minutes* or for calibrated airspeed (CAS). The inner scale graduations represent hours and *minutes* only.

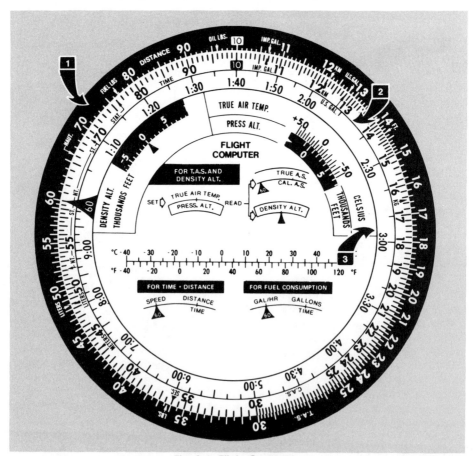

Fig. 9-1. Flight Computer

CHANGING VALUES

In order to accurately read the calculator side of the computer, the changing values of the scale graduations must be understood. When using these scales to solve problems, common sense must be used to determine the value of the number. In figure 9-2, for example, the number 25 might be 250 or even 2,500 miles. If a short distance is involved, 25 might be read as 2.5 miles. If the number 14 is used as 14, each graduation between 14 and 15 is equal to 0.1. If these numbers are used as 140 and 150, each graduation is equal to 1. If used as 1,400 and 1,500, they represent 10.

There are only five graduations between the numbers 15 and 16, shown in figure 9-3, as compared to the 10 graduations between 14 and 15. When the numbers are used as 15 and 16 respectively, each graduation between them is equal to 0.2; when used as 150 and 160, each unit represents 2.

The changing values on the inner scale are somewhat different from those on the other two scales. These graduations always represent minutes and are equal to 5 or 10 minutes, as shown by the arrows in figure 9-4. For example, between 1:50 and 2:00, the graduations are equal to 5 minutes; between 2:00 and 2:30, they represent 10 minutes.

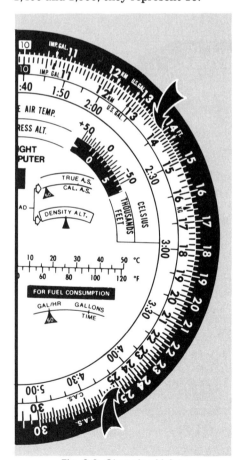

Fig. 9-2. Changing Values

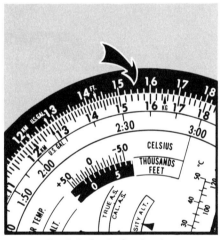

Fig. 9-3. Scale Graduations

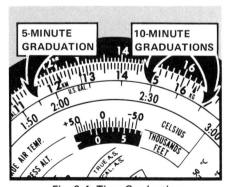

Fig. 9-4. Time Graduations

TIME, SPEED, AND DISTANCE

The speed index, shown in figure 9-5, is the large black triangle across the middle and inner scales. It is used as a reference in time and distance problems. The speed index always represents 60 minutes or one hour. There are three items to solve for in time and distance problems — time, speed, and distance. Two of these must be known to solve for the third.

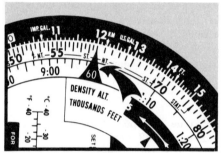

Fig. 9-5. Speed Index

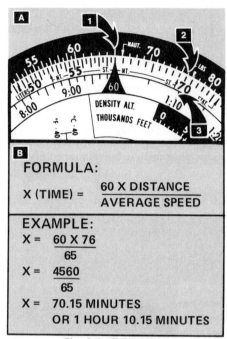

FORMULA:

$$X \text{ (TIME)} = \frac{60 \times DISTANCE}{AVERAGE\ SPEED}$$

EXAMPLE:

$$X = \frac{60 \times 76}{65}$$

$$X = \frac{4560}{65}$$

$$X = 70.15 \text{ MINUTES}$$

OR 1 HOUR 10.15 MINUTES

Fig. 9-6. Finding Time

Solving for Time

If a sailplane is flying at an average speed of 65 m.p.h., how long will it take to fly 76 miles? The steps involved in solving this problem using the computer are shown in figure 9-6, part A.

1 Rotate the computer disc until the speed index is located directly under 65, which represents 65 m.p.h.

2 Look clockwise on the outer scale to 76.

3 The answer is read from the middle scale, directly below 76. It takes 70 minutes, or 1 hour and 10 minutes, as read from the inner scale, to travel 76 miles at 65 m.p.h.

Should a calculator be unavailable, the same problem can be solved using the formula shown in figure 9-6, part B.

Solving for Distance

Use the steps illustrated in figure 9-7, part A to solve a distance problem using the flight computer. If the sailplane flies at 57 m.p.h. for a two-hour period, how many miles will it fly?

1 Place the speed index under 57 on the outer scale. As noted, this setting denotes that the sailplane is flying 57 miles in one hour.

2 Move clockwise on the inner scale to 2:00 (two hours), or 120 minutes.

3 Look directly above 2:00 and find 114 on the outer scale. The 114 is interpreted by noting the 10 graduations between 11 and 12 on the outer scale. Each one of these graduations represents one mile.

The same problem also can be solved using the formula illustrated in figure 9-7, part B.

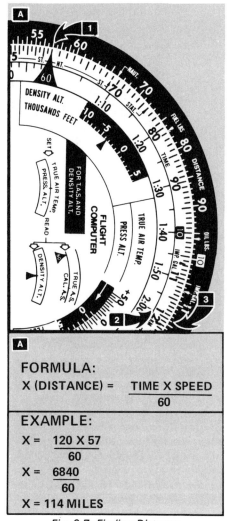

FORMULA:

X (DISTANCE) = $\dfrac{\text{TIME X SPEED}}{60}$

EXAMPLE:

$X = \dfrac{120 \times 57}{60}$

$X = \dfrac{6840}{60}$

X = 114 MILES

Fig. 9-7. Finding Distance

AIRSPEED CORRECTIONS

An error in the airspeed instrument occurs due to inherent errors in the position of the static source on the fuselage. The sailplane manual may have a calibration table to show this error if it is significant. The result of the correction produces *calibrated airspeed*. However, *indicated airspeed*, which is read directly from the airspeed indicator, and calibrated airspeed will be synonymous in this discussion.

True Airspeed

The airspeed indicator is a pressure instrument which indicates different values with changes in pressure and temperature. The correction of indicated airspeed to allow for pressure, altitude, and temperature variations results in a value called *true airspeed*. In a no-wind condition, true airspeed and the actual speed across the ground, or *groundspeed*, are equal.

True airspeed and indicated or calibrated airspeed are identical on a standard day at sea level. As a general rule, true airspeed increases above indicated airspeed by approximately two percent per thousand feet above sea level. For example, if a sailplane were indicating 70 m.p.h. at 9,000 feet, the true airspeed would be approximately 83 m.p.h., or 18 percent higher (9 x .02 = 18% x 70 m.p.h. = 12.6 m.p.h. + 70 m.p.h. = 82.6 m.p.h.).

Indicated and calibrated airspeed can also be converted to true airspeed using the computer. For a hypothetical problem, assume the sailplane is flying at an altitude of 9,000 feet, the temperature is + 10° Celsius, and the calibrated airspeed is 70 m.p.h. Pressure altitude is read on the altimeter when the barometric pressure is set to 29.92. If the sailplane is not equipped with an outside air temperature gauge, the temperature can be obtained by calling a flight service station, or by copying a winds and temperatures aloft forecast before takeoff. Figure 9-8 specifies the steps used to solve for true airspeed.

1 In the small window labeled "PRESSURE ALTITUDE THOUSANDS OF FEET," place the pressure altitude, 9,000 feet, under the temperature 10°C on the scale labeled "AIR TEMPERATURE °C" (Celsius).

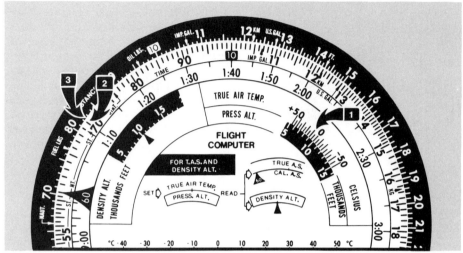

Fig. 9-8. True Airspeed

2 Without moving any scales, locate the calibrated airspeed 70 m.p.h. on the middle scale.

3 Find the true airspeed, 82 m.p.h., on the outer scale immediately above the calibrated airspeed value.

GROUNDSPEED

Groundspeed relates to the aircraft's progress over the ground as it is affected by wind. Groundspeed directly correlates to the motion of the airmass in which the sailplane is moving.

For example, if a sailplane has a true airspeed of 70 m.p.h. and is flying in an airmass which is moving in the same direction at 20 m.p.h., the sailplane is considered to have a 20 m.p.h. tailwind assisting its progress over the ground. Its groundspeed, as illustrated by figure 9-9, part A, is then 90 m.p.h.

Conversely, if the same sailplane is moving against a 20 m.p.h. airmass, the headwind is deducted from the sailplane's 70 m.p.h. true airspeed. Its groundspeed is reduced to 50 m.p.h., as seen in figure 9-9, part B.

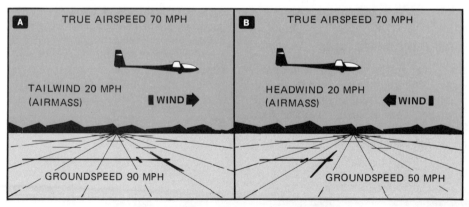

Fig. 9-9. Effect of Wind on Groundspeed

Solving for Groundspeed

To find groundspeed, consider the next problem. If a sailplane flies 64 miles in 1 hour and 10 minutes, what is the groundspeed? The computer solution is shown in figure 9-10, part A.

1 Position 64 miles on the outer scale directly over 1:10 on the inner scale.

2 Directly over the speed index, read the answer — 55 m.p.h.

The mathematical solution is found by using the formula illustrated in figure 9-10, part B.

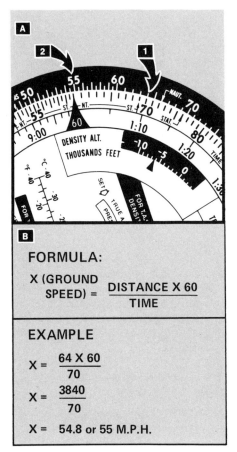

FORMULA:

$$X \text{ (GROUND SPEED)} = \frac{\text{DISTANCE} \times 60}{\text{TIME}}$$

EXAMPLE

$$X = \frac{64 \times 60}{70}$$

$$X = \frac{3840}{70}$$

$$X = 54.8 \text{ or } 55 \text{ M.P.H.}$$

Fig. 9-10. Finding Groundspeed

CONVERSION INDEX

The slide rule side of the computer can be used to convert statute miles to nautical miles or vice versa. If kilometers are being used, they also can be converted to statute or nautical miles. The first conversion is facilitated by aligning the appropriately labeled arrows on the outer and inner scales, as shown in figure 9-11, part A. The conversion is made by reading directly across the two scales. The tables shown in part B also may be used.

OTHER COMPUTER FUNCTIONS

A pilot can increase the utility of any flight computer by learning to do a few simple multiplication and division operations. Many of the preflight and inflight mathematical problems can be simplified with efficient use of the flight computer.

MULTIPLICATION AND DIVISION

When the computer is used to multiply and divide, the reference indices are the small enclosed "10s" on both the middle and outer scale. For example, to find the altitude gained in a 450 f.p.m. rate of climb during an eight minute period, 450 must be multiplied by eight. To use the computer for multiplication, follow the steps shown in figure 9-12.

1 Place 450 on the outer scale over 10 on the middle scale.

2 Find 8 on the middle scale, representing 8 minutes.

3 The answer is found on the outer scale, directly above 8; 3,600 feet of altitude.

Division problems are performed in reverse. In figure 9-13, the steps are shown to calculate the time in minutes it would take for a sailplane to descend from 3,000 feet AGL to the ground at a sink rate of 200 f.p.m.

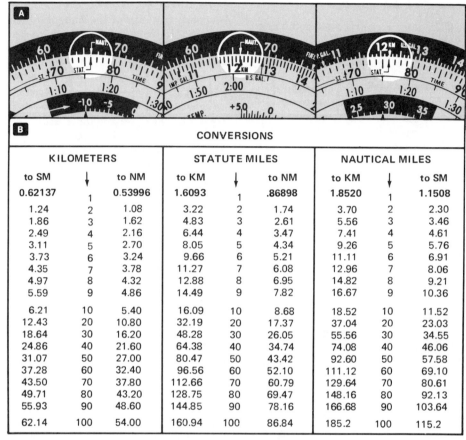

A

B

CONVERSIONS

KILOMETERS			STATUTE MILES			NAUTICAL MILES		
to SM	↓	to NM	to KM	↓	to NM	to KM	↓	to SM
0.62137	1	0.53996	1.6093	1	.86898	1.8520	1	1.1508
1.24	2	1.08	3.22	2	1.74	3.70	2	2.30
1.86	3	1.62	4.83	3	2.61	5.56	3	3.46
2.49	4	2.16	6.44	4	3.47	7.41	4	4.61
3.11	5	2.70	8.05	5	4.34	9.26	5	5.76
3.73	6	3.24	9.66	6	5.21	11.11	6	6.91
4.35	7	3.78	11.27	7	6.08	12.96	7	8.06
4.97	8	4.32	12.88	8	6.95	14.82	8	9.21
5.59	9	4.86	14.49	9	7.82	16.67	9	10.36
6.21	10	5.40	16.09	10	8.68	18.52	10	11.52
12.43	20	10.80	32.19	20	17.37	37.04	20	23.03
18.64	30	16.20	48.28	30	26.05	55.56	30	34.55
24.86	40	21.60	64.38	40	34.74	74.08	40	46.06
31.07	50	27.00	80.47	50	43.42	92.60	50	57.58
37.28	60	32.40	96.56	60	52.10	111.12	60	69.10
43.50	70	37.80	112.66	70	60.79	129.64	70	80.61
49.71	80	43.20	128.75	80	69.47	148.16	80	92.13
55.93	90	48.60	144.85	90	78.16	166.68	90	103.64
62.14	100	54.00	160.94	100	86.84	185.2	100	115.2

Fig. 9-11. Mileage Conversions

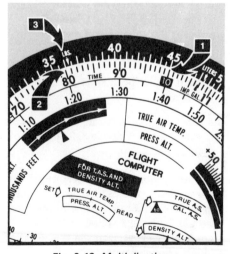

Fig. 9-12. Multiplication

1 Place 3,000 feet on the outer scale directly above 200 on the middle scale.

2 Locate the 10 index on the middle scale and read the answer directly above it on the outer scale. The time it would take to descend from 3,000 feet to the ground is 15 minutes.

ALTITUDE VS. DISTANCE TO GLIDE

Most sailplane pilots are aware of the glide ratio at best L/D speed for the sailplane being flown. This ratio can be expressed as miles covered horizontally

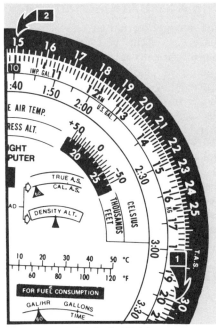

Fig. 9-13. Division

per mile of altitude lost. A more useful comparison is miles of distance versus *feet* of altitude, which can be set up on the computer for a known glide ratio.

Since a nautical mile scale is easiest to find on a sectional chart, being marked along each longitude line, nautical miles will be used as the basis for this comparison. A nautical mile contains 6,080 feet, which can be rounded off to 6,000 feet.

To set up miles traveled versus feet of altitude lost, set the speed index under the known glide ratio, as shown in figure 9-14, part A, item 1. In this example, the glide ratio of 23:1 is stated as 23 nautical miles traveled horizontally for each 6,000 feet of altitude lost. With this ratio set on the computer, any distance on the outer scale can be related to altitude loss on the inner scale.

For the practical application of this problem, suppose the sailplane is 10 miles from the field. How many feet of altitude will it lose at the 23:1 glide ratio previously set on the computer? To find the answer look under 10, representing 10 miles, on the outer scale, in figure 9-14, part A, item 2, and

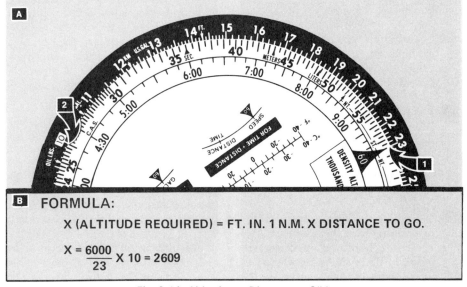

B FORMULA:

X (ALTITUDE REQUIRED) = FT. IN. 1 N.M. X DISTANCE TO GO.

$$X = \frac{6000}{23} \times 10 = 2609$$

Fig. 9-14. Altitude vs. Distance to Glide

see that it will take about 2,600 feet of altitude to glide the 10 miles. An additional 1,000 feet of altitude would have to be added for the traffic pattern. The mathematical solution is shown in part B.

The figure derived from the foregoing calculation is the minimum amount of altitude required to glide a given distance in still air at the best L/D speed. Many factors can work against actually achieving this ratio, such as turbulence, sink, headwinds, maneuvering, and inaccurate airspeed control. However, only two factors tend to increase the ratio relative to the ground — lift or a tailwind. It is usually wise to be very conservative in the use of figures derived from this computation and add extra altitude as a safety margin.

Some manufacturers also produce computers which are used to determine the amount of altitude required and the speed to fly for the final glide. Figure 9-15 illustrates how this particular computer is used.

1 Set wind on rate of climb. In this example set 10 knots headwind on the 400 f.p.m. curve, the estimated rate of climb in the next thermal.

2 Read the distance in miles left to travel — 10 miles. Opposite the distance read the altitude required — approximately 3,800 feet. (1,000 feet should be added for the traffic pattern, if required.)

3 Determine the correct speed to fly by entering with the known wind — 10 knots headwind. The correct speed to fly is the point where the wind intersects the curve — 71 m.p.h.

THE NAVIGATION PLOTTER

The navigation plotter, developed to assist in flight planning, combines many functions into one compact and convenient device. The most conventional style of navigation plotter is shown in figure 9-16. It is a precision instrument made of clear plastic so chart details can be viewed through the plotter. Since it is made of plastic, care should be taken to keep it from being exposed to high temperatures or direct sunlight, which could cause the plotter to warp or shrink.

STRAIGHTEDGE

The straightedge portion of the plotter is used to measure distance and draw the course from the departure point to the destination point. This line, when measured from true north, is called the true course. On one side of the straightedge, the mileage scale matches that of a sectional chart with a scale of 1:500,000. This scale is shown in figure 9-16, item 1. The scale along the bottom of the straightedge (item 2), is graduated in statute miles, while the scale along the top of the straightedge (item 3), is graduated in nautical miles. The opposite side of the plotter displays both statute and nautical scales for the WAC charts, which have a scale of 1:1,000,000. Concise instructions on how to use the plotter are sometimes printed on the plotter as shown in item 4.

PROTRACTOR

The course direction is measured by the protractor or semicircular scale of the plotter. It is labeled from 0° to 180° on the outside scale, and 180° to 360° on the inside scale, as illustrated in figure 9-17. The reference point index is drilled to accept a pencil point or other sharp instrument for use as a pivot point when aligning the plotter with the true course.

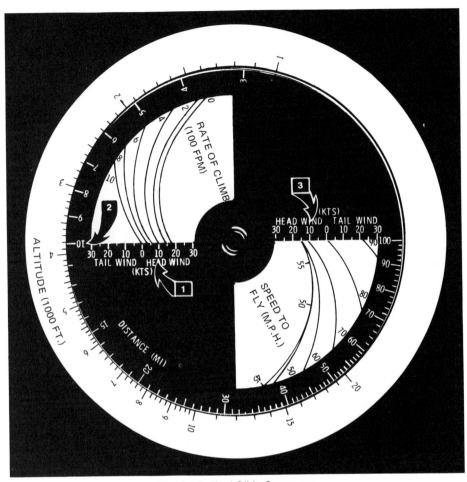

Fig. 9-15. Final Glide Computer

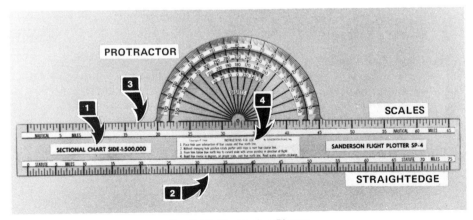

Fig. 9-16. Navigation Plotter

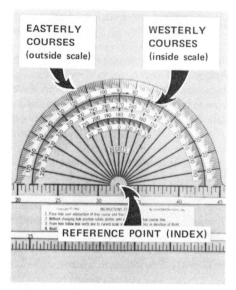

Fig. 9-17. Protractor Portion of Plotter

USING THE PLOTTER

Consider the planning of a hypothetical flight from the Black Forest Gliderport northeast to the Ramah Reservoir. The plotter is used to measure the true course, as illustrated in figure 9-18.

1 Place the small hole in the center of the plotter directly over an intersection of the true course line and one of the longitude lines printed on the chart.

2 Next, align the edge of the plotter adjacent to the protractor with the true course line, being careful to keep the hole in the plotter over the intersection of the longitude and the true course lines.

3 Read from the scale graduation of the protractor that lies directly over the longitude line. The outside scale is used to measure easterly courses, and the inner scale is used to measure westerly courses. In this case, the true course line is easterly and measures 072°.

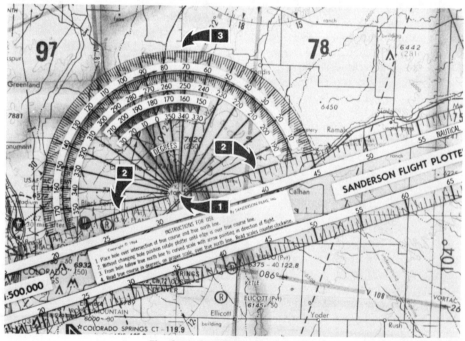

Fig. 9-18. Measuring True Course

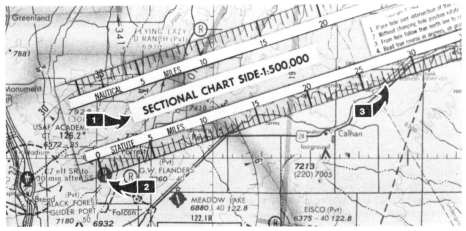

Fig. 9-19. Measuring Chart Distances

The plotter is used to measure the course distance from the gliderport to the reservoir, as shown in figure 9-19.

1 Determine the correct side of the plotter (in this case, the sectional chart side) and scale to use for measurement.

2 Place the statute miles scale parallel to the true course line, and align the zero mile mark with the center of the point of departure.

3 Read the statute mile mark closest to the center of the point of destination. In this example, the distance from the Black Forest Gliderport to the reservoir is 27 statute miles.

USING THE NORTH-SOUTH SCALES

Sometimes a true course is laid out so directly northerly or southerly that the course does not cross a meridian. In this flight, suppose a turn was made to the south at the reservoir to continue on a course to Truckton. Rather than extend the course until it intersects a meridian, a parallel of latitude and the

innermost scale of the plotter may be used instead. With a southerly course, as shown in figure 9-20, the edge of the plotter is aligned with the course line. The intersection of the course line and the latitude line is directly under the small index hole of the plotter. The true course of 175° is read at the point where the south scale directly overlies the latitude line.

TRUE HEADING

It has been demonstrated that a headwind or tailwind has an effect on the speed of a sailplane relative to the ground. In like manner, a crosswind affects the sailplane's path over the ground, so that it doesn't always travel in the direction it is heading.

The sailplane in figure 9-21 is heading east in an airmass which is moving from the south at 20 m.p.h. Without the crosswind, the sailplane would follow the true course line, but here, the crosswind will move the sailplane 20 miles north of course by the end of one hour. A true heading may be calculated to compensate for the effect of wind so that the path over the ground, called *track*, will coincide with the desired course.

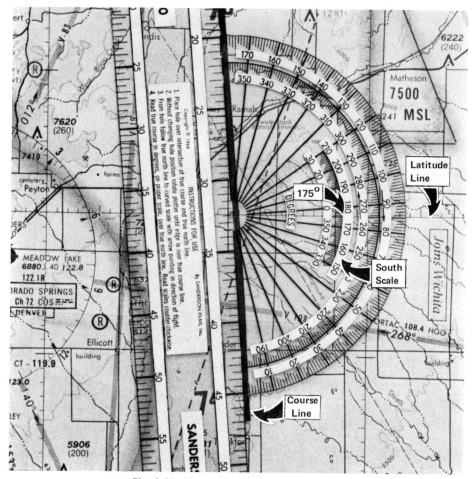

Fig. 9-20. Measuring North-South Tracks

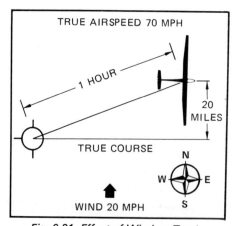

Fig. 9-21. Effect of Wind on Track

PROBLEM SOLVING

The solution to the variations of speed and flight path caused by wind direction and velocity is effected through the use of a wind triangle. A wind triangle may be drawn on the sectional chart, thereby providing a graphic depiction of the corrective actions to be anticipated in flight. To determine the total effect of wind on a flight, *true course, true airspeed, wind direction,* and *velocity* must be known. Figure 9-22 can be used as a reference while working the following sample problem.

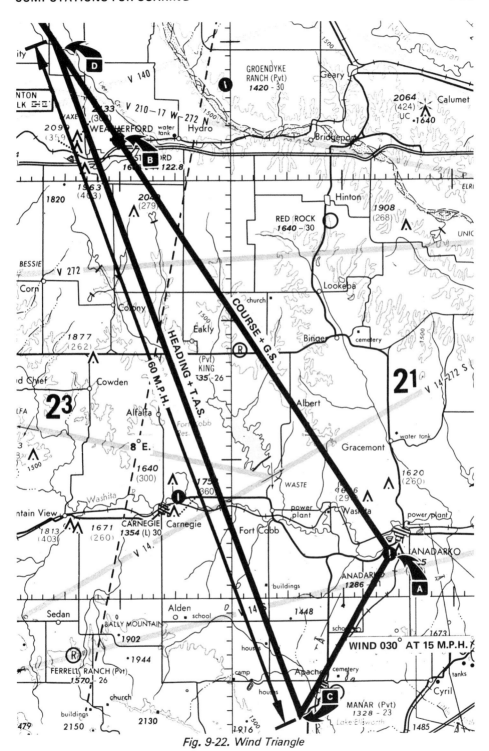

Fig. 9-22. Wind Triangle

Given:

> True course (Line A-B) . . . . . . 326°
> True airspeed . . . . 60 m.p.h.
> Wind direction . . . . 030°
> Wind velocity . . . . 15 m.p.h.

Determine:

> True heading
> Magnetic heading
> Groundspeed
> Time enroute

1 First, draw the true course line (A-B) from Anadarko to Stafford.

2 Next, plot the wind line (A-C) by measuring a 030° line from true north. The length of the wind line is determined by wind velocity. For a 15 m.p.h. wind, extend the wind line 15 miles on the straightedge of the plotter

3 Then, noting a true airspeed of 60 m.p.h., draw a line from point C until, at 60 miles of length, it intersects the true course line (A-B). Line A-B may be extended as necessary to permit interception by line C-D.

4 The true heading is obtained by measuring line C-D, here, 338°.

5 Magnetic heading is calculated by subtracting magnetic variation (shown on the isogonic line in the illustration) from the true heading (338° - 8° = 330°)

6 Groundspeed is shown by measuring line A-D. In this problem, groundspeed is 52 miles per hour.

7 Time enroute may be computed by measuring the distance between points A and B (41 miles), using the groundspeed of 52 m.p.h., and working the problem normally on the slide rule face of the flight computer. At 52 m.p.h., the time required to fly 41 miles would be 47 minutes.

This chapter has presented the methods for solving navigation problems with the aid of the flight computer and plotter. It takes only a little practice to learn to use them with speed and accuracy.

SOARING

Chapter
Ten

Personal
Equipment

INTRODUCTION The need for personal
equipment in soaring operations has been
accelerated in recent years by the considerable
increase in high altitude and cross-country
soaring. Flights covering long distances over
varying terrain and changing climatic conditions
often require the use of several types of personal
equipment.

Professional pilots prepare themselves for all
contingencies by becoming familiar with all
equipment that may be needed in an
emergency. This chapter highlights the use of
oxygen, parachutes, and survival equipment.

OXYGEN SYSTEM COMPONENTS

An aviation oxygen system generally consists of three major components: storage tank, pressure-reducing system, and mask assembly. Oxygen systems usually are installed in the sailplane, but small, portable systems also are available.

Most civilian aircraft oxygen systems use high-pressure cylinders, such as the one shown in figure 10-1, for oxygen storage. These cylinders normally are filled to 1,800 p.s.i. The duration of the oxygen supply depends on the flight altitude, the capacity in cubic feet of the storage cylinder, and the oxygen flow system being used.

Fig. 10-1. Oxygen Cylinder

Many oxygen storage systems have an external filler valve which permits filling the cylinder without removing it from the sailplane. The specific operating procedures should be followed carefully when the cylinder is being filled. Cylinders should be filled only with *aviator's breathing oxygen*. Hospital and welder's oxygen often contain water and other impurities which can cause the sailplane's oxygen system to freeze up at altitude or the valves to become clogged.

Certain safety precautions are absolutely necessary when servicing or using the oxygen system. The cylinders, for example, should be handled carefully to avoid accidental damage to the cylinder or the valve. Also, an oxygen-rich atmosphere is highly conducive to combustion, if both combustible materials and a source of heat are present. Smoking should *never* be allowed when the oxygen system is being serviced on the ground or used in flight.

OXYGEN FLOW SYSTEMS

There are three types of oxygen flow systems in common use — *continuous-flow, diluter-demand*, and *pressure-demand*. Each type uses one or more pressure-regulating components and a compatible mask.

CONTINUOUS-FLOW SYSTEM

A continuous-flow system uses a high-pressure storage cylinder and a pressure-reducing regulating valve to reduce the pressure at the mask. The oxygen flow is continuous and steady as long as the system is operating. Some systems, however, have manual adjustments for controlling the flow, or automatic regulators that vary the oxygen flow with altitude.

The mask used in the continuous-flow system is the rebreather type and may be made of rubber for permanent use or disposable plastic. Both types are shown in figure 10-2. When a rebreather mask is placed correctly over the nose and mouth and the oxygen is turned on, the rebreather bag fills with oxygen. As the oxygen is inhaled, the breather bag collapses and

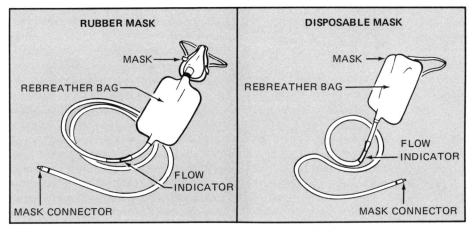

Fig. 10-2. Continuous Flow Oxygen Masks

is refilled with fresh oxygen from the system. The exhaled air, which contains unused oxygen, mixes with the pure oxygen and is rebreathed with the next inhalation. A porous section in the rebreather bag permits excess air to be expelled during exhalation and make-up air to enter when the bag does not contain sufficient quantity for a full inhalation. The rebreather mask helps conserve oxygen by reusing the exhaled oxygen that might otherwise be wasted with a continuous-flow system.

The oxygen pressure reaching the outlet is constant with some systems and manually adjusted with others. The manual system enables the pilot to adjust the flow rate according to flight altitude. With a properly-fitted mask the continuous-flow system may be used up to about 25,000 feet.

DILUTER-DEMAND SYSTEM

The diluter-demand oxygen system uses the same type of storage cylinder as the continuous-flow system. Instead of a continuous flow of oxygen, however, the diluter-demand regulator automatically dilutes the oxygen with atmospheric air and supplies the mixture when the user inhales. The

oxygen-to-air ratio is automatically adjusted according to flight altitude. As altitude increases, the percentage of oxygen increases until, at about 32,000 feet, the regulator supplies 100 percent oxygen. This system may be used safely up to about 35,000 feet.

PRESSURE-DEMAND SYSTEM

A pressure-demand regulator is needed for flights above 35,000 feet. Because of low atmospheric pressure at higher altitudes, positive pressure is needed to force sufficient oxygen into the lungs. The regulator operates the same as the diluter-demand type except at higher altitudes, where oxygen is delivered to the mask at higher than atmospheric pressure. Positive pressure may be activated manually or automatically, depending on the regulator.

The pressure-demand mask is designed to provide a positive seal against the face to hold the pressure and eliminate leaks. Although inhalation is effortless, a conscious effort must be exerted to exhale because of the positive pressure. This method of breathing may seem unnatural, but it can be learned with practice. A diluter-demand mask may be used with the pressure-demand regulator up to about 32,000 feet, or where the positive pressure begins. Above that altitude, a pressure-demand mask must be used. The pressure-demand flow system is adequate up to about 45,000 feet.

A sailplane oxygen system is illustrated in figure 10-3. A control valve on the regulator permits selection of 100 percent oxygen at any time. As a safety precaution, the valve should be turned to 100 percent when the sailplane reaches 28,000 feet and returned to normal at lower altitudes. Another safety feature is a blinker flag, shown in the upper right next to the pressure gauge. Each time the user inhales, the blinker flag operates to indicate that oxygen is flowing.

Fig. 10-3. Oxygen Installation

The mask used with the diluter-demand regulator has intake and outlet valves so that, during exhalation, the breath passes out of the mask. If the selector is set to NORMAL and the oxygen supply is depleted, it is still possible to breathe atmospheric air from the regulator. For this reason, the pilot should check the blinker flag periodically and descend to a lower altitude if the oxygen is not flowing properly.

OXYGEN SUPPLY AND DURATION

An important preflight consideration is to determine how much oxygen is available and how long it will last. The determining factors are the cylinder storage capacity, measured in cubic feet, bottle pressure, and the rate of consumption. The oxygen supply should be monitored continuously while in flight.

The table in figure 10-4 is used to estimate oxygen duration for a continuous-flow oxygen system. If either a diluter-demand or pressure-demand system is in use, the oxygen supply normally will last longer, especially at lower altitudes, since oxygen is supplied only on demand. These two systems control oxygen flow more efficiently than a continuous-flow system.

OXYGEN DURATION TABLE		
VOLUME	DURATION	
(CUBIC FEET AT 1,800 P.S.I.)	(1 PERSON)	
	(TIME IN HOURS)	
	12,000 feet	16,000 feet
11	3.0	2.4
15	4.1	3.3
22	5.9	4.8
30	8.1	6.5
38	10.3	8.3
48	13.0	10.4

Fig. 10-4. Oxygen Duration

EMERGENCY OXYGEN

A "bailout" bottle, as shown in figure 10-5, should be carried on any flight expected to exceed 20,000 feet. Although it is designed for use during a parachute descent from high altitude, it also serves as an emergency oxygen supply, should the main system malfunction or become prematurely

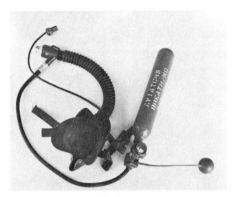

Fig. 10-5. Bailout Bottle

Fig. 10-6. Oxygen Mask Test Stand

exhausted. The bailout bottle may be secured in the cockpit, strapped to the pilot's leg, or stowed in a pocket of the parachute harness. A typical bailout bottle provides a five-to-ten minute oxygen supply, which normally is sufficient for a rapid descent to a safe altitude where supplemental oxygen is not required.

A normal bailout bottle may not be adequate for emergency replacement of the main system at a very high altitude. For such flights, it is wise to provide an auxiliary system. It may be as complete as the main system or as simple as a larger bailout bottle installation.

OXYGEN SYSTEM PREFLIGHT

All oxygen equipment to be used for a high altitude flight should be given a thorough preflight. This includes the primary system and any back-up systems. A few gliderports have an oxygen mask test stand, as illustrated in figure 10-6, to check the mask for proper fit and leaks before going out to the sailplane.

One method used for the inspection of diluter and pressure-demand systems is the "PRICE" check. Applicable items also are used to check a continuous-flow system. Each letter of the acronym

"PRICE" stands for a particular item. The check is performed as follows:

1. P — PRESSURE
    Turn oxygen system on. The pressure gauge should read between 1,500 and 1,800 p.s.i. for a high-pressure system.

2. R — REGULATOR
    Perform a blowback check on the regulator hose on both the NORMAL and 100 percent OXYGEN positions. Little or no resistance to blowing indicates a leaking regulator diaphragm, or a leak between the regulator and quick-disconnect.
    Hook up the mask and perform a pressure check, if applicable. Turn the regulator pressure dial to the SAFETY position, take a deep breath, and hold it. If the mask leaks, as indicated by the blinker flag, readjust it and reaccomplish the check. The oxygen should stop flowing. If the mask appears to be properly fitted, but the oxygen continues flowing, the outlet valve is not holding pressure and should be replaced. Return the regulator pressure lever to NORMAL. If you cannot exhale, the outlet valve is obstructed, defective or improperly seated and should be corrected or replaced.

3. I — INDICATOR
    With the diluter lever in the 100 percent OXYGEN position, check the blinker for proper operation.

4. C — CONNECTIONS
    Check connection for security at the regulator. Check the regulator hose for kinks, cuts, or cover fraying. Check the male part of the quick-disconnect to insure it is not warped and the rubber gasket is in place. A 10- to 20-pound pull should be required to separate the two parts. Make sure the mask hose is properly installed to the connector.

5. E — EMERGENCY
    Insure the bailout bottle is properly connected and has a minimum pressure of 1,800 p.s.i. This gauge should be checked during the parachute preflight.

PARACHUTES

Parachutes are required to be carried on all sailplane flights in SSA sanctioned contests and on all aerobatic flights. The types most commonly used by soaring pilots are the standard canopy backpack and the chair type (canopy in back.) The most suitable type depends on the sailplane cockpit and seat configuration and the pilot's personal preference. A chair type chute is illustrated in figure 10-7.

PARACHUTE PREFLIGHT

Federal Aviation Regulations require that parachutes be repacked every 60 or 120 days, depending on the type. A repacking record, usually stored in a small pocket in the canvas pack, can be checked to verify the chute has been repacked within the required time. Then, the chute can be inspected for the following items:

1. STAINS AND DETERIORATION — Foreign substances such as salt, water, oil, grease, acids,

Fig. 10-7. Chair Type Parachute

and ammonia are harmful to the chute fabric and can cause rapid deterioration.

2. HARDWARE — Check for corrosion, rust, cracks, abrasive wear and look of shine on metal parts. The flap covering the ripcord pins should be opened for inspection. The pins should be checked to be sure they are not bent and have been pushed fully into their studs. The seal should be unbroken. The ripcord cable should be checked to make sure there are no sharp bends which could cause any type of binding.

FITTING THE CHUTE

The chute is fitted after the preflight inspection. The straps should be adjusted so that the pack is in a position which will be comfortable when seated in the sailplane. Then the harness straps should be tightened with the wearer in a standing position. This procedure assures comfort while seated, yet minimizes risk of injury when the chute opens.

BAILOUT

If an emergency dictates leaving the sailplane, the bailout should be expedient and methodical. Under most circumstances, if the sailplane is under control, an emergency landing is preferable to bailing out. Once the decision has been made to leave the sailplane, the following sequence should be followed:

1. If bailout is above 14,000 feet, disconnect the oxygen, if it is being used, and activate the emergency "bailout" bottle.
2. Jettison the canopy.
3. Release the safety belt and shoulder harness.
4. Dive out and down, head first, keeping the feet together.
5. When clear of the sailplane, pull the ripcord. If the bailout is made from high altitude, this step should be delayed since the emergency oxygen supply is limited and the pilot could suffer from oxygen starvation while descending.

DESCENT AND LANDING

When the "D" ring is pulled, the parachute opens to reduce the falling speed to approximately 16 to 18 feet per second. Some parachutes can be steered while descending by pulling a rear suspension line on the side of the desired direction of turn. Others have steering vents, with control lines installed in the risers.

The landing fall should be made as shown in figure 10-8. It is a method of landing which permits the landing shock to be distributed throughout the entire body, thus minimizing possible injury. The body should be relaxed before landing to allow it to absorb the shock evenly. All bone joints should be unlocked, and the legs should be bent slightly. The checklist for parachute landings, illustrated in figure 10-9, should be memorized and the procedure mentally practiced.

CONTINGENCY PLANNING

Preflight preparation should include not only the clothing and equipment to be used during normal flight, but also those items that may be needed in a contingency situation. For example, such items as sturdy walking shoes, a hat, a light jacket, sunglasses, and adequate clothing for the season and area should be worn on every flight. Additionally, a minimum amount of survival equipment should be carried in case of an off-field landing or a bailout.

Every sailplane pilot should carry a small, compact survival kit that will fit into a pocket of the flight clothing or the parachute pack. It is essential that the kit be on the pilot's person in case of bailout. The contents of a personal survival kit depend on the area of flight, the season, and the pilot's own knowledge of survival techniques. Some suggested items include a small knife, waterproofed matches, small candle, thermal space blanket, pocket compass, dehydrated food packet, aspirin, bandaids, and a signal mirror. For mountainous or wilderness areas, the kit should always include fishing line, fishhooks, snare wire, and a needle and thread. Several types of personal survival kits are available from commercial sources. Sometimes, however, it is more practical for pilots to make their own personalized kits.

Some emergency gear should be stowed aboard the sailplane for use after an off-field landing. Such items as a first aid kit, tie-down kit, flashlight, and extra water supplies could be very valuable. This is by no means a complete list of useful items, but it does suggest that contingency planning deserves more than casual attention.

This chapter has dealt with common items of personal equipment and with

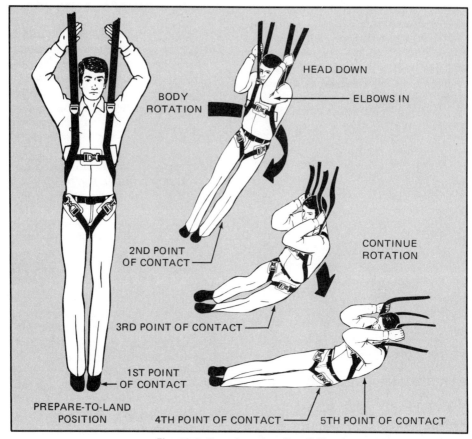

Fig. 10-8. Parachute Landing Fall

CHECK LIST FOR PARACHUTE LANDINGS

Face into the wind on landing.

Head erect, eyes on the horizon until moment of impact.

Feet and knees together when landing.

Make initial contact with ground on the balls of the feet.

Stay off the heels!

Drop chin to the chest and bring elbows and hands in front of chest and
    head upon contact with ground.

Keep body muscles tense enough to absorb the initial part of the landing shock.

Recover quickly and run around your canopy to collapse it.

Collapse the chute by pulling the bottom risers and suspension lines

Fig. 10-9. Parachute Landing Checklist

some important preflight preparation and contingency planning considerations. It is always wise, however, to consult pilots familiar with a specific area to benefit from their experience regarding local practice and conditions.

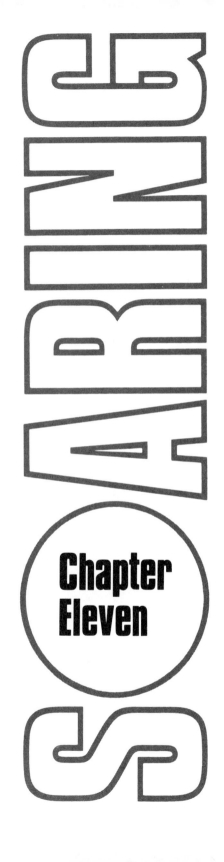

Preflight and Ground Operations

INTRODUCTION Preflight and other ground procedures have an important impact on sailplane operations. Among the best assurances for a safe flight are the proper assembly of the sailplane, and the use of a checklist for preflight inspections.

This chapter is designed to introduce and explain the basics of sailplane preflight procedures and ground operations. Assembly and disassembly procedures are discussed first, followed by trailering, tiedown, and the preflight inspection. The procedures involved with the launch effort, including ground handling, are then presented and explained in an orderly sequence.

ASSEMBLY AND DISASSEMBLY

Sailplane assembly and disassembly should be introduced prior to cross-country training. Unless an un-scheduled off-field landing is made during the initial phase of training, the first opportunity to learn how to disassemble a sailplane and retrieve it by trailer usually occurs after early cross-country flights. A typical disassembly and loading procedure is shown in figure 11-1.

The actual assembly and disassembly procedures usually are included in the sailplane flight handbook. If a checklist is not included, one should be developed. It is also important to use the proper tools to avoid damaging the parts or the surrounding structure.

There are a few general rules which should be followed when assembling or disassembling a sailplane. One of the most important considerations is to work in a location which is sheltered from wind, and to avoid exposing large, flat areas to the wind by keeping the sailplane components streamlined.

At least two people and sometimes more are required to disassemble or assemble a sailplane. Use of wing stands or a fuselage cradle can make the task considerably easier.

A small supply of spare parts, such as nuts, bolts, washers, and cotter pins should be kept on hand in case a part is misplaced. A good way to insure that parts are not lost is to always replace each item in the hole from which it is removed as the sailplane is disassembled. Small parts should *never* be placed on the ground. A small metal pie tin or pan may be used to contain them during disassembly. A non-

Fig. 11-1. Sailplane Disassembly and Loading

breakable container with a secure lid should be used for storage.

Prior to assembly, all spar pins and control connections should be cleaned with a solvent and then lubricated. Major components should be handled with care and rested on level ground or padded surfaces during assembly or disassembly. When assembly is complete, all tools, parts, and rags should be accounted for to prevent items from becoming jammed in the flight controls.

The use of a checklist is strongly recommended during assembly to insure all required steps are performed. A thorough preflight inspection should be given to the sailplane after it is assembled. During this inspection, all fittings, attachments, and safeties should be checked carefully. A positive control check should also be performed to insure the controls are connected and travel freely in the proper direction. The positive control check is performed as follows:

1. Hold the stick firmly in the neutral position.
2. Have a ground crewman hold the control surfaces firmly as the pilot attempts to move the stick, as shown in figure 11-2.

If the pilot is able to move the stick while the control surface is being held stationary, the controls are *not* hooked up properly. This check should be repeated for each individual control surface, including the rudder. Divebrakes, spoilers, flaps, and wheel brakes also should be checked.

The preflight assembly of a sailplane is not classified as preventive maintenance in FAR Part 43, so this activity need not be recorded. However, the pilot in command is responsible for proper assembly of the sailplane according to FAR 91.7.

TRAILERING

Several types of trailers are available to transport sailplanes, including both the open and closed types illustrated in figure 11-3. The open type allows for easier loading and unloading, while the closed type provides storage and better protection.

Fig. 11-2. Positive Control Check

Fig. 11-3. Open and Closed Trailers

The trailers used to transport sailplanes are longer than most other types of trailers, so special care must be taken when traveling or parking. Handling becomes easier, however, with a little practice.

After the trailer is parked for either loading or unloading, it may be removed from the tow vehicle and the wheels blocked or brakes set to prevent it from rolling. The tongue end of a rear-loading trailer may be raised and blocked in position with a sawhorse or jack to aid in removing or loading the sailplane parts. Care should be taken to insure the trailer will not fall off the support. Some trailers have ramps and do not require removing the tongue from the vehicle.

TIEDOWN

A sailplane is a valuable piece of equipment that needs maximum protection from the elements. Since high winds or hail can cause a great deal of damage, a sailplane should not be left unattended for even a short time unless it is tied down.

The proper equipment and procedures should always be used to secure the sailplane. Chains or ropes may be used for this purpose. The tiedown ropes should be able to withstand two to three thousand pounds of tension before breaking and should be replaced periodically due to natural deterioration.

The size and style of ground anchor depends on soil composition and the type of sailplane. Ground anchors should be able to withstand a minimum vertical pull of 2,000 to 3,000 pounds, or two to three times the sailplane's gross weight.

A rudderlock should be installed to prevent wind damage to the rudder. If control locks are not used, the ailerons and elevator should be secured with the seatbelt around the control stick.

In a relatively sheltered area, the sailplane can be secured with the tail down using rope or chain tiedowns at the wings and tail. This procedure is illustrated in figure 11-4.

In unsheltered areas, a different technique must be used. The sailplane should be faced into the direction of the prevailing wind, and adequate tiedowns used for the wings and tail with an additional tiedown fastened to the release hitch.

Unsheltered, high wind areas require even greater security. In this situation, the tail is supported on a stand and secured with two tiedowns. The wings are tied down tightly and a short chain is used to secure the nose, as illustrated in figure 11-5.

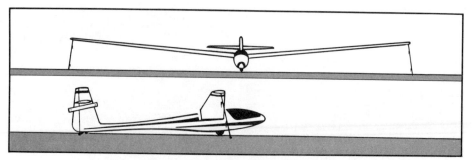

Fig. 11-4. Sheltered Area Tiedown

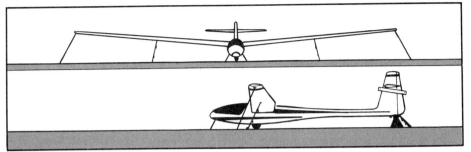

Fig. 11-5. Unsheltered Area or High Wind Tiedown

Once the sailplane is secured, its parts which are susceptible to damage from the elements must be covered. The pitot tubes and total energy venturi tubes should be protected by suitable covers with red streamers. These red streamers serve as a reminder to remove the covers prior to flight. The canopy should be latched and may be covered for protection.

GROUND HANDLING

The movement of a sailplane on the ground requires special handling procedures, especially during high or gusty wind conditions. A sailplane normally is handled on the ground by either pushing, pulling by hand, or towing with a vehicle. The instructor will point out the parts on the sailplane which may be used for this purpose, since application of pressure in the wrong place could cause structural damage. The trailing edge of the wing, for example, is one location that is particularly susceptible to this type of damage.

Several precautions should be taken when a sailplane is moved by a car or truck. A towline that is no longer adequate for launch is excellent for ground towing. The minimum rope length should be at least five feet longer than half the wing span. The driver should take up the slack very slowly because a sudden jerking movement can damage the sailplane or injure one of the crewmembers.

The ground movement of a sailplane is a slow, deliberate process. The driver of the tow vehicle should be alert for signals from the wingwalkers, as well as other landing or takeoff traffic. The tow vehicle should *never* move at a speed faster than a slow walk.

The number of crewmembers required around the sailplane to assist with the ground movement is dependent on the existing conditions. During light wind conditions and on level ground, usually only one wingwalker is required. Downhill towing should be done with a wingwalker on each wingtip. The dive brakes should be open, the flaps up, and the stick secured forward for upwind towing in high wind conditions. These procedures reduce lift and preclude an involuntary takeoff. The pilot may be seated in the cockpit, to monitor the controls, if desired.

An additional person should be stationed at the tail when moving downwind or crosswind during high wind conditions to prevent it from being blown upward or sideways. The controls should also be secured to prevent them from being blown against the stops. These procedures are shown in figure 11-6.

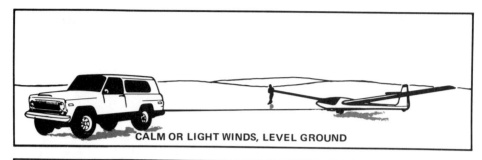
CALM OR LIGHT WINDS, LEVEL GROUND

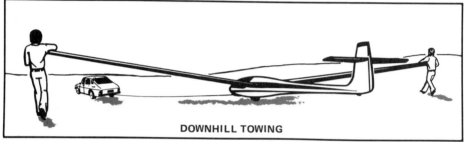
DOWNHILL TOWING

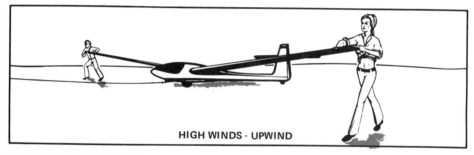
HIGH WINDS - UPWIND

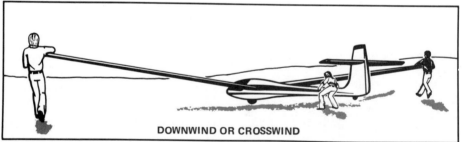
DOWNWIND OR CROSSWIND

Fig. 11-6. Ground Towing Procedures

PREFLIGHT INSPECTION

A thorough preflight inspection is good insurance for a safe soaring flight. A comprehensive preflight inspection should be accomplished before the first flight each day; then, an abbreviated "walk-around" inspection may be used for each subsequent flight. Three types of equipment require inspection — personal, sailplane, and launching. Each is discussed separately in the following paragraphs.

PERSONAL EQUIPMENT

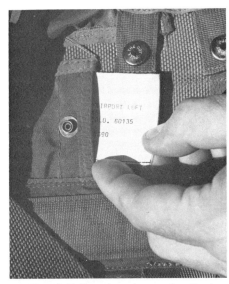

A pilot's safety, comfort, and enjoyment depend on adequate preparation of personal equipment. For example, if a *parachute* is carried, the instructor will demonstrate the proper procedure to inspect it for tears, wet spots, grease spots, or unpacked areas. The harness should be checked to make sure all attachments are secure. The inspection card, illustrated in figure 11-7, shows whether the parachute has been packed within the time required by FAA regulations. The flap on the outside of the pack can be opened to expose the pins, as shown in figure 11-8. They should be in the proper place and safetied with a thread and lead seal.

Fig. 11-7. Parachute Inspection Card

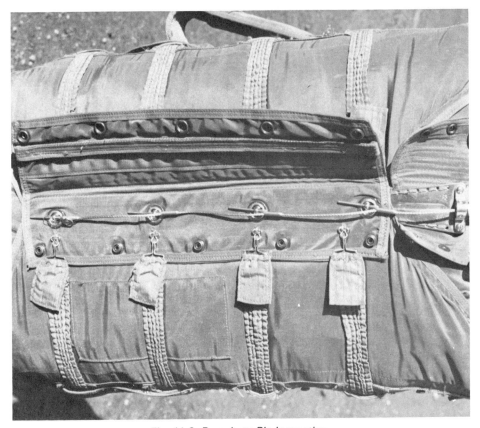

Fig. 11-8. Parachute Pin Inspection

The parachute is fitted by putting it on and snugly adjusting the harness. The parachute fits comfortably when the pilot is seated, but it will not allow the pilot to stand up straight. Part of the parachute indoctrination includes the procedures for jettisoning the canopy, getting out of the sailplane, opening the parachute, and making a proper descent and landing.

If an *oxygen mask* is used, it should be checked for general condition, cleanliness, fit, and valve operation. The proper fit of the mask is important in preventing leakage around the sides and assuring comfort.

The proper *clothing* varies with the type of flight being made. The primary consideration for training flights, however, is comfort. For example, even in the summer, high altitude soaring may require warm clothing.

Food and *water* usually are not a factor during training, but certainly are considerations for flights of long duration. Dehydration is a major factor during long flights; therefore, adequate water should be carried, especially in warm areas.

SAILPLANE PREFLIGHT

Preflight inspections are similar for most sailplanes, but each requires that special items be checked. The sailplane's flight manual usually outlines the minimum number of items to be inspected to insure a safe flight. Additional items can be added, as necessary.

The airworthiness of the sailplane rests solely with the pilot accepting it for flight. Ideally, the preflight inspection should be performed just prior to the launch.

The preflight inspection begins with a check of the cockpit area, including the following items.

INTERIOR INSPECTION CHECKLIST

1. **REGISTRATION AND AIRWORTHI-NESS CERTIFICATE** -- IS SAILPLANE LEGALLY FLYABLE?
2. **OPERATIONS PLACARD** -- GROSS WEIGHT AND C.G. WITHIN LIMITS
3. **BALLAST** -- SECURED IN PLACE (IF REQUIRED)

Additionally, the following items should be inspected for condition, operation, signs of wear, security, and proper assembly.

---

4. **FLIGHT CONTROLS** -- FREEDOM OF MOVEMENT IN PROPER DIRECTION
5. **SPOILERS, DIVE BRAKES, OR FLAPS** PROPER OPERATION AND RE-TRACTION
6. **TRIM CONTROL** -- PROPER OPERA-TION AND SET FOR TAKEOFF
7. **INSTRUMENTS** -- SET, WOUND, AND CHECKED
8. **SEATBELT AND SHOULDER HAR-NESS** -- SECURITY AND CONDITION
9. **CANOPY** -- CLEANLINESS
10. **WING AND FLIGHT CONTROL AT-TACHMENTS** -- PROPER AND COM-PLETE INSTALLATION
11. **OXYGEN SYSTEM** -- "PRICE" CHECK AS DETAILED IN CHAPTER 10
12. **BAROGRAPH** -- SECURITY, WOUND, SEALED, AND READY FOR OPERA-TION
13. **BATTERIES** -- CHECKED AND SE-CURED
14. **LOOSE ITEMS** -- REMOVED FROM COCKPIT AND STORED PROPERLY

The canopy can then be closed and latched, and the "walk-around" inspection begun. A recommended procedure is to start at the nose, work around either side of the sailplane to the empennage, then along the other side back to the nose, as illustrated in figure 11-9.

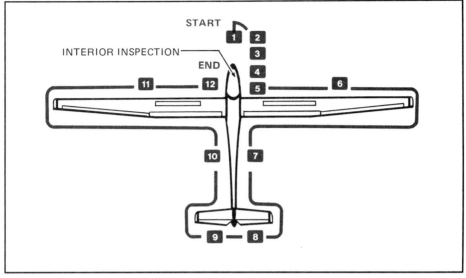

Fig. 11-9. "Walk-Around" Inspection

The following exterior checklist is an example. It should be modified, as necessary, to suit a particular model sailplane. If the sailplane has just been assembled, a positive control check should be performed, as described earlier in this chapter, in addition to the exterior inspection.

EXTERIOR INSPECTION CHECKLIST

1 NOSE -- DAMAGE, PITOT TUBE AND STATIC PORTS CLEAR, VENTILATOR CLEAR, AND YAW STRING FREE

2 TOW HITCH -- SECURITY, PROPER OPERATION, AND GENERAL CONDITION

3 SKID -- SECURITY AND CONDITION

4 WHEEL AND TIRE – PROPER INFLATION, GENERAL CONDITION, FREEDOM FROM MUD OR OBSTRUCTIONS, AND THE BRAKE WORKING

5 UNDERSIDE OF FUSELAGE -- GENERAL CONDITION

6 RIGHT WING –
(a) DAMAGE, DENTS, TEARS, WRINKLES, AND POPPED RIVETS
(b) WING STRUTS IN PLACE AND SECURE
(c) TIP WHEELS OR SKID FOR SECURITY AND CONDITION
(d) AILERON SKIN, HINGE, AND LINKAGE, FOR FREEDOM OF MOVEMENT AND SECURITY
(e) SPOILERS, DIVE BRAKES, OR FLAPS FOR SECURITY AND DAMAGE

7 FUSELAGE SKIN – SIGNS OF STRESS OR DAMAGE

8 EMPENNAGE –
(a) FOR GENERAL CONDITION
(b) BOLTS AND STRUTS SAFETIED
(c) HINGES AND LINKAGE CHECKED AND SAFETIED
(d) FREEDOM OF RUDDER AND ELEVATOR
(e) ELEVATOR SAFETIED

9 TAIL WHEEL OR SKID -- FOR GENERAL CONDITION

10 LEFT SIDE AND UNDERSIDE OF FUSELAGE – FOR GENERAL CONDITION

11 LEFT WING – AS ACCOMPLISHED IN ITEM 6

12 LEFT SIDE OF NOSE – FOR GENERAL CONDITION

LAUNCH EQUIPMENT INSPECTION

In addition to the personal equipment and the sailplane inspections, the launch equipment should be checked to make certain it will function properly. The tow pilot should perform a normal preflight inspection for the airplane. The procedures listed in the launch equipment inspection checklist are presented as a guideline for the inspection of the towing equipment.

Throughout this chapter, the various types of checklists used for ground operations have been presented. While these checklists can be memorized, the preferred procedure is to use them for each operation. This is a prime consideration for the safety of every flight.

LAUNCH EQUIPMENT INSPECTION CHECKLIST

1. **TOW HITCH AND RELEASE CABLE** — EXAMINED AND RELEASE TESTED
2. **TOW ROPE** -- EXAMINED FOR
   (a) PROPER LENGTH, STRENGTH AND MATERIAL
   (b) CONDITION, WEAK SPOTS, BROKEN OR FRAYING OF ROPE STRANDS
   (c) CONDITION OF SPLICES, THIMBLES AND RINGS
3. **WEAK LINK** -- SIZE, STRENGTH, AND PROPER LOCATION
4. **RADIO** — CHECKED WITH RADIO OF SAILPLANE FOR PROPER OPERATION

Aero Tow
Launch Procedures

INTRODUCTION The most commonly used method of launching sailplanes today in the United States is with a powered towplane. This places lighter structural loads on the sailplane during the launch and is more flexible than either the auto or winch tow methods. It also provides a greater opportunity to find a lift area once airborne.

An aero tow normally is performed at an airport or gliderport. It is fast and convenient and requires fewer ground crewmembers. Perhaps the greatest advantage is that it uses a normal flight attitude for takeoff which makes it preferred for training.

This chapter discusses the aero tow knowledge areas required for safe flight, the FAA written examination, and flight test. Included in this discussion are the aero tow signals, tow equipment, prelaunch checks, takeoff procedures, tow positions, turns on tow, tow releases, and emergency procedures.

SOARING

Chapter
Twelve

VISUAL SIGNALS

A safe aero tow requires adequate communications between the sailplane pilot, the ground crew, and the tow pilot. Radio is the best means, since the tow pilot can receive and acknowledge verbal instructions. In the absence of radio equipment, however, visual signals are the primary means of communication.

PRELAUNCH SIGNALS

The numbered items below define the prelaunch signals shown in figure 12-1.

1 **Check Controls.** The ground crewmember will signal the pilot to check control travel and freedom of movement with a "thumbs up" signal, rotated in a circle.

2 **Open Tow Hitch.** Ground crewmember holds an open hand vertically.

3 **Close Tow Hitch.** This signal follows the open hitch signal and is performed by closing the hand.

LAUNCH SIGNALS

The following signals, illustrated in figure 12-2, are used during launch.

1 **Take Up Slack.** Ground crewmember signals towpilot to take up slack by moving arms from side to side (as shown). If a wingrunner is not available, closing the canopy of the sailplane may be used instead. Either signal should only be given when the sailplane pilot is ready for takeoff.

2 **Hold.** Ground crewman signals towplane to hold position by holding arms outstretched to his side.

3 **Pilot Ready, Level Wings.** The sailplane pilot signals to the ground crewmember he is ready and wants

the wings leveled by giving the "thumbs up" signal.

4 **Begin Takeoff.** Pilot waggles the sailplane's rudder while in a wings level position. A circular motion of the wingrunner's arm also may be used for this signal.

5 **Stop Engine/Release Towline.** Ground Crewmember signals towpilot by moving hand back and forth across the throat.

6 **Stop Operation or Emergency.** The signal to stop operation is made by waggling the arms back and forth above the head swiftly. The sailplane pilot also may stop the launch by releasing the towline.

AIRBORNE SIGNALS

Signals can be used while airborne to communicate with the tow pilot. They are shown in figure 12-3.

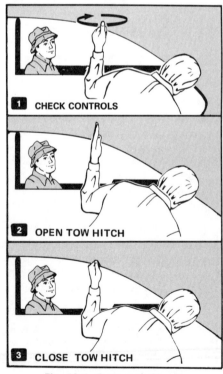

1 CHECK CONTROLS

2 OPEN TOW HITCH

3 CLOSE TOW HITCH

Fig. 12-1. Prelaunch Signals

1 Turn Right. Pilot maneuvers the sailplane to the left of the towplane and pulls its tail gently to the left.

2 Turn Left. Opposite the right turn.

3 Increase Speed. Indicated by rocking the sailplane's wings when positioned directly behind the towplane.

4 Decrease Speed. Sailplane is fishtailed using the rudder. Sailplane should be aligned directly behind the towplane when this signal is given.

1 TAKE UP SLACK

4 BEGIN TAKEOFF

2 HOLD

5 STOP ENGINE/RELEASE TOWLINE

3 PILOT READY, LEVEL WINGS

6 STOP OPERATION OR EMERGENCY

Fig. 12-2. Launch Signals

AIRBORNE EMERGENCY SIGNALS

The use of the radio, if available, is recommended to declare an emergency exists. However, if the radio cannot be used for any reason, the signals shown in figure 12-4 can be used to express emergencies.

1 **Release Now.** Tow pilot signals for an immediate release by rocking the wings. *It is mandatory for the sailplane pilot to release.*

2 **Sailplane Cannot Release.** Sailplane pilot moves into visual range of the tow pilot and rocks the wings. After making sure the tow pilot understands the signal, the sailplane pilot should return to the normal tow position.

3 **Towplane Cannot Release.** Towplane pilot indicates the towline cannot be released by making an obvious yawing motion back and forth.

4 **Warning—Spoilers Out.** The towplane pilot indicates to the sailplane pilot that the spoilers are extended by a rapid "waggling" of the towplane rudder. This is distinctive from "towplane cannot release" in that the towplane does NOT yaw obviously back and forth.

LAUNCH EQUIPMENT

Prior to flight, the pilot should inspect the equipment to be used. For aero tow, this equipment normally includes the tow rope, safety links, tow rings, and tow hitch.

TOW ROPE

Several types of ropes are now being used for aero tow operations. The ideal tow rope should be slightly elastic, rotproof, easy to splice, quick-drying, resistant to abrasion, and of a high strength-to-weight ratio. Most ropes

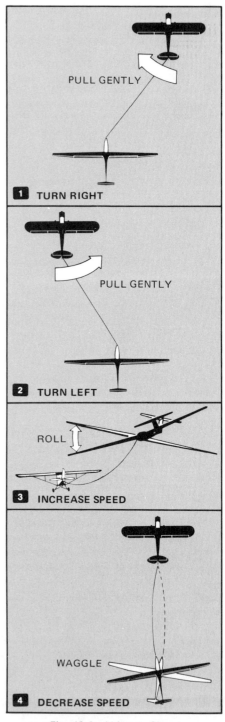

Fig. 12-3. Airborne Signals

suitable for towing are made of nylon, dacron, polyethylene, or polypropylene.

Each rope type has its own advantages and disadvantages. Figure 12-5 gives the size and approximate strength of each type, although breaking strength

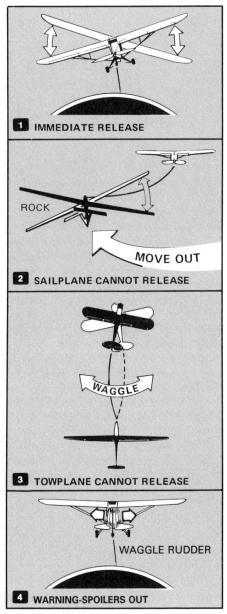

Fig. 12-4. Emergency Airborne Signals

varies with manufacturer. Sisal and cotton ropes are not adequate for tow operations because of low strength-to-weight ratios and should *not* be used.

The most common rope length used for operations from an airport or gliderport is approximately 150 to 200 feet. Short ropes usually are used for an aero tow retrieve out of a small field. The shorter ropes require more precise pilot technique, since there is less margin for error during tow operations.

The tow rope should be stored on a small hand reel or in a small bucket or box, arranged in a criss-cross random pile to permit smooth and rapid extension. A hand-coiled rope is more easily snarled or knotted.

The tow rope is equipped with rings at each end which are attached by splices to preserve the rope's strength. Knots are not recommended since they bend the fibers and weaken the rope. They are also subject to excessive wear.

The entire tow rope should be inspected before the day's towing for cuts, broken strands, excessive abrasions, worn splices, and knots. Knots should be removed and worn portions of the tow rope respliced or replaced, if necessary.

SAFETY OR WEAK LINKS

FAR 91.309 requires the towline to have a breaking strength not less than 80 percent of the maximum certificated operating weight of the sailplane, and not more than twice this operating weight. However, the towline may have a breaking strength more than twice the maximum certificated operating weight of the sailplane if the following conditions are met:

1. A safety link is installed at the point of attachment of the towline

TYPICAL ROPE STRENGTHS
NOTE: Breaking strengths may vary with the manufacturer.

SIZE		AVERAGE TENSILE STRENGTH				
Dia.	Cir.	Nylon	Dacron	Poly-ethylene	Polypropylene	
					Monofil.	Multifil.
3/16"	5/8"	960	720	700	800	870
1/4"	3/4"	1,500	1,150	1,200	1,300	1,200
5/16"	1"	2,400	1,750	1,750	1,900	2,050
3/8"	1-1/8"	3,400	2,450	2,500	2,750	2,700
7/16"	1-1/4"	4,800	3,400	3,400	3,500	3,280

Fig. 12-5. Typical Rope Strengths

to the sailplane. It must have a breaking strength *not* less than 80 percent of the maximum certificated operating weight of the sailplane, and not more than twice this operating weight.

2. A safety link is installed at the point of attachment of the towline to the towing aircraft. It must have a breaking strength greater, but not more than 25 percent greater, than that of the safety link at the towed sailplane end of the towline and not greater than twice the maximum certificated operating weight of the sailplane. This feature prevents the rope from breaking at the towplane end and entangling itself on the wing or some part of the sailplane.

The safety link, or "weak link" as it is commonly called, is approximately 10 to 15 inches in length and has a ring at one end attached by a braided loop. The ring attaches to the sailplane's tow mechanism. The other end of the weak link also has a spliced loop which attaches to the ring of the tow rope. Figure 12-6 illustrates the tow rope and weak link as they commonly are attached to the sailplane. A similar arrangement is used for attachment of the second weak link to the towplane.

TOW RINGS

Two types of tow rings are illustrated in figure 12-7. The larger ring is used primarily for American-built sailplanes, while the smaller ring is used on most European-built sailplanes. The ring should be made of a steel alloy, because mild steel rings are susceptible to stretching or elongating which, in turn, could cause jamming of the release mechanism. Certain types of rings which might be purchased in a hardware store can break quite easily, resulting in a premature release or a lost tow rope. Most American-built sailplanes require a two-inch diameter ring made of high grade, one-quarter-inch steel, magnafluxed, and with a good weld.

TOW HITCHES

The hitch installed on the towplane must be an approved type which meets the specification of FAA Advisory Circular 43.13. The tow hitch on the sailplane is an approved type if the sailplane has a standard airworthiness certificate. The sailplane tow hitch is typically located well forward of the center of gravity and below the nose like the type illustrated in figure 12-8,

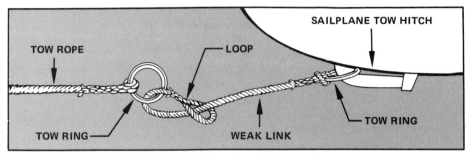

Fig. 12-6. Tow Rope/Weak Link

item 1. Some sailplanes have hitches under the fuselage near the center of gravity and well to the rear of the nose, as shown by item 2 of figure 12-8. This type of hitch is most effective for auto or winch launches. When both nose and CG hitches are installed, the nose hitch should be used for aero tow.

PRELAUNCH CHECKS

One of the most important prelaunch or pretakeoff checks is that of the sailplane equipment and controls. Many sailplane pilots use the letters ABCCCD as a memory aid for the items which must be checked. Each letter represents a different item.

A — *Altimeter* — The altimeter should be set to the field elevation and the other flight instruments checked for proper indications or settings.

B — *Seat Belts and Shoulder Harness* — The seat belts and shoulder harness should be fastened and adjusted. On dual flights, this must be accomplished by both occupants. If a seat is unoc-

Fig. 12-7. Tow Ring Types

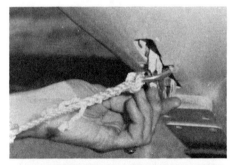

Fig. 12-8. Types of Sailplane Tow Hitches

cupied, the seat belt, shoulder harness, and seat cushion should be secured.

C — *Canopy* — Canopy and emergency canopy release should be locked.

C — *Controls* — The rudder, elevator, ailerons, dive brakes/spoilers, and flaps should be checked to insure complete freedom of movement. Dive brakes/spoilers should then *be locked* in the closed position. Sailplanes equipped with flaps may require some flaps for takeoff.

C — *Cable* — The towline should be hooked up and the cable release checked.

D — *Direction of Wind* — The nearest windsock should be observed to verify the wind direction and velocity. This information is required to position the controls correctly during takeoff.

LAUNCH PROCEDURES

The sailplane should be parked at the downwind end of the runway. The tow rope, if not connected to the towplane, should be stretched from the sailplane's position to the point where the towplane will be positioned for the beginning of the takeoff run. Some slack should be left in the line, and the wingrunner should check it to make sure it is free from snags on the takeoff surface. Usually, however, the tow rope remains attached to the towplane and is connected to the sailplane when the tow pilot has taxied into position.

HOOKUP

A typical sequence of events for hookup involves the following steps. First, the towplane taxis into position, laying the towline as close as possible to the sailplane but with enough slack to permit hookup. The sailplane pilot

should ask the crewmember to show the towline ring end and/or weak link for inspection. If there are excessive abrasions, worn splices, or broken strands, the sailplane pilot should reject it and request a new one.

When the sailplane pilot is ready, the crewmember hooks up the towline to the sailplane, applies tension to the line, and signals the pilot to activate the release mechanism. Then, the crewmember can complete the second hookup and check tension a final time.

TAKEOFF

Prior to giving the takeoff signal, the wingrunner should clear the area of all people who are not directly involved in the launch. When ready for takeoff, the pilot gives a thumbs-up signal to the wingrunner. The wings should then be leveled and slack removed by the tow pilot. Just prior to takeoff, both pilots should make a final check of the area for conflicting traffic.

During the initial portion of the takeoff roll, the wingrunner supports the wing to prevent it from tipping or dragging, as shown in figure 12-9. During a crosswind, the wingrunner should hold the upwind wing slightly low. This will prevent the wind from lifting the wing and weathervaning the sailplane before adequate control is available.

If there are obstructions close to the runway, or if strong crosswind conditions are present, it may be advisable to position the wingrunner on the downwind side of the sailplane. This permits the wingrunner to hold the downwind wing back to prevent the sailplane from weathervaning and swerving into obstructions near the takeoff path.

Fig. 12-9. Normal Wingrunner Position

Normally it is not necessary for the wingrunner to run a long distance in an attempt to keep up with the sailplane, since control surfaces usually become responsive at very low speeds. The wingrunner should support the wing tip of a high performance sailplane as long as possible since the controls do not become effective as rapidly.

An inexperienced wingrunner should be cautioned not to grip the wing tips or tip wheels. It could cause the sailplane to swerve as it accelerates. Rather, a gentle supporting force should be provided with one hand under the tip. The hand can be removed safely when the sailplane controls become effective.

The stick should be positioned during acceleration to raise the nose skid off the ground as soon as possible. It should then be adjusted to keep the sailplane in a slight nose-up attitude. As the speed increases, the sailplane's controls will become effective quite rapidly. However, it is not unusual to use full control deflection during the initial portion of the takeoff.

A wings-level attitude is maintained using the ailerons, and directional control is accomplished with the rud-der. The sailplane pilot should verify that the flight controls and airspeed indicator are functioning normally during the early portion of the takeoff roll. If anything unusual is noticed, the takeoff should be discontinued immediately by releasing the towline.

The takeoff technique differs slightly in a sailplane whose tail normally rests on the ground with the pilots on board. The stick initially is positioned forward to raise the tail. Then, a takeoff attitude is maintained until liftoff.

If the proper pitch attitude is maintained, the sailplane will become airborne when sufficient speed has been attained. *The sailplane should not be forced into the air; it will fly when it is ready.* Unless the sailplane is quite heavy, it normally leaves the ground before the towplane.

Immediately after takeoff, the initial climb should be made to position the sailplane just above the towplane's wake. The correct position for a *normal takeoff*, illustrated in figure 12-10, is *directly* behind the towplane and no higher than the top of the towplane's fuselage. This position should be

2 to 5 feet

Fig. 12-10. Sailplane Liftoff

maintained until after the towplane has taken off.

A common error is the application of too much back pressure on the control stick during takeoff. This can cause the sailplane to "kite" into the air and become excessively high above the towplane.

When the sailplane is too high, it can pull the tail of the towplane up, making it difficult, if not impossible, for the towplane to take off. In an extreme situation, the propeller may be forced into the ground, causing the towplane to nose over. If corrective action is not taken, the only alternative for the tow pilot is to release the towline.

CROSSWIND TAKEOFFS

Crosswind takeoffs require coordinated action by the wingrunner and the pilot to prevent the sailplane from weathervaning. The wingrunner should hold the upwind wing slightly low and continue to do so as the takeoff ground roll begins. Before starting the ground roll, the pilot should position the control stick into the wind to keep the wing from lifting, and apply downwind rudder. As the takeoff progresses, the controls become more effective and less input is required. The ailerons will then keep the upwind wing down and op-

posite rudder will prevent weathervaning.

A crosswind takeoff requires a higher than normal takeoff airspeed to allow a clean break with the ground. This prevents the sailplane from settling back to the runway while drifting, causing excessive side loads.

If the towplane is still on the ground immediately after liftoff, crab should be applied to maintain a position directly behind it. If crab is not applied, the sailplane will drift to the downwind side. This makes it extremely difficult for the tow pilot to maintain directional control and may prevent a safe takeoff.

Once the towplane is airborne, the tow pilot should apply the necessary crab to maintain the runway centerline. The sailplane should then be maneuvered directly behind the towplane, as shown in figure 12-11.

The *only* exception to this procedure is when towing down a runway with side obstructions. Under these circumstances the sailplane should be crabbed into the wind to maintain a track over the runway.

There are few universal guidelines as to the maximum acceptable crosswind

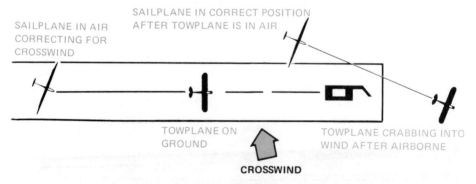

Fig. 12-11. Alignment Following Crosswind Takeoff

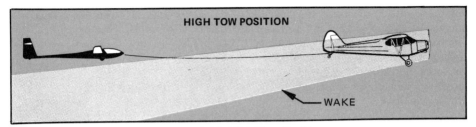

Fig. 12-12. High Tow Position

component for attempting a takeoff. In training situations, the instructor normally establishes a maximum crosswind component based on student proficiency and safety considerations.

TOW POSITIONS

Aero tow is a form of formation flying. Although there is a towline connecting the two aircraft, achieving proper position and maintaining it requires special techniques and practice.

Two recognized tow positions are in common use. They are called the *high* or *normal tow*, and *low tow* positions. Both have certain advantages, and a sailplane pilot should be able to fly in either position.

HIGH TOW

The high tow position, illustrated in figure 12-12, is used by a majority of sailplane pilots in their day-to-day operations. While in the high tow

position, the sailplane flies above the wake of the towplane. This permits better visibility for both pilots and provides the added safety feature of an immediate release by either aircraft without a danger of the tow rope becoming entangled on the sailplane.

LOW TOW

The low tow position is used at some soaring schools and can be used for cross-country retrieves. The correct low tow position is located beneath the wake, as illustrated in figure 12-13. This position can be maintained by reference to two or more points on the towplane. The primary lateral reference is the fuselage of the towplane. A vertical reference is the relationship between the horizontal stabilizer and the upper surface of the wing.

WAKE

The *wake* is the turbulent airstream behind the towplane caused by the

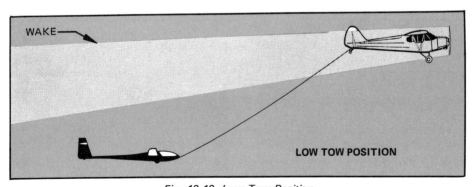

Fig. 12-13. Low Tow Position

combined effect of wing downwash, wingtip vortices, and the propeller slipstream. When the sailplane is directly behind the towplane and within the wake, both wings are more or less equally affected by downwash and wingtip vortices.

If the sailplane is slightly off center, the propeller slipstream and wingtip vortices tend to roll the sailplane. The rolling tendency is removed when the sailplane moves to a position outside the wake.

One of the maneuvers practiced while on tow is transitioning from the high tow position, through the wake, to the low tow position. The purpose of this maneuver is to enable the pilot to recognize and locate the wake, know how to correct for its effects, and learn how to transition from one position to the other.

The high-to-low maneuver is performed by aligning the sailplane with the centerline of the towplane. The nose is then lowered so it can move smoothly and positively through the wake. If the sailplane moves *too* rapidly through the wake, slack line could develop, causing the sailplane to become entangled.

After proficiency in this maneuver is gained, the student should practice moving around the wake from various lateral positions. This gives the sailplane pilot a better feel for the aerodynamic effects of the wake.

HOLDING VERTICAL POSITION

Several techniques are used to hold proper vertical position while on tow. One technique is to keep the towplane in a fixed position on the windshield. Once the proper position is determined, a "bullseye" aimed at the towplane can be drawn on the canopy plexiglass with

a grease pencil. This technique is particularly useful when towing in very turbulent air or when the horizon is obscured.

Another technique is to align the vertical fin within the upper center portion of the wing, or greenhouse area, as shown in figure 12-14, or to align the horizontal stabilizer with the main landing gear. The exact picture differs according to the pilot's seat position and the type of towplane used, but the references should be similar. This technique may also be used when the horizon is obscured.

A third technique, used over relatively flat land areas with a prominent horizon, is to place the towplane on the horizon, as depicted in figure 12-15. This position can be maintained by keeping the towplane's wings on the horizon while using its fuselage for lateral alignment.

A common problem is allowing the sailplane to drift down into the wake.

Fig. 12-14. Holding Vertical Position

Fig. 12-15. Holding Position with Horizon

The rolling effect of the wake may cause overcontrolling in an attempt to correct back to the proper position, illustrated in figure 12-16. The overcontrolling problem can be corrected by pulling up out of the wake into the proper high tow position. If the problem occurs out of the wake, an attempt should be made to "freeze" the sailplane's position by leveling the wings and easing slowly back into the proper position.

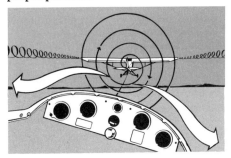

Fig. 12-16. In the Wake

TURBULENCE

Atmospheric turbulence can have a significant effect on a sailplane on tow. The chop associated with turbulence occasionally makes it extremely difficult to maintain the proper tow position, especially the vertical position.

The proper technique is to fly precise formation with the towplane. Any vertical displacement by the towplane is immediately compensated for by matching the towplane's movement. If the sailplane gains an excessive amount of height and a slack line results, the proper recovery techniques should be used to remove the slack.

HOLDING LATERAL POSITION

Once the sailplane is aligned with the towplane, it should remain in a relatively constant lateral position unless it is disturbed by vertical gusts or turbulence.

Student pilots may have difficulty holding the proper lateral position. This usually is the result of being slow to recognize any sideward movement, and then using uncoordinated control inputs or excessive control inputs while attempting to get back into position By using the fuselage of the towplane for reference and correcting position as soon as displacement from center is noted, large lateral displacements can be avoided.

After the initial attempt to recover position, the pilot must anticipate when to apply an opposite correction to stop the glider from overshooting the desired position, and use coordinated control pressures to do so. The use of either aileron *or* rudder to correct position is not good technique and should be avoided.

TURNS ON TOW

The first turn is initiated at a safe altitude above the ground, depending on local traffic pattern requirements. The use of a shallow bank angle (10° to 12°) by the tow pilot greatly aids in maintaining the proper position during the turn.

It is important to fly the same arc as the towplane and roll into the same bank angle as the towplane. In a turn on tow, the nose of the sailplane should be pointed slightly to the outside of the turn toward the towplane's high wing tip, as shown in figure 12-17.

One common problem during turns on tow is turning too early or too late. If the turn is begun too soon, or at a bank angle greater than the towplane's, the towplane's nose is pulled to the outside of the turn. This situation is corrected by shallowing the bank angle until the sailplane is in the proper position, and then matching the bank angle of the towplane.

Fig. 12-17. Position During Turns

If a turn is initiated too late, or with an insufficient bank angle, the result can be an acceleration to the outside of the turn. This can result in slack line if an attempt is made to turn back toward the towplane too rapidly. If this happens, a correction should be made using the procedure for slack line recovery.

TOW RELEASE

The release should be made from the high tow position with normal tension on the towline. This enables the tow pilot to feel the release as the handle is pulled. Release from low tow usually is not recommended.

Before pulling the release handle, the sailplane's position should be noted and the area cleared for other air traffic. When the pilot is ready, the release handle is pulled and the release confirmed visually. A level right turn is then made to clear the towline and towplane. This turn should never be made before release. The tow pilot normally makes a descending left turn away from the sailplane.

If for any reason, the sailplane pilot loses sight of the towplane, he should release immediately.

SLACK LINE

The sailplane normally follows the towplane at a distance determined by the length of the towline. Changes in relative airspeed by either aircraft can cause slack in the towline. If the difference in airspeed becomes substantial, it is possible for a large loop to develop. This presents an immediate hazard to the sailplane pilot since a loop of sufficient size could reach back far enough to entangle the wing or control surfaces. It is important for a sailplane pilot to know some of the factors which cause a slack line.

The primary cause of slack line is acceleration, which can occur in any of the ways illustrated in figure 12-18.

1 If the sailplane gets too high, descending to correct position too rapidly can cause the sailplane to accelerate, resulting in slack line.

2 A sudden acceleration of the towplane can cause a slingshot effect, making the sailplane accelerate faster than the towplane. The elasticity of the towline makes this possible.

3 An unexpected deceleration of the towplane can cause the sailplane to overrun the towline.

4 If the sailplane is too far to the outside of a turn, it accelerates. Slack results if the pilot turns back toward the towplane too rapidly.

Corrective action should be taken at the first indication of slack developing in the towline. This can be accomplished by using one of several techniques. For example, the slack may be removed by yawing the nose away from the slack. When the slack is

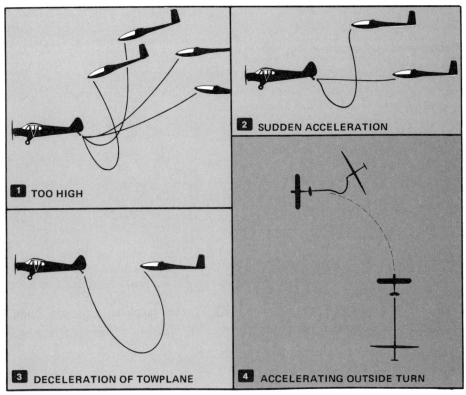

Fig. 12-18. Causes of Slack Line

almost out, the sailplane should be yawed back into alignment with the towplane and the sailplane's nose lowered momentarily. This prevents excessive stress on the towline and the possibility of the sailplane being rapidly accelerated into a climb when the line becomes taut. Excessive stress on the towline could cause the towline or weak link to break.

A climb caused by acceleration can result in a secondary slack as the pilot noses down. This is shown in figure 12-18, item 1. The sailplane should *not* be allowed to descend into the slack line.

Another technique is the careful application of divebrakes or spoilers. When the slack is almost out, the divebrakes should be closed and the nose lowered momentarily. It is im-

portant to remember to close the divebrakes before all of the slack is removed, otherwise, the towline or weak link could break.

Slack line which has been caused by turning back too rapidly from an acceleration to the outside of a turn on tow may be corrected using the following procedures:

1. Adjust the bank angle to coincide with the bank angle of the towplane.
2. Hold position by flying formation on the towplane.
3. Allow the sailplane to decelerate.
4. Slip back into normal position by banking *toward* the towplane on the inside of the turn and applying opposite rudder.
5. Remove the slip when the sailplane is in the proper position.

6. Match the bank angle of the towplane.

Divebrakes may be used along with a slip in an extreme situation where considerable slack has developed. However, they should be closed before the slack is completely out. In the event a large uncontrollable loop develops in the towline, or it appears the towline is about to be entangled on any part of the sailplane, a release should be made immediately.

BOXING THE WAKE

One of the maneuvers included in the FAA flight test is demonstration of ability to fly around the wake. The objective of the maneuver is to move from one tow position to the other, forming a rectangular or box-like pattern, and then return to the original position while avoiding the wake.

Although different methods may be used, the maneuver is usually accomplished using the steps illustrated in figure 12-19, with a two to three-second pause at each position.

1 Use a slight amount of bank or rudder to slide out to a point just beyond the towplane's wing tip.

2 While holding rudder (to keep from being pulled in), descend to the lower position. After the lower position is reached, hold the position with rudder and elevator.

3 Release the rudder and initiate a slight bank to move back to the center, and continue to move to the opposite side just beyond the towplane's wing tip.

4 While holding enough rudder to maintain lateral displacement, raise the nose slightly and slowly climb to high tow position.

5 Slowly release the rudder to allow the sailplane to move into the high tow position directly behind the towplane.

Emphasis should be on keeping the sailplane's wings generally parallel to those of the towplane. This may be

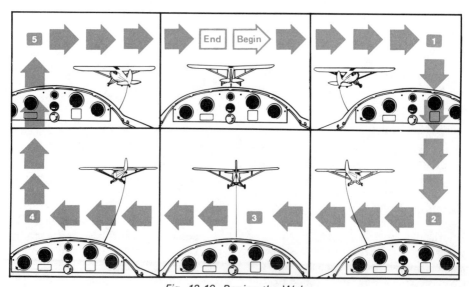

Fig. 12-19. Boxing the Wake

accomplished by using slight aileron turns or rudder only for lateral movements and elevator for vertical movements. A *slight* application of divebrakes may be used to keep the line taut should any slack develop. The most common errors during this maneuver are the tendency to over-control, to rush the maneuver, or to move out too far. As proficiency increases, the sailplane pilot will be able to move from one position to the next without having to pause at each corner.

AERO TOW EMERGENCIES

One of the most important rules concerning towing of sailplanes is formulation of a planned course of action for possible emergencies. The pilots of the towplane and sailplane must function as a team. Specifically, FAR 91.17 requires that, "the pilots of the towing aircraft and the glider have agreed upon a general course of action including takeoff and release signals, airspeeds, and emergency procedures for each pilot."

Anytime there is an emergency, both pilots have an obligation to do everything possible to assist each other. Under most circumstances, the tow pilot will indicate either by rocking the wings or by radio that there is an emergency. The sailplane pilot should release immediately and provide the necessary separation. As long as the sailplane is on tow, it compounds the tow pilot's problem.

Prior to every takeoff, the sailplane pilot should plan for a course of action in case of an emergency. The sailplane pilot must know exactly what to do if the towplane loses power, has insufficient runway or obstacle clearance, or if a break occurs in the towline.

If the towplane loses power, the sailplane pilot should immediately release, maneuver to the right of the towplane, and stop as quickly as possible. The tow pilot can then discontinue the takeoff and maneuver to the left side of the runway.

Prior to takeoff, an emergency release point should be selected that leaves plenty of room to land straight ahead using normal stopping techniques. If this point is reached before the towplane becomes airborne, the same procedure used for a power loss on takeoff is employed.

If the towplane is airborne and it appears it will be unable to clear an obstacle, the tow pilot should release the sailplane. In all probability, the tow pilot will not have sufficient altitude or speed to signal for an immediate release.

If the towline breaks during the takeoff sequence, the course of action to be taken by the sailplane pilot depends on the altitude, airspeed, wind, and local terrain, as shown in figure 12-20. If a break occurs during or shortly after liftoff, the sailplane should land straight ahead on the runway (item 1).

At an altitude below 200 feet AGL and/or low airspeed, the only alternative may be slight turns in order to reach a suitable landing area (item 2). Between 200 and 800 feet, it usually is possible to make a turn back toward the runway for a downwind landing (item 3). Above 800 to 1,000 feet, a normal or modified pattern usually can be flown.

The wind velocity may be the deciding factor in the selection of alternatives. For example, it may be better to land straight ahead from altitudes of 200 to

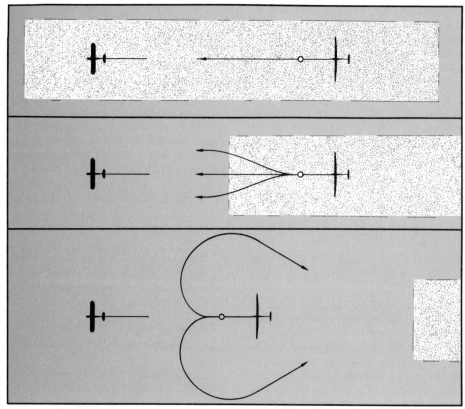

Fig. 12-20. Emergency Landing Alternatives

300 feet if the wind is over 20 m.p.h., since 20 m.p.h. usually is considered the maximum downwind landing component. Also, in crosswinds where there is a discernible crab correction on the part of the towplane, the sailplane pilot should insure adequate separation following release or a rope break, and then turn into the wind for the maneuver back to the field, as illustrated in figure 12-21.

Normal approach airspeed should be maintained during the turn back to the runway. There is a tendency to be too slow by holding the stick back in an effort to conserve altitude.

POWER FAILURE AT ALTITUDE

If the tow pilot experiences a power failure at altitude, the sailplane pilot

should be informed visually by the pronounced rocking of the towplane's wings or by radio. The sailplane pilot should then release immediately.

SAILPLANE RELEASE FAILURE

If the sailplane's release mechanism fails, the tow pilot should be notified over the radio, if available. Without radio communication, the pilot can signal by moving into a position where the sailplane can be seen easily by the tow pilot and then deliberately rocking the wings. After the sailplane pilot is sure the tow pilot has received the signal, the sailplane should be maneuvered into the proper high tow position for return to the gliderport.

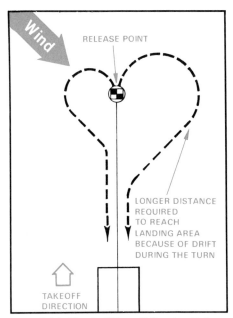

Fig. 12-21. Upwind Turn Following Release

1. Sailplane pilot is informed by the yawing of the towplane's tail, or by radio.
2. Sailplane should move to the low tow position.
3. A slow descent is begun for a wide pattern at the airport. Divebrakes may be used, as necessary, to avoid overrunning the towplane.
4. The tow pilot should allow sufficient altitude on final approach for both planes to avoid any obstacles.
5. The sailplane should land first, since it is lower than the towplane.
6. A stable position should be maintained after touchdown, using only divebrakes during the rollout, while the tow pilot descends the last few feet and lands.

The tow pilot should release the sailplane at a safe altitude over the field. The sailplane can then maneuver to an unobstructed area on the airport. A higher-than-normal final approach should be planned to avoid snagging the towline.

FAILURE OF BOTH RELEASES

Although failure of both release mechanisms is extremely rare, it is wise to be prepared for such an emergency by using the following procedure:

The nose skid should not be allowed to contact the ground since the excessive drag could cause the towplane to stall or contact the ground with excessive force. The sailplane pilot should make every attempt to land first to prevent overrunning the towplane.

This chapter has presented the aero tow knowledge required for the FAA written examination and flight test. Only after this information is thoroughly understood and all prelaunch checks have been completed should an aero tow launch be attempted.

SOARING

Chapter Thirteen

Ground Launch Procedures

INTRODUCTION The earliest form of ground launch used was a bungee cord. The sailplane was launched like a rock out of a slingshot from the top of a hill into the wind. Unless lift conditions were ideal, however, the ride to the bottom of the hill was of short duration.

Sailplane pilots used their ingenuity and began to experiment with other launch methods. Out of these experiments came the auto and winch launches using shock cords and later wire or rope. These procedures are still used extensively in many parts of the world.

This chapter will present the equipment, signals, towlines, emergency procedures, and distinctive features of auto and winch tows.

AUTO AND WINCH TOW

Auto and winch tows are, for all practical purposes, very similar in technique. Both offer advantages to the sailplane enthusiast.

Auto and winch tow equipment usually is more economical to purchase and operate than a tow plane, and the equipment can be used in most fields away from congested airport traffic patterns.

A few of the disadvantages of auto or winch tow include:
1. a limited maximum release altitude
2. lack of flexibility
3. less time and altitude for thermal search
4. requirement for additional ground crewmembers
5. interference with other traffic in the immediate vicinity of busy airports.

GROUND LAUNCH SIGNALS

Radio is the preferred method of communication between the launch crew and the pilot. Even small, hand-held CB radios are useful.

Some of the visual signals used in aero launch also can be used in ground launch. The length of the towline, however, makes some of them difficult to see, so special signals should be used instead. These signals must be clearly visible, easily understood, and not subject to misinterpretation. The following signals have been found to be effective, and are illustrated in figure 13-1.

1 One wing should be held on the ground by the starter until the pilot is ready for takeoff.

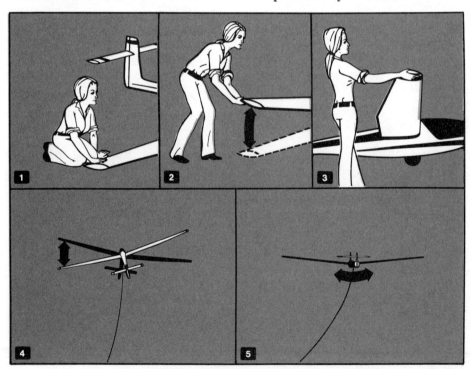

Fig. 13-1. Ground Launch Signals

2 Once the towline has been hooked up by the ground crew, the signal to remove slack is made by raising and lowering the wing as far as possible until all of the slack line has been removed.

3 The sailplane's wings are leveled when the pilot is ready for takeoff. To signify *hold*, return the wingtip to the ground.

4 In flight, if the tow is too slow, the signal to increase the towing speed by increments of five miles per hour is made by a pronounced rocking of the wings. Sufficient time should be allowed for the driver to take action before repeating the signal. If the speed is close to the stall speed, however, the pilot should lower the sailplane's nose and release immediately, rather than using this signal.

5 The signal used to indicate a reduction in speed of five miles per hour is made by fishtailing or yawing the sailplane using the rudder.

Alternate signals which have also been found effective are made with either flags or paddles, as depicted in figure 13-2.

1 The signal to take up slack is made by crossing the paddles back and forth below the waist.

2 When all of the slack has been removed, the paddles are crossed above the crewmember's head.

3 If an emergency exists and the crewmember wishes to stop all operations, both paddles should be held vertically together over the crewmember's head.

In all cases, as a safety consideration, the tow car should have an observer to watch the sailplane and relay the signals to the driver. There also must

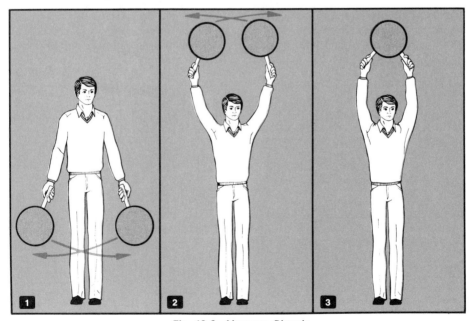

Fig. 13-2. Alternate Signals

be a crewmember at the sailplane to assist with the towline hookup, and to relay signals to the launch vehicle. It is extremely important that everyone involved with the launch *completely* understand the visual signals and procedures.

SAFETY LINKS

A safety link is required in the towline for all ground launches. It prevents overstressing the sailplane if excessive tension is applied to the tow cable.

The safety link is similar to those used for aero tow except its breaking strength should be between one and two times the gross weight of the sailplane. If the towline is too weak, premature breaks can cause an emergency situation and, if it is too strong, it may not break at all.

The safety link, as in aero tow, must always be attached directly to the tow hitch of the sailplane. A 5- to 10-foot length of good five-sixteenths inch manila or synthetic fiber rope with a breaking strength of 1,000 pounds should be adequate for most sailplanes

up to the 1,000-pound category. Stronger ropes are required for heavier sailplane categories. A parachute is used with wire or cable towlines, and it should be placed ahead of the weak link as illustrated in figure 13-3.

TOW HITCH

The tow hitches used for ground launches are similar to those used for aero tow. The tow hitch should be one with an automatic release which opens when the towline reaches aft of the vertical. Figure 13-4 illustrates a typical tow hitch which may be used for auto or winch tow.

The ideal location of the tow hitch used for ground launches is closer to the sailplane's center of gravity than those used for aero tows. These locations are illustrated in figure 13-5. When both an aero tow and CG hitch are installed, they should have a common release handle to prevent pulling the wrong release.

If a nose hitch is used for either an auto or winch launch, the downward pull of the cable on the sailplane's nose limits both the climb angle and the release

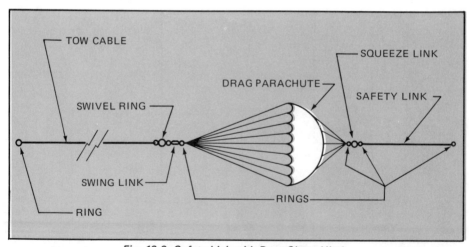

Fig. 13-3. Safety Link with Drag Chute Hitch

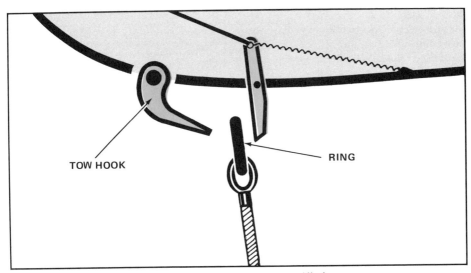

Fig. 13-4. Vertical Release Tow Hitches

altitude. In addition, the control stick forces and structural loading on the sailplane's tail are greater.

The distinct advantage of a CG hitch is that the sailplane can gain a greater altitude with a given line length. The CG hitch also reduces the pitch-up tendency should the cable or a safety link break.

AUTO TOW

It is possible for a sailplane to attain an altitude of 1,500 feet during an auto tow with a 2,000-foot towline. The power required to launch a sailplane by automobile depends on the gross weight and aerodynamic characteristics of the sailplane. A full-sized car with an automatic transmission is recommended for most operations because it is better to have too much power available than to have too little. Pickup trucks and station wagons usually are preferred because they offer a better view of the sailplane.

Auto tow requires the use of certain types of equipment. The release

mechanism and towline require careful selection to insure that they function properly and to provide all of the desired safety features.

AUTO TOW RELEASES

A good method of installing a suitable release hitch is by attaching it to an automobile trailer hitch having at least a 2,000-pound rating. If one is not available, a release hitch capable of withstanding a minimum pull of 2,000 pounds should be installed on the rear of the car. A tow hitch used in aero tow operations also can be adapted for auto tow.

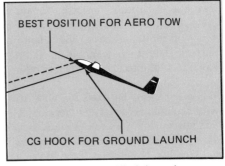

Fig. 13-5. Tow Hitch Locations

It is absolutely imperative to incorporate a dependable system for releasing the towline if the pilot is unable to release. It should be rigged in a position where the observer or driver can release the towline, if necessary. A simple system is illustrated in figure 13-6. A pair of cable cutters or an axe also should be available in case the normal emergency release system malfunctions.

A tensiometer is a useful accessory which improves the performance and safety of car and winch towing. This device indicates the tension in the cable so it can be monitored and adjusted as necessary. Maintaining the proper tension prevents the cable from breaking or possibly overstressing the sailplane. A tensiometer can be constructed using an automobile master brake cylinder, similar to the one shown in figure 13-7. This illustration also shows how a tensiometer is used with a winch.

Different sailplanes require different pressure tension on the towline. It is advisable to make several experimental launches to determine which pressure tension gives the best launch speeds. This tension can then be maintained on subsequent tows.

TOWLINE

The length of the wire or rope used is dependent on the length of the runway and the altitudes desired. In most cases, 600 feet is the minimum altitude which permits a safe 360° landing pattern. The towline should be at least 1,000 feet long to attain this altitude.

While rope can be used for auto tow, wire or cable is preferable because it is less susceptible to wear. An advantage of rope is that it absorbs surges, will not conduct electricity, and does *not* require a drag chute.

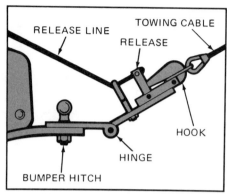

Fig. 13-6. Car Release System

One-eighth inch diameter hard wire also can be used as a towline, but it has many drawbacks. Wire has low aerodynamic resistance, but tends to kink and snarl after being dropped, breaks easily, is difficult to repair, and is also very difficult to roll up for storage.

Perhaps the best towline to use for auto tow is one-eighth inch diameter steel cable. Drag chutes are recommended when using either wire or cable to keep it from falling too fast and kinking.

CAUTION: Great care must be exercised when working around towlines, especially when removing slack. Any type of towline but, especially, wire or cable can cause serious injury. Also, wire or cable towlines should never be used in the vicinity of an electrical storm or powerlines.

CHOOSING A SITE

A suitable extended roadway or an airport with little or no power plane traffic and a runway 4,000 feet or greater is probably the best site for auto towing. High altitude sites require a proportionally longer field. If an airport is unavailable, a long level field may be used instead. If necessary, a 15-foot wide straight roadway aligned

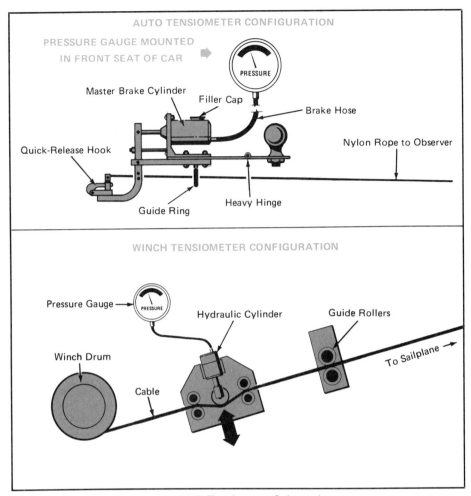

Fig. 13-7. Tensiometer Schematic

with prevailing winds could be scraped smooth enough for automobile speeds of up to 60 m.p.h. The approach ends of the runway should be clear of any obstructions, away from powerlines, and far enough from airports to avoid interference from their traffic.

TOW SPEEDS

The pilot must determine and advise the driver what towing speed to use. Four things should be considered when estimating the speed to be used by the automobile for the launch — surface wind velocity, sailplane speed increase during the climb, wind velocity gradient, and maximum placard speed.

The tow speed for *straight auto tow* may be calculated as follows:

1. Subtract the surface wind from the placard speed.
2. Subtract an additional five miles per hour as a safety factor.
3. After the sailplane has climbed to an altitude between 100 and 200 feet, the tow speed should be reduced an additional 10 m.p.h.

4. Subtract the surface wind again to accommodate wind gradient increases.

A sample problem is illustrated in figure 13-8.

Sailplane's Maximum Auto/Winch	
Tow Speed	65 m.p.h.
Less Surface Wind	- 5
	60 m.p.h.
Less Safety Factor	- 5
Initial Vehicle Tow Speed	55 m.p.h.
Speed Reduction (After Sailplane Climbs Between 100-200 Feet of Altitude)	
Climb Effect	- 10
	45 m.p.h.
Wind Gradient	- 5
Reduced Vehicle Tow Speed	40 m.p.h.

Fig. 13-8. Vehicle Tow Speed Computations

AUTO LAUNCH PROCEDURES

Two common methods of auto tow used in the United States incorporate the simplest procedures. The *straight car tow* method utilizes a towline attached directly between the automobile and the sailplane. As the car moves forward and gains speed, it pulls the sailplane into the air and permits a climb. The speed of the sailplane is governed by the speed of the car.

If the road or runway is too rough to permit the car to operate at normal launch speeds, the *auto pulley tow* method may be used. This method, described later in this chapter, permits the automobile to operate at speeds approximately one-half the speed of a straight auto tow.

INSPECTION OF TOW VEHICLE

It is as important to inspect the tow vehicle prior to launch as it is to preflight the sailplane. The following checklist is offered as a guide to some of the items which should be checked. The list may be modified, if necessary.

1. Automobile — for general condition, fuel supply, temperature, tires
2. Tow hook — for condition and operation of emergency release
3. Tow wire — for weak spots and kinks, condition of rings on end
4. Weak link — for size and condition, and location at sailplane end
5. Drag chute — for condition, orientation and proper position between weak link and wire
6. Pulley and stake (for pulley tow) — for condition
7. Qualified driver thoroughly familiar with auto tow procedures and an observer in car

STRAIGHT AUTO TOW

Prior to launch, the sailplane and tow equipment should also be given a thorough preflight inspection. The prelaunch checks and hookup are identical to those used in aero tow.

In a direct headwind, the towline should be laid out directly behind the automobile. If a crosswind is present, the towline should be laid out downwind of the car, as shown in figure 13-9. When the pilot is ready for takeoff, a signal is given to the ground crewmember to "connect the towline." The ground crewmember then moves to the wing and gives the signal to remove slack.

After the line is taut, the starter, pilot, and driver make a last check of the area for traffic. The wings of the sailplane are leveled when the pilot is ready for takeoff.

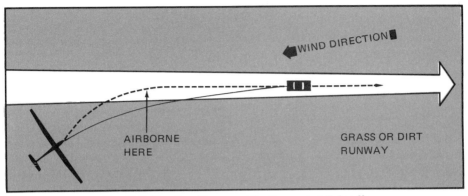

Fig. 13-9. Towline Placement for Crosswind Takeoffs

PILOT TAKEOFF TECHNIQUES

The driver applies power smoothly, increasing speed with full acceleration until the desired tow speed or the proper towline tension is obtained. The starter supports the wingtip, holding it level until the sailplane is moving too fast to keep up with it.

With the initial pull, the pilot positions the control stick to keep the wings and nose in a level flight attitude. If any difficulty is experienced during the initial portion of the takeoff, the pilot should release immediately. As minimum flying speed is attained, the pilot gradually applies necessary elevator control pressure to ease the sailplane into the air. Under certain circumstances, and especially when using a CG hitch, forward control stick pressure may be required. Once airborne, the pilot should apply crab if a crosswind is present, and initiate a gentle climb while maintaining a safe climb speed. This sequence occurs quite rapidly.

After the proper climb speed is attained, the pilot should continue a shallow climb making sure that the pitch attitude is not too steep until the sailplane has reached an altitude of at least 200 feet. In case of a cable break,

lowering the nose to prevent a stall is of primary importance.

Above 200 feet, the pilot should begin increasing the climb angle. Since the climb attitude of the sailplane is steep, the nose hides the horizon. The wingtips should be used to determine the climb angle. As a guide, the pitch angle should *not* exceed 15° at 50 feet of altitude, 30° at 100 feet, and 45° at 200 feet, as illustrated in figure 13-10. The rate of climb is quite rapid and the altimeter will lag behind the actual altitude.

Airspeed must be monitored closely during the entire launch sequence to prevent the sailplane from exceeding the placard speed. Under most circumstances, the best way to reduce airspeed is to raise the nose. During ground launch, however, the opposite is true. The steeper the sailplane's climb angle, the more its speed exceeds that

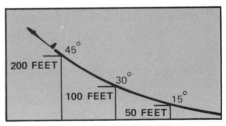

Fig. 13-10. Climb Profile

of the towing vehicle. Therefore, pulling the nose up results in an increase in airspeed, assuming the launch vehicle has adequate power. One of the dangers of attempting a ground launch using an *under-powered* automobile or winch is that pulling the nose up to increase airspeed could have the opposite effect. The additional tension on the towline tends to decrease the speed of the launch vehicle, instead of increasing the airspeed of the sailplane.

When the sailplane is at a low altitude and a slow airspeed, it is usually not wise to add back pressure to gain airspeed. The pilot should maintain a safe climb angle and signal the tow vehicle to increase speed. If the sailplane is at a safe altitude, the pilot may either increase the climb angle, signal for the car to increase its speed, or use a combination of the two.

As the sailplane approaches the top of the climb, the rate of climb begins to decrease. When the pilot is ready to release, the sailplane is nosed down slightly to reduce tension on the line. After the tension has been relieved, the release control is pulled at least twice to insure separation. The release also must be confirmed visually.

If there is any doubt that the release has been made, the sailplane should be maneuvered straight ahead past the car so the backward pull of the cable will automatically open the release. The driver of the car should continue straight ahead until the cable has dropped to the ground.

GROUND CREW PROCEDURES

The primary concern of the ground crew is the safety of the sailplane and pilot. It is wise to have a minimum of three crewmembers for auto tows — a driver, observer, and starter. The starter is responsible for assisting the pilot with the prelaunch checks, relaying signals, and supporting the wing during the initial portion of the launch. The observer is responsible for relaying the signals to the driver and releasing the towline in an emergency. The observer also should notify the driver when the sailplane has released and monitor the descent of the towline. The towline may be released from the car just before the drag chute hits the ground to prevent damage to the chute. The observer also assists with the towline retrieve.

The driver has perhaps the most important job. The automobile must be operated smoothly and positively to avoid jerking the sailplane. The car must be accelerated to the agreed-upon tow speed quickly. The driver must then apply the predetermined speed reductions unless the pilot signals otherwise. If a tensiometer is used, it is the driver's responsibility to maintain the proper tension. At the first indication of a release by the sailplane, the driver should slow the car and move to the side of the runway. This allows the sailplane to land on the runway, if necessary.

AUTO-PULLEY PROCEDURE

The auto-pulley procedure may be used when the runway is rough or less than 3,500 feet long. This method allows the car to operate at about half speed, therefore decreasing the driving distance. This type of launch is more complicated and hazardous than the straight tow because of the danger of the towline fouling in the pulley.

As with the straight tow, either rope, wire, or cable can be used. The cable to be used for an auto-pulley launch should be a minimum of 3,000 feet long. The towline is placed over and through

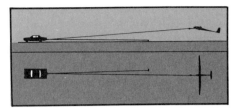

Fig. 13-11. Auto-Pulley Launch

the pulley, as shown in figure 13-11. One end of the towline is then anchored into the ground. The pilot techniques used for the launch are the same as those used for straight tow.

The greatest hazard involved with this type of launch is the inability to release the towline immediately in case of an emergency. Bolt cutters or some other suitable cutting tool should be placed in the automobile and as near the anchor as possible in case of an emergency.

WINCH LAUNCH

Winch launches are an effective way of getting a sailplane airborne. They are currently used more in Europe than in the United States. A winch is a large engine-driven reel much like a large fishing reel, as illustrated in figure 13-12. As with the other forms of ground

Fig. 13-12. Winch

launch, winch launching provides a rapid acceleration at takeoff with an early transition to a climb attitude. It is not uncommon to climb as high as 1,500 to 2,000 feet in two minutes when the proper techniques are applied by the pilot and winch operator.

The winches which provide the best results use 3,000 to 6,000 feet of towline. If the towline is too short, it is almost impossible to gain sufficient altitude for an adequate traffic pattern. On the other hand, excessively long towlines (over 6,000 feet) are not recommended because the added weight of the towline tends to reduce the total climb altitude.

Winches may be purchased in the United States or in Europe, or may be built from easily available parts. A satisfactory winch should have the following components:

1. Chassis
2. Engine (200 h.p. minimum)
3. Automatic power transmission
4. Drive system
5. Large spool (3,000 to 6,000 feet of cable)
6. Level-wind mechanism (insures the cable is wound evenly)
7. Guillotine to cut the towline in an emergency
8. Brake for the spool
9 .Operator's controls
10. Instruments
11. Screened cab for operator

WINCH INSPECTION

The winch should be inspected prior to the first launch. The following checklist is provided as a guideline. It may be modified, as necessary, for the type of winch being used.

1. Engine — sufficient fuel, oil and water; general condition, warmed up

2. Drum and level wind — for condition and operation
3. Wire — condition, weak spots, and freedom from kinks at sailplane end
4. If a radio is available at the winch, it should be checked with the radio of the sailplane.
5. Guillotine — for proper operation
6. Controls — functioning, secure
7. Static electricity wire — for grounding
8. Weak link — for proper size, strength, condition and location at the sailplane end
9. Drag chute — for condition and proper position between weak link and wire
10. Position of winch
11. Communication system
12. Presence of qualified winch operator.

WINCH LAUNCH PROCEDURES

After a thorough preflight of the sailplane and the winch, the winch should be warmed up while the sailplane is towed into position for takeoff at the downwind end of the takeoff area. When the pilot is ready, the cable is hooked up to the sailplane and the wingrunner or starter signals the winch operator to remove slack. A final check for traffic is made and then the starter levels the sailplane's wings.

As the takeoff signal is given, the winch operator applies full power smoothly and rapidly until the proper tensiometer reading has been reached, or the sailplane has climbed to about a 30° angle. Power is then reduced slowly until the sailplane is at a 60° angle, where only 20 percent of takeoff power should be used. As the sailplane reaches the 70° angle, the remaining power is cut to idle to signal the pilot to release.

The pilot should use the same technique during the climb and for making the release as is used in auto tow. As the sailplane approaches the vertical, the nose is lowered and the release control pulled twice. These procedures are illustrated in figure 13-13.

EMERGENCY PROCEDURES

The emergency procedures for both auto and winch launches are the same. As with all emergencies, there is an element of surprise when they occur because they are rare. It is the *pilots* reponsibility to fly the sailplane, analyze the problem, and take corrective action. In most cases, all three actions occur simultaneously so each situation must be mentally rehearsed before each flight and practiced during dual flights.

OVERRUNNING THE TOWLINE

Overrunning the towline can occur during the initial phase of the launch. If the initial pull of the towline is too hard, the sailplane may accelerate ahead of the towline. If this occurs, the takeoff should be discontinued by pulling and holding the release control

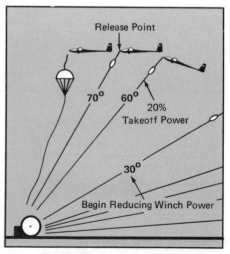

Fig. 13-13. Winch Procedures

open to prevent the sailplane from becoming entangled in the towline or drag chute. When the starter sees that the line has been released, a prearranged signal should be given to the tow vehicle or winch operator to discontinue the launch.

LOSS OF TOWLINE TENSION

Loss of towline tension or a cable break can occur at anytime during the launch, and the sailplane's altitude determines the course of action to be taken. As with an aero tow, the pilot must have a definite plan of action in mind in case problems develop during the launch. The procedures are depicted in figure 13-14.

1 *If the power fails or the towline breaks below 200 feet, the pilot should quickly and smoothly lower the nose, pull the release handle, and land straight ahead making turns only to avoid objects on the ground.*

2 *If the sailplane is too high to land straight ahead and too low to make a 180° turn back to the field, the*

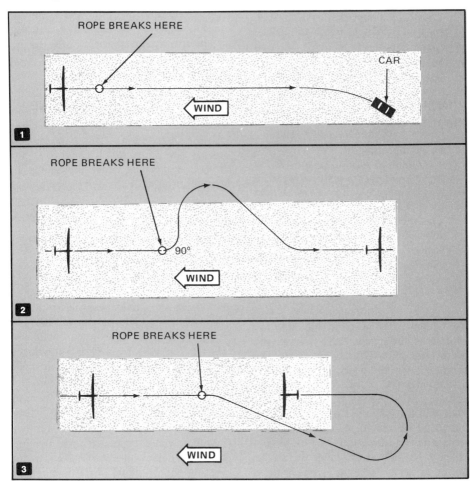

Fig. 13-14. Ground Launch Emergency Patterns

pilot should turn crosswind and then into the wind in order to lose altitude. Sufficient airspeed should be maintained to avoid stalling the sailplane during the turns. The use of slips, dive brakes, spoilers, or a combination of these increases the sink rate and aids in losing altitude.

3 *Between 200 and 400 feet,* a 180° turn to the landing area may be possible, if the winds and available runway permit. *If the loss of tension occurs between 400 and 600 feet above ground,* a modified 180° pattern may be accomplished. The normal approach speed should be used for the approach and landing. An initial turn is made for lateral spacing from the runway, followed by a second turn in the opposite direction to position the sailplane for a downwind landing on the landing area.

Between 600 and 800 feet a modified or normal pattern may be flown depending on several factors. *If the tension loss occurs above 800 feet,* a normal pattern can be flown. Under these circumstances, the sailplane should be immediately turned to the downwind leg after release, and the pattern adjusted for altitude on the base leg.

INABILITY TO RELEASE TOWLINE

The inability of a sailplane pilot to release is uncommon but, if it should occur, the pilot should maneuver the sailplane over the winch or tow vehicle at a good speed in an attempt to allow the automatic release to function. The pilot will feel the nose of the sailplane being pulled down if the automatic release fails to function. In this case, a steep turn should be made in an attempt to circle the launch vehicle while the ground crew severs the tow cable. A

modified pattern should then be flown. The pilot should maneuver to land in an unobstructed area with a higher-than-normal final approach, to avoid snagging the towline on any obstructions.

OVER OR UNDERSPEEDING

The pilot should know the minimum and maximum tow speeds to be accepted prior to the launch. If the speed is outside the desired range, back pressure should be relaxed and the appropriate signal given. If the airspeed remains too high or too low, a release should be made and the appropriate landing pattern flown.

PORPOISING

Porpoising, or a rapid pitch oscillation may occur as the sailplane approaches the top of the climb. This phenomenon occurs as a result of the horizontal stabilizer stalling and unstalling in combination with the downward pull of the tow cable. If the pilot attempts to correct the porpoising by making control inputs, the situation may become so aggravated that the safety link may break.

The recommended corrective action is to release some back pressure to reduce the climb angle until the oscillations stop, and then resume a shallower climb. The use of a CG hitch reduces the porpoising problem, since it is most noticeable when using a nose hitch.

This chapter has discussed the equipment, procedures, and techniques involved with a ground launch. Ground launch provides an additional means of getting the sailplane airborne to enjoy soaring.

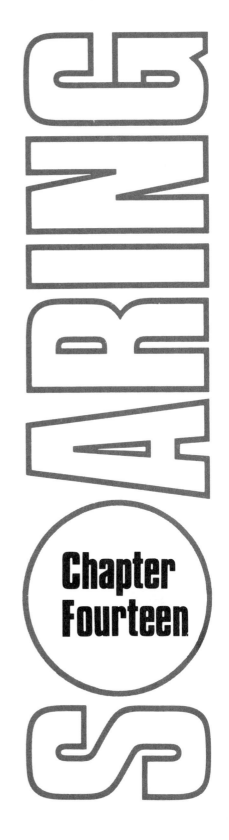

SOARING

Chapter
Fourteen

Basic Flight Maneuvers and Traffic Patterns

INTRODUCTION The first three chapters of Part Two have discussed ground handling procedures and the methods of launching the sailplane. This chapter introduces the basic maneuvers to be used in the air and presents the procedures required to control the sailplane effectively, recover from stalls and spins, and conduct traffic pattern operations.

There are few experiences in soaring which are more rewarding than making the sailplane do exactly what you want it to do, flying a precise traffic pattern, and finishing the flight with a smooth landing. Practicing the maneuvers in this chapter will build confidence and increase enthusiasm for the sport of soaring.

USE OF FLIGHT CONTROLS

The flight controls used in a sailplane are similar to those used in most other airplanes. The respective control surfaces produce motion about each of the three axes. Before discussing maneuvers, let's review briefly the functions of the flight controls.

The control of pitch is accomplished by the use of the *elevator,* which is operated by fore and aft movement of the control stick. Back pressure on the stick causes the nose of the sailplane to rise, and forward pressure causes it to descend. The ailerons create movement, called *roll,* about the longitudinal axis. The ailerons are operated by moving the stick to the left or right. Movement about the vertical axis is referred to as *yaw.* The rudder, a movable surface on the fin, controls rotation around the vertical axis. It is operated through pressure on either rudder pedal.

INFLIGHT MANEUVERS

The practice of inflight maneuvers increases the pilot's confidence and the knowledge and skills required to safely operate a sailplane. The following pages outline the procedures, limitations, and the areas in which safety must be emphasized when performing each maneuver.

CLEARING TECHNIQUES

Today's airspace is full of activity at all altitudes; therefore, great care must be exercised to see and avoid other aircraft. For this reason, all pilots should "clear the area," by looking in the direction of a planned turn much as an automobile driver checks for other traffic before changing lanes.

Clearing turns should be made prior to performing any maneuver which results in a change in altitude. Two acceptable clearing maneuvers are the use of two 90° turns in opposite directions or a single 180° turn.

AIRSPEED AND ATTITUDE CONTROL

The safety and performance of a sailplane depends on adherence to prescribed airspeeds. Therefore, it is important to develop techniques and habits for good airspeed control. Airspeed is controlled by pitch. Lowering the nose increases airspeed, while raising the nose causes a decrease in airspeed, as shown in figure 14-1. The pitch attitude required to maintain a certain airspeed will be learned through practice. Accurate attitude control is stressed because during soaring flight, attention must be directed outside the

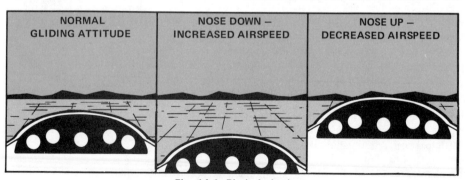

| NORMAL GLIDING ATTITUDE | NOSE DOWN — INCREASED AIRSPEED | NOSE UP — DECREASED AIRSPEED |

Fig. 14-1. Pitch Attitude

cockpit to check traffic, look for lift indications, and assess weather.

The airspeed indicator lags behind a pitch change because it takes time for the sailplane's mass to change airspeed. Therefore, concentration on the airspeed indicator alone can cause the pilot to chase it without ever establishing the desired airspeed. The proper technique is to adjust the pitch attitude using the horizon as a reference, as shown in figure 14-1, and then cross-check the airspeed indicator. After a pitch adjustment has been made, a few moments should be allowed for the airspeed to stabilize before any additional corrections are made. A difference in the sound of the slipstream passing over the sailplane at different speeds and configurations can be used as an indicator in identifying certain relationships between pitch and airspeed. After attaining proficiency in maintaining airspeed in a clean configuration, practice may be conducted with the dive brakes, spoilers, or flaps extended.

STRAIGHT GLIDES

It is necessary to understand the meaning of three terms before discussing the techniques used for performing straight glides. *Heading* pertains to the direction the sailplane is pointed, while *track* refers to the path of the sailplane over the ground. *Crab*, or wind correction angle, is the angle between heading and track.

The purpose of learning straight glides is to develop the ability to maintain a desired track while holding a constant airspeed. A straight glide is performed by selecting a prominent landmark and gliding directly toward it at a specified airspeed. Usually, it is not possible to maintain a perfectly straight line because of wind and turbulence, so a

straight flight path requires a series of small corrections. In most cases, the principal factor is the wind. The effect of wind can be seen by observing the drift, or sideward motion over the ground. Once the direction of the wind has been determined, the sailplane should be crabbed into it in order to maintain a desired track. Several small corrections usually are required to establish the proper crab angle. Once the amount of crab needed has been determined, the sailplane's wings should be held level by use of outside references, as shown in figure 14-2.

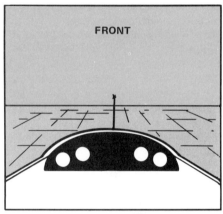

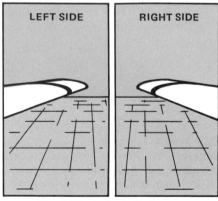

Fig. 14-2. Attitude References

A predetermined airspeed should be maintained while tracking a straight line. This requires attention to be divided between the landmark, pitch, and airspeed indicator, while watching for air traffic.

GLIDING TURNS

Coordination of all three controls is required to make gliding turns. They are performed by applying coordinated aileron and rudder in the desired direction of turn. Ailerons are used to establish and maintain the bank angle, and rudder pressure is required to overcome adverse yaw. Back pressure is required to keep the nose the same distance below the horizon and maintain the desired airspeed, compensating for the loss of the portion of the lift which is diverted to turning force. The steeper the bank, the more back pressure is needed. Bank angle is judged by the angle of the horizon.

The pilot should continue to scan the area for other traffic, while checking the attitude and airspeed with brief glances. Also, the yaw string, depicted in figure 14-3, should be checked to make sure the turn is coordinated.

Fig. 14-3. Coordinated Turn

The rollout from a turn to a particular heading must be lead by a few degrees. As the sailplane approaches the desired point, opposite aileron and rudder are used to level the wings. After proficiency is attained by practicing gentle, shallow turns, bank angles can be increased to 30°, 45°, and then 60°. The procedures for performing the steep banked turns are identical to those used for shallower banked turns, except that a noticeable increase in the amount of back pressure

is required to keep the nose up and maintain the desired airspeed.

SPIRAL DIVES

Some students may have the tendency to overbank the airplane while performing steep turns. A high-speed spiral can result if the bank angle becomes too steep and the nose of the sailplane is allowed to fall well below the horizon. If this should occur, the correct recovery procedure, illustrated in figure 14-4, should be used. The first step is to relax back pressure and shallow the bank angle to less than 45°. Next, back pressure can gradually be increased while the sailplane is rolled out of the turn. Caution must be exercised to avoid overstressing the sailplane.

SLOW FLIGHT AND STALLS

It is important for the pilot to recognize the different sensations experienced as the sailplane is slowed to thermalling speed and below. Slow flight in sailplanes is attained by maneuvering at minimum control speed. Recognizing when a sailplane is approaching a stall or actually stalled is paramount in avoiding excessive rates of sink or spins.

MANEUVERING AT MINIMUM CONTROL AIRSPEED

One of the purposes of learning to control a sailplane by reference to a pitch attitude is to develop the ability to operate in a narrow airspeed range such as used for thermalling. During maneuvers at minimum control airspeed, the sailplane is flown at a speed just above stall, where any increase in the angle of attack or load factor, or a decrease in airspeed, would cause an immediate stall. In turbulent air, a slight increase in airspeed will be required to prevent the sailplane from stalling. This maneuver permits the pilot to develop a "feel" for control responses at airspeeds near a stall.

Flight at minimum control airspeed is performed in straight flight and in shallow or medium banked turns. The maneuver is entered from straight flight by applying and gradually increasing back pressure on the

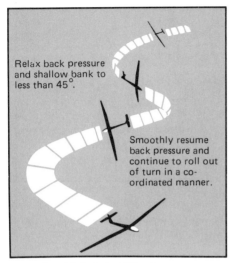

Relax back pressure and shallow bank to less than 45°.

Smoothly resume back pressure and continue to roll out of turn in a co-ordinated manner.

Fig. 14-4. Spiral Dive Recovery

control stick until the airspeed is just above a stall. As the sailplane nears the desired airspeed, the nose is lowered to a pitch attitude which will maintain this air-speed.

After the airspeed has stabilized, the area should be checked for other traffic; then, gentle, shallow turns may be initiated. At slow airspeeds, there is a noticeable dif-ference in the amount of aileron control deflection required to enter and maintain a turn. The controls often feel mushy, so control inputs should be careful, slow, and coordinated to prevent the sailplane from stalling. If a wing begins to drop during a turn, the nose of the sailplane should be lowered before applying coor-dinated pressure to the opposite aileron and rudder. Attempting to raise a nearly stalled wing with opposite aileron will only aggravate the stall, causing the wing to drop even more.

Recovery from maneuvering at minimum control airspeed is made by lowering the nose, and, if the sailplane is in a turn, by slowly rolling the wings level. Then the sailplane can be accelerated to the desired speed.

STALLS

The primary purpose of practicing stalls is to become familiar with stall symptoms in order to react quickly with the proper recovery techniques. A stall is a safe maneuver, but it should be practiced at an altitude at least 2000 feet above the ground.

An unintentional stall can happen during any phase of flight, at any airspeed or pitch attitude, but is most likely to occur during thermalling or in the landing pattern. There are several indications that a stall is imminent. They may not be present for every type of stall, but should be learned to insure prompt recognition and recovery. They include:

1. a nose-high attitude,
2. decreasing airspeed,
3. a decay in control effectiveness, especially the ailerons,
4. vibration or buffeting in the tail area,
5. decreasing wind noise, and
6. aft control stick.

Straight ahead, turning, accelerated, and secondary stalls should be prac-ticed with and without dive brakes. Before beginning any stall series, clearing turns should be made.

A straight-ahead stall simulates conditions during final approach or an attempt to stretch the glide. It is performed by establishing a straight glide, then raising the nose slightly above the horizon and holding this attitude until the sailplane is stalled, as shown in figure 14-5. Recovery is made by reducing the angle of attack of the wing to allow it to begin flying again. The nose should be lowered below the horizon to regain sufficient airspeed for a normal glide and then adjusted to a normal glide attitude.

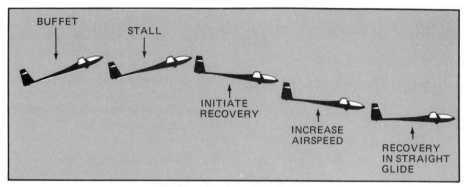

Fig. 14-5. Straight-Ahead Stall

Another type of straight-ahead stall simulates a cable break during a ground launch, where the sailplane's nose is excessively high. It should be practiced with the dive brakes closed. This stall is performed like the normal straight-ahead stall, except the nose is raised much higher. The recovery is similar, but the nose must be lowered further to allow the sailplane to accelerate to a safe flying airspeed. Caution should be exercised during the recovery to avoid over-controlling and imposing negative G-loads.

A turning stall simulates a stall while thermalling. It is accomplished by rolling the sailplane into a 15° to 30° banked turn, establishing a nose-high pitch attitude slightly above the horizon, and holding it by increasing back pressure. This stall is illustrated in figure 14-6. The recovery is made by lowering the nose, then applying opposite rudder. When the stall is broken, coordinated aileron and rudder are used to level the wings.

An accelerated stall simulates over-shooting final approach during a turn from the base leg, and tightening the turn in an attempt to turn back to the runway. It is performed by rolling into a 45° banked turn at an airspeed well below maneuvering speed, and applying back pressure on the control stick. The

recovery procedure is the same as a turning stall.

The secondary stall, shown in figure 14-7, occurs during the recovery from another stall. It is caused by raising the nose too quickly before the sailplane has gained sufficient flying speed. Recovery from a secondary stall is made by using normal stall recovery procedures.

An imminent stall may be practiced using any of the stalls previously discussed. However, recovery is initiated at the first sign of buffeting or rapid decay of control effectiveness

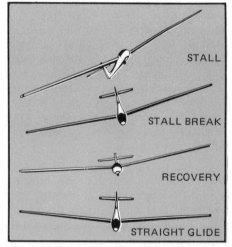

Fig. 14-6. Turning Stall

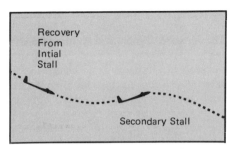

Fig. 14-7. Secondary Stall

instead of allowing the sailplane to stall.

Recovery procedures should be practiced until a pilot can recognize an approaching stall and initiate corrective action. The proper procedures to be used for all stall recoveries are as follows:

1. Lower the nose by moving the control stick forward.
2. Close the dive brakes or spoilers.
3. Apply full opposite rudder to level the wings and counteract any tendency to spin.
4. When the sailplane has sufficient flying speed, apply light back control pressure until the nose is in normal glide attitude.
5. When practicing stalls with flaps, the flap setting should not be adjusted until the sailplane is fully recovered from the stall.

The use of ailerons to level the wings is discouraged when the wing is in a stalled condition. The use of this procedure can have the opposite effect, due to adverse yaw, and cause an inadvertent entry into a spin. A safe procedure is to use the rudder to pick up the wing until the stall is broken and then introduce coordinated aileron inputs when a safe flying speed is attained.

SPINS

Although spins are not a requirement for the recreational, private, or commercial FAA flight tests, stall/spin aware-

ness training (both flight and ground) is required. The regulations require additional ground training pertaining to stall and spin awareness, including academic information on spin entry, spins, and spin recovery. For the flight portion, students receive additional instruction in slow flight with realistic distractions which exposes them to situations where inadvertent stalls are likely. An inadvertent spin can occur during stall recovery, or when thermalling or during the turn from base leg to final approach. An attempt to flatten the turn with the nose too high could result in a spin from too low an altitude for recovery.

Spins should be practiced at a minimum of 3,500 feet above the ground. The first step in performing the maneuver is to clear the area around and below the sailplane. The normal entry into a spin is made from a shallow turning or straight-ahead stall. The dive brakes and flaps should be fully retracted. Just before the nose drops, the control stick is brought to the aft stop and full rudder is applied in the desired spin direction. Rotation begins immediately and continues as long as the controls are held in this position. The indicated airspeed will remain stabilized during the spin. The recovery is made first by applying full opposite rudder and then forward control stick pressure until rotation stops. The rudder should then be neutralized, and careful recovery made from the ensuing dive.

The entry into an incipient spin is identical to that of a full spin. The only difference between the two is that recovery from an incipient spin is initiated at the first sign of a spin.

Some sailplanes are stable and very difficult to spin. If back pressure is relaxed when flying this type of sailplane, it will enter a spiral dive, even though it appears to be spinning. A *spiral dive*, in contrast to a spin, is recognized by rapidly increasing speed with high "G" loading. If recovery is delayed, the speeds and "G" loading become dangerously high. The differences in sailplane loading in a spin and in a spiral are illustrated in figure 14-8.

SLIPS

There are two types of slips, which are aerodynamically the same, but which differ in the way the sailplane is maneuvered with respect to the ground. As shown in figure 14-9, the pilot can execute either a *forward slip* or a *side slip*.

FORWARD SLIP

The forward slip is used to increase the angle of descent without causing an increase in airspeed. It is used to lose excess altitude during landing or to land short over an obstacle. This is accomplished by exposing as much of the sailplane surface to the oncoming air as possible, so that the sailplane's frontal area produces considerable drag. This allows a steeper angle of descent without acceleration. Normally, forward slips are performed with dive brakes or spoilers fully open.

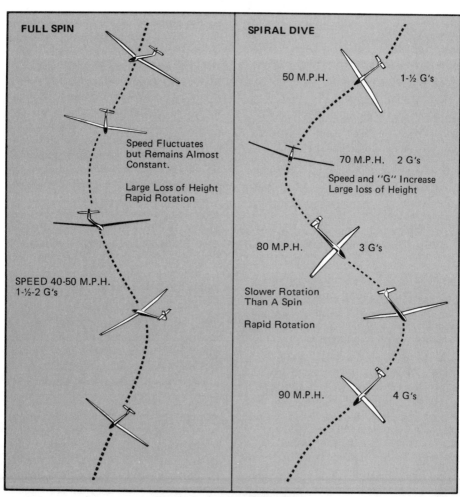

FULL SPIN

Speed Fluctuates but Remains Almost Constant.

Large Loss of Height Rapid Rotation

SPEED 40-50 M.P.H. 1-½-2 G's

SPIRAL DIVE

50 M.P.H.   1-½ G's

70 M.P.H.   2 G's

Speed and "G" Increase Large loss of Height

80 M.P.H.   3 G's

Slower Rotation Than A Spin

Rapid Rotation

90 M.P.H.   4 G's

Fig. 14-8. Spin and Spiral Dive

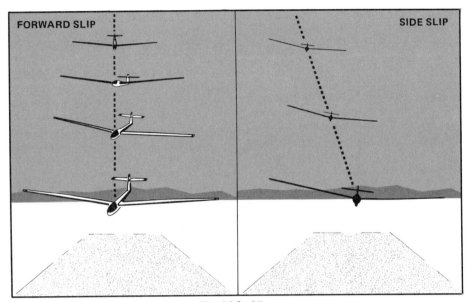

Fig. 14-9. Slips

To initiate a forward slip, one wing is lowered using aileron control, and opposite rudder is applied simultaneously to keep the sailplane from turning in the direction of the lowered wing. The forward slip should be executed *toward* any crosswind which may exist. This procedure keeps the sailplane's ground track in alignment with the extended centerline of the landing area, but allows the sailplane's nose to angle away from the landing area. To prevent the airspeed from increasing, the nose is raised slightly above the normal approach attitude. In this attitude, the glide path steepens, even though the airspeed remains constant.

As soon as sufficient altitude is lost, the recovery is accomplished by raising the low wing and simultaneously easing rudder pressure as the wings are leveled and pitch attitude is adjusted to the normal approach attitude. If the control force on the rudder is removed abruptly, the nose will swing too

quickly into line and the sailplane will tend to acquire excess speed.

SIDE SLIP

The side slip normally is used to compensate for drift during crosswind landings. During a side slip in a no-wind condition, the nose of the sailplane remains on the same heading throughout the maneuver, but the ground track is sideways in the direction of the low wing. However, when a crosswind is present, and a side slip is performed *into* the wind, the resulting ground track is a straight line. This line is parallel to the longitudinal axis of the sailplane.

To maintain a constant heading and a straight flight path during a slip, the aileron and rudder control pressures must be balanced properly. Too much aileron or too little opposite rudder causes a turn in the direction of bank. In contrast, too much rudder or too little opposite aileron causes a yaw away from the bank. To steepen the descent, both aileron and rudder must be increased in a coordinated, proportionate manner.

TURNING SLIPS

A turning slip may be used to dissipate excess altitude during the turn from base leg to final approach. It is accomplished by applying rudder opposite to the turn while maintaining the bank angle with aileron.

Caution should be exercised during slips since the airspeed indicator is not accurate. The reason for this situation is that the air does not flow directly into the pitot tube in uncoordinated flight. References, such as the position of the nose with respect to the horizon, and sound are usually more reliable.

THE TRAFFIC PATTERN

The primary purpose of a traffic pattern is to make certain there is adequate traffic spacing and all pilots are flying the same pattern. All pilots entering a traffic pattern have an obligation to observe certain courtesies and to follow prescribed procedures. If a radio is available, it is a good operating practice to inform other pilots of your position, especially when entering the pattern and prior to turning on base leg. Pilots should constantly scan the pattern for other traffic and adjust their own pattern accordingly.

The traffic pattern and the height of the traffic pattern may vary from airport to airport due to terrain, obstructions, or other considerations, but most have similar characteristics. A typical traffic pattern is illustrated in figure 14-10. It consists of an entry point, usually over some landmark, an entry leg, downwind leg, base leg, and a final approach.

The pattern is meant to represent the flight path of the sailplane over the

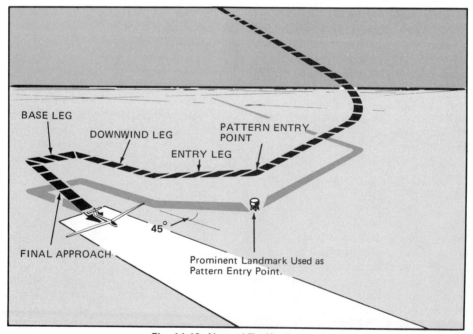

Fig. 14-10. Normal Traffic Pattern

ground under *ideal* conditions. These conditions rarely exist and it is up to the pilot to adjust the pattern accordingly. Target altitudes at designated points also may be used, but it is desirable to be able to fly a pattern and judge altitude by visual references in the event an off-field landing is required.

Should strong lift or sink be encountered in the pattern, immediate action must be taken to adjust the pattern so a desired position and altitude can be met. Any delay may result in the inability to land in the desired area.

Emphasis must be placed on making sure all turns are coordinated, and a frequent check of the yaw string or inclinometer is required. Though slips and turning slips have a definite use in the traffic pattern, any tendency to skid turns must be overcome, especially in the traffic pattern where the danger of skidding turns cannot be overemphasized. Any tendency to turn the sailplane with rudder, rather than with coordinated pressures, must be eliminated.

THE ENTRY LEG

A pilot should be aware of wind conditions and the traffic pattern in use prior to reaching the entry point. While clearing the area for other traffic, the sailplane is maneuvered to provide spacing and to arrive over the entry point approximately 1,000 feet above the ground.

Normally, the entry leg is made at a 45° angle to the downwind leg. A pre-landing checklist is performed while looking for other traffic and obtaining the proper spacing.

A "pre-landing" checklist should be used so all required checks can be recalled quickly to memory. For example, the acronym "U-STALL," illustrated in figure 14-11, could be

U — UNDERCARRIAGE — Extend Gear and Check.
S — SPEED — Increase Airspeed to Proper Pattern Speed.
T — TRIM — Adjust for Landing.
A — AIRBRAKES — Divebrakes, Spoilers or Flaps as Desired.
L — LOOKOUT — Check Wind, Traffic, and Landing Area Clear of People and Vehicles.
L — LAND — Full Concentration on Landing. After Downwind, Do Not Use Radio.

Fig. 14-11. Pre-Landing Checklist

used to recall necessary checks. The important aspect of using a memory aid such as "U-STALL" is that it allows concentration on flying the sailplane instead of reading a checklist. It also calls attention to the most dangerous occurrence at low altitude, *the stall.*

THE DOWNWIND LEG

The purpose of the downwind leg is to position the sailplane for a safe turn to base and final approach. The turn to downwind should be made between 700 and 800 feet above the ground. Figure 14-12 illustrates a visual method for determining the proper downwind position. The landing area should appear approximately 25° below the horizon. This angular relationship exists when the sailplane is approximately twice as far from the runway as its altitude. If the reference angle is maintained, variations in altitude will be automatically compensated for by adjustments in distance from the field.

As the downwind leg is entered, the touchdown and stop points should be selected. The proper approach speed should be established, as specified in the sailplane's flight manual. The calm

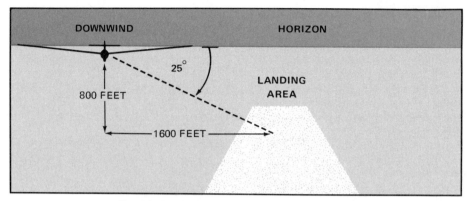

Fig. 14-12. Visual Angle for Downwind Position

wind approach speed is usually equal to 1-1/2 times the stall speed. One half of the estimated wind speed is added to compensate for the tendency to lose airspeed as wind velocity decreases near the surface. The airspeed must be monitored carefully and maintained until the flare, because wind shear near the surface normally causes a loss in airspeed.

While on downwind, attention should be divided among the desired landing point, airspeed, drift, and other traffic. Further references to the altimeter are *not* recommended, so the pilot can concentrate on the pattern and landing. If the sailplane is high on downwind, the pattern should be widened or the dive brakes extended to lose altitude. Conversely, if the sailplane is low, the pattern should be moved closer to the runway and the dive brakes retracted. An early turn also can be made to the base leg, if necessary.

THE BASE LEG

The turn to the base leg should be made when on downwind, approximately 45° to the landing area. This turn is illustrated in figure 14-13. The base leg is used to adjust the sailplane's position and altitude to a point where a safe final approach can be made. If too high, altitude may be lost by opening the dive brakes to increase the rate of

descent or by making the base leg wider. "S" turns or 360° turns should *never* be used to lose altitude.

The worst situation is to get too low on the base leg to allow a safe turn to final. Should this occur, there is no alternative but to land out of the base leg or angle across the runway and land. Raising the nose in an attempt to conserve altitude or hurrying the turn with excessive rudder compounds the problem by increasing the sink rate and the danger of a stall or spin. The proper action is to close the dive brakes and make a nose-low turn toward the new landing area.

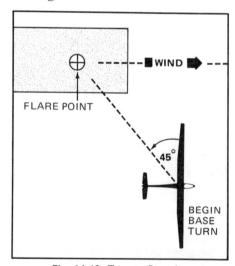

Fig. 14-13. Turn to Base Leg

FINAL APPROACH

The turn to final should be made so the sailplane rolls out on an extension of the center of the landing area. The turn should be made slightly nose low, using a bank angle no greater than 45°. A medium bank angle is preferred since it reduces the possibility of an accelerated stall. If a tailwind is present on base leg, the turn to final should be initiated early to avoid overshooting the runway.

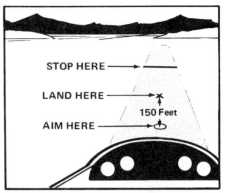

Fig. 14-14. Final Approach

After rolling out on final approach, attention should be focused on the selected landing point. An "aim" point should be chosen about 150-200 feet short of the selected landing spot, as shown in figure 14-14, or adjusted as necessary for existing wind conditions.

The elevator is used to maintain a constant airspeed, and dive brakes, spoilers, or flaps are used to control the glide path. These devices should be opened and adjusted to maintain the proper glide angle, as shown in figure 14-15. The importance of accurate airspeed control cannot be overemphasized. Fluctuations in airspeed make it difficult to judge and control the approach.

The sailplane should be aligned with the aim point while maintaining a constant glide angle so the apparent shape of the landing area remains constant, as illustrated in figure 14-16,

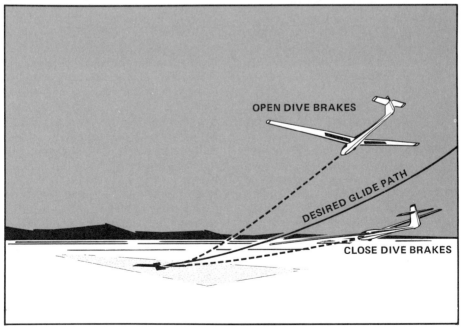

Fig. 14-15. Glide Path Adjustments

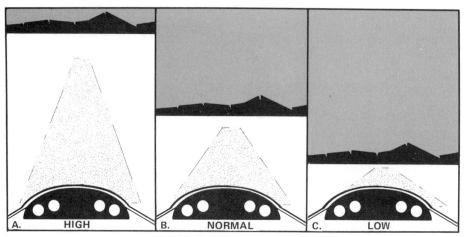

Fig. 14-16. Runway Appearance

item B. If the approach is too high, the landing area appears longer and steeper, as shown in item A, and the aim point appears to move down the canopy toward the sailplane. Conversely, if the approach is too low, the landing area appears to shorten and become wider, as depicted in item C, and the aim point moves up the canopy and appears to move farther away. Therefore, if a constant approach angle is maintained, the sides of the landing area hold the same relationship and the aim point remains in a fixed position in relation to the sailplane's canopy.

Flaps also may be used as a means of controlling the approach and landing. After about 25° of downward deflection of the flaps, the increase in lift is offset by much greater drag, and the glide angle becomes steeper. The lowered stalling speed with flaps down allows a slower approach speed. If the flaps are lowered to more than 45°, even steeper

approach angles may be used. Flaps should not be lowered until the pilot is absolutely certain of making the landing area. Another rule to be followed is that flaps should *never* be retracted when the sailplane is close to the ground because there will be a sudden loss of lift, causing the sailplane to sink rapidly, and make a hard landing.

Precise airspeed control is required, because excess airspeed can result in overshooting or ballooning on the flare for landing. Too slow an airspeed can cause high sink rates or a stall. In either case, a hard landing may result. The flare should be initiated as the sailplane approaches the aim point at an altitude of approximately 5 feet. When the flare is completed, the sailplane will be *slightly* nose high, as illustrated in figure 14-17. Too much back pressure and airspeed will cause the sailplane to balloon, while too little airspeed and a high flare may cause a

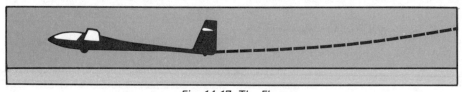

Fig. 14-17. The Flare

hard landing. Should the sailplane balloon, the dive brakes should be closed and a new landing initiated.

The sailplane will continue to float in ground effect after the flare. The dive brakes or spoilers should be partially opened, while maintaining a slight nose-high pitch attitude. They may be adjusted, as necessary, to either extend or reduce floating distance.

LANDING AND ROLL-OUT

The landing should be made without further adjusting the pitch attitude. The sailplane will gradually settle to the landing surface. Once the sailplane is on the landing surface, the pilot should continue to fly it along the ground with the wings level until the controls become ineffective. If dive brakes were not used during the landing flare, they should be partially opened after touchdown. Then, the brakes can be applied smoothly to bring the sailplane to a straight stop.

CROSSWIND LANDING

The traffic pattern for crosswind landings is the same up to the final approach using crab to maintain pattern alignment. In light to moderate crosswinds, a wing-low side slip or crab may be used on final to maintain runway alignment. A strong crosswind usually requires a combination of the two. Since the slip increases the rate of descent, less dive brake normally will be used.

If the crab or a combination method is used, the sailplane is straightened with the rudder just before touchdown. The wing should be kept slightly low into the wind throughout the touchdown and roll-out to prevent it from being lifted, and directional control maintained with rudder.

If a difficult crosswind landing due to high crosswinds is anticipated, and the runway is wide enough, an acceptable procedure is to align the sailplane with the downwind side of the runway on final approach, and land as shown in figure 14-18.

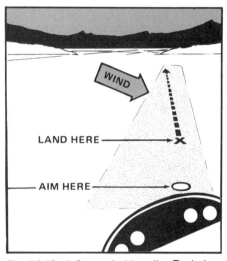

Fig. 14-18. A Crosswind Landing Technique

DOWNWIND LANDING

Downwind landings should be the exception rather than the rule and, except in an emergency situation, they should not be attempted in tailwinds exceeding 20 m.p.h. There are few differences between landing in light tailwinds and light headwinds. However, the technique used in moderate tailwinds (between 15 and 20 m.p.h.) is different. The downwind leg should be extended to permit a longer final approach and the aim point must be moved farther back from the desired touchdown point.

The final approach, flare, and landing are made like a normal headwind landing, but at a higher groundspeed. Care must be taken to maintain the proper approach speed, since there is a tendency to attempt to slow the sailplane to compensate for the higher groundspeed.

After touchdown, the pilot should continue to fly the sailplane directly down the center of the landing surface, keeping the wings as level as possible. The wheel brake is used to slow the sailplane as long as it is going straight. The nose skid also helps to slow the sailplane as soon as it drops to the surface. Swerves should be stopped as soon as possible.

The maneuvers and traffic patterns discussed in this chapter provide the foundation for all aspects of soaring. They should be practiced until each can be performed smoothly and with precision.

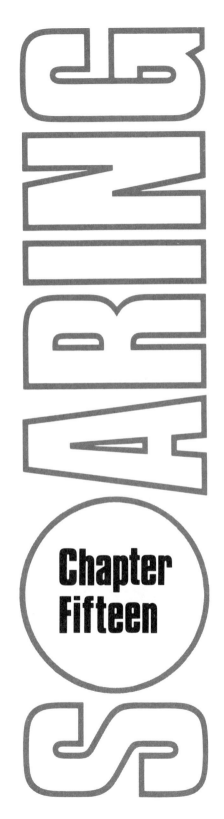

SOARING

Chapter
Fifteen

Soaring Techniques

INTRODUCTION The success of a sailplane flight is measured by whether it stays aloft long enough to accomplish the purpose of the flight. The ability to find and work the different sources of lift largely determines the length of the flight.

This chapter presents the techniques used to locate and take advantage of the lift generated by thermals, ridges, waves, and mountains. The meteorological aspects of these sources of lift were discussed in the weather chapter and will be mentioned only briefly here.

THERMAL ACTIVITY

Thermals are rising bodies of warm air varying in size and shape. They are rarely stationary, since they are moved about, tilted, or broken up by wind shear.

Two general weather conditions are required to generate the convection currents necessary for natural thermal production. First, the sky must be clear enough for the sun to warm the earth's surface. Second, atmospheric conditions generally must be *unstable*.

Unfortunately, thermals cannot be seen by the naked eye. Soaring pilots must, therefore, recognize the various indicators of thermal activity. A cumulus cloud in its building stage, as illustrated in figure 15-1, is probably the most important indicator because it represents rising heat and moisture. Other indicators of thermal activity include dust columns (dust devils), swirls of dust on the ground, and rising smoke.

Fig. 15-1. Cumulus in Building Stage

When atmospheric indicators are insufficient or totally absent in dry air, it is necessary to look for thermal-producing ground features. Dark, smooth surfaces, such as paved highways and parking lots, radiate large amounts of solar heat. They are ideal for generating convective currents. Brown fields, dry river beds, industrial areas, and cities usually produce more thermal activity than areas covered with vegetation.

Although thermals may extend as high as 50,000 feet in extreme conditions such as thunderstorms, they normally reach a peak usable height of 5,000 to 10,000 feet AGL on a typical good day. The actual usable peak height varies with such factors as regional climate, cloud formations, and other general weather conditions. If a temperature inversion is present, the thermal will be capped by the inverted layer.

Thermal activity normally begins in mid-morning and diminishes in late afternoon. The strongest activity typically occurs in mid-afternoon, but can be influenced by sudden airmass changes or other factors. A weather forecaster usually can predict when thermal activity will begin and how strong it will be. If a forecast is not available, the thermal index can be used to predict probable conditions.

THERMAL SOARING

Working a thermal is somewhat like groping around in a dark room trying to find the light switch. The strongest lift, like the light switch, can be found only by exploration. First, however, it is necessary to locate a thermal.

Initial entry into a thermal may be felt as a mild bump. At other times, the sailplane may enter a high sink area just before reaching the thermal. The transition from sinking to rising air may be characterized by a bump or it may be relatively smooth. Once a thermal has been entered, a high degree of concentration is required to find the best lift.

Immediate decisions must be made while analyzing the thermal structure, such as when and in which direction to turn. "Is the lift stronger to the left or to the right?" is the first question that must be answered. The best indication is an induced roll away from the side with the stronger lift. It may be very slight, so the pilot must be aware of involuntary, or instinctive aileron corrections.

If a turn has been made in the wrong direction, as indicated by an immediate decrease in climb rate, the technique shown in figure 15-2 is used. After approximately 270° of turn, the sailplane should be rolled level. A few seconds after the lift is encountered, it should be turned in the original direction.

The best indication of *when* to turn should come from the variometer. It peaks out in the strongest lift area and falls off in weaker areas. If the variometer has a constant upward reading, probably the sailplane is well within the thermal. When a climb is first indicated, a turn should be initiated after a slight delay. An early turn can cause the sailplane to miss the thermal entirely.

When a turn has been made in the proper direction but is too late or too shallow, the pattern is corrected using the procedure illustrated in figure 15-3. A late or shallow turn may be indicated by the disappearance of lift before 90° of turn has been completed. In this event, the turn should be continued until the thermal is reentered. Then, a short period of straight flight is used to adjust the turning pattern so the sailplane will remain in the thermal.

An early turn, shown in figure 15-4, is indicated if the lift loss occurs between

90° and 180° of turn. In this event, a full 360° turn should be made before rolling out. After a few seconds of straight-and-level flight, a second turn should be started in the original direction. This procedure moves the turning circle closer to the thermal core.

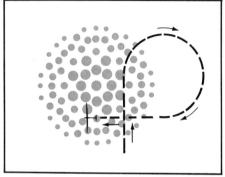

Fig. 15-2. Turning the Wrong Way

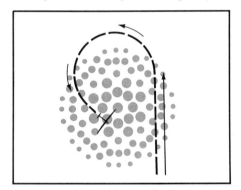

Fig. 15-3. Late Turn

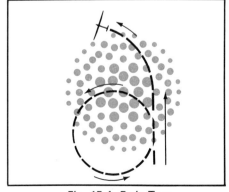

Fig. 15-4. Early Turn

Normally, it is necessary to repeat the orientation procedure each time the thermal is entered. After several adjustments, the location, size, and intensity of the thermal become more evident. It is important to maintain a uniform circling pattern while exploring the thermal. Otherwise, the pilot may become disoriented and lose the thermal. The direction of turn usually should not be reversed, as this can cause the sailplane to fly out of the lift area.

If more than one sailplane is circling in the same thermal, all must turn in the same direction. The *first sailplane in the thermal establishes the direction of turn*. Each pilot must constantly be alert for other traffic while thermalling.

The best airspeed to use while thermalling is the minimum sink speed for the bank angle being flown. Faster or slower speeds reduce the rate of climb. If the thermal is turbulent, however, a slightly higher airspeed may be necessary to maintain adequate control.

Cross-country thermalling requires special techniques to take maximum advantage of lift areas, while avoiding or minimizing areas of sink. It is wise to fly downwind of potential lift-producing areas and on the sun side of hills or ridges. Lines of cumulus clouds, called "cloud streets," may produce a continuous source of lift and should be used when available. On the other hand, blue sky areas with no clouds should be avoided, unless lift indicators are visible on the ground.

When flying between thermals or in high sink areas, it is important to fly at best L/D speed or faster, depending on sailplane performance. Speed is reduced when lift is encountered and minimum sink speed is flown while thermalling.

SHEAR LINE SOARING

A shear line is an area where two opposing airmasses converge, as shown in figure 15-5. These airmasses are much smaller than the ones that create the frontal systems displayed on weather maps. The lift of a convergence zone usually is rather narrow, and if one of the airmasses contains moisture, it may be marked by a line of small cumulus. Often, a shear line is too short to take a sailplane any significant distance, but it provides adequate lift for local soaring.

WARM   COLD

Fig. 15-5. Shear Line

RIDGE AND SLOPE SOARING

Ridges and slopes provide a different type of lift than thermals. As the wind strikes a hillside, it is deflected up the slope, creating orographic lift. Then, it moves downward after passing over the ridge, or crest. If the slope is steep, there is a possibility of turbulence on the downwind side.

The technique used in ridge soaring, illustrated in figure 15-6, is to fly parallel to the upwind slope, crabbing into the wind as necessary. Entry into the ridge lift area should be at a shallow angle, rather than directly toward the ridge. This will permit a safe turn away from the ridge, if the lift is not as strong as anticipated.

The best speed to fly varies with the distance from the slope. When close to the ridge, a faster speed is used to give better control response. As the sailplane moves away from the slope or slightly above it, minimum sink speed will help to attain the maximum height above the ridge.

If the sailplane enters an area where lift ends, the pilot should turn back to the area of known lift. There is no guarantee new lift will be found farther down the ridge. Flying over the crest or on the downwind side should always be avoided because of the danger of strong downdrafts and turbulence.

Ridge soaring in the United States offers great possibilities for cross-country flight because of the abundance of mountain ranges. Many flights have been made in excess of 500 miles using ridge lift. However, several general rules must be obeyed when flying ridges. They may be modified under certain circumstances to fit local situations. The general rules, illustrated in figure 15-7, are as follows:

1 Never fly directly over or under another sailplane.

2 When overtaking slower sailplanes, pass on the inside toward the ridge.

3 Make all turns away from the ridge into the wind.

4 Sailplanes approaching each other head-on give way to the right.

THE WAVE

A *wave* is caused by a stable airmass and strong winds blowing across a

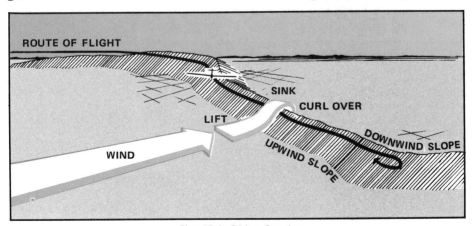

Fig. 15-6. Ridge Soaring

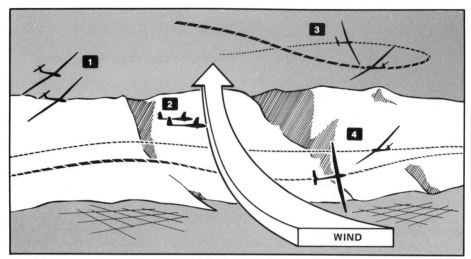

Fig. 15-7. Ridge Soaring Rules

mountain range or other obstruction. These waves may be called mountain waves, standing waves, or lee waves, but they are all the same type of rising air phenomena. Wave effects caused by wind shear occasionally may be observed over flat areas.

Unlike ridge lift, the smooth, strong updrafts of wave lift are on the *downwind* side of the obstruction. The activity may occur at any time of year, but it is more marked in winter than in summer.

Waves have been the source of lift for most altitude records, and flights above 30,000 feet are common in certain areas. The potential of wave lift is in excess of 50,000 feet, limited only by physiological constraints.

The situation most conducive to waves is an extended barrier, such as a mountain range, with a steep drop on the downwind side. For waves to form, the wind along the tops of the mountains must have a velocity of at least 25 knots, nearly perpendicular to the mountain range. Figure 15-8 illustrates the basic airflow pattern. As the wind passes over a mountain range, it begins a series of harmonic motions, forming waves, much as waves develop on a

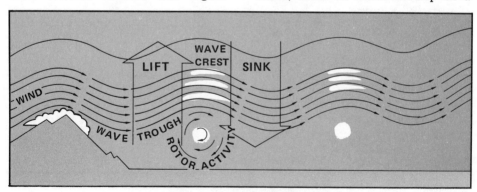

Fig. 15-8. Mountain Wave

disturbed water surface. The result is alternate areas of lift at the wave crests and sink in the wave troughs.

Wave crests often may be identified by lenticular, or lens-shaped clouds, shown in figure 15-9, which form when sufficient moisture is present. An area of rotor activity and turbulence is located beneath each wave crest. This area often is identifiable by the presence of a rotor, or roll cloud. An area of strong lift usually may be found just upwind from the rotor cloud.

WAVE SOARING

Normally, the sailplane is towed into the smooth lift of the wave, avoiding the rotor area, if possible. After release, the sailplane should be turned into the wind and slowed to minimum sink speed. Wave lift is worked by maintaining position over the ground, since the best lift area usually remains stationary with respect to the ground. If the sailplane drifts upwind from the lift, reduced speed or "S" turns can be used to regain position. Full 360° turns are not recommended, unless the winds are very light. A typical wave *flight profile* is depicted in figure 15-10.

Fig. 15-9. Lenticular Cloud

As the climb continues, the wind may become strong enough to keep the sailplane stationary in relation to the ground. Then it may become necessary to speed up to keep from being blown back away from the area of best lift.

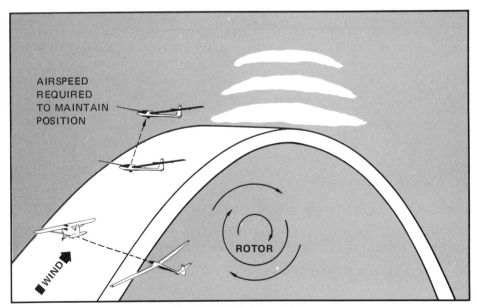

AIRSPEED
REQUIRED
TO MAINTAIN
POSITION

ROTOR

WIND

Fig. 15-10. Working a Wave

A more difficult method of entering the wave is by climbing in the rotor area. A low release can be made on the upwind side of the rotor, although the air is very turbulent and difficult to work until contact is made with the wave.

MOUNTAIN SOARING

Mountain soaring should be attempted only after becoming proficient in thermal, ridge, and wave soaring. All three of these types of lift frequently are produced by mountains, although not necessarily at the same time or as close together as shown in figure 15-11. The experienced pilot can take advantage of each type, soaring from one to another, while avoiding undesirable areas.

The sunny side of the mountain radiates more heat than the shady side. This normally results in thermal lift on the sunny side, often marked by cumulus clouds, and sink over the shaded areas. The sailplane pilot can use this source of thermal lift by flying close to the ridge on the sunny side.

Orographic, or ridge lift, is created when the wind flows upward toward the mountain slopes. The opposite side of the ridge will have sink as a result of the wind curl-over. Mountain waves may exist on the lee side of the ridge, downwind from the mountain range. Extreme caution is required because of the roller-coaster pattern of lift and sink associated with mountain waves. If the wave activity is intense or winds are high, cross-country flights into the mountains should be avoided.

The uneven structure of a mountain range encourages moderate to severe turbulence as the wind is deflected in different directions. The pilot must constantly plan a defensive strategy. For example, when attempting to cross over a ridge from the upwind side, the approach should be made at an angle. With this technique, a turn can be

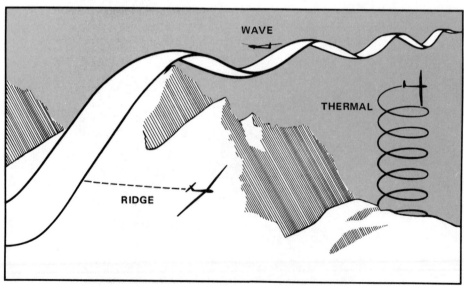

Fig. 15-11. Mountain Soaring

made away from the high terrain, if the sailplane has attained insufficient altitude to safely cross the ridge.

When approaching a ridge from the downwind side, the sailplane must have sufficient altitude and airspeed to pass through the high sink area with a safe margin. This approach also is made at an angle to facilitate a turn away from the ridge, if necessary. Both techniques are illustrated in figure 15-12.

Mountain weather often changes very rapidly and with little warning. Thunderstorms and heavy rain or snow showers can suddenly build up and effectively block a planned or alternate escape route. Pilots should be aware of changing weather conditions and leave the mountains at the first sign of severe activity.

The most important consideration for mountain soaring is to be *at all times* within safe gliding distance of a suitable landing area. Also, an extra margin of altitude should be allowed for the sailplane to transit safely any unexpected downdrafts. Valleys usually provide the only safe landing areas, unless the flight is near the edge of the mountain range.

Another important requirement for mountain soaring is a thorough knowledge of speeds to fly. Minimum sink speed should be used only when well clear of a slope and in lift. At other times, sufficient airspeed must be maintained to insure adequate control response.

This chapter has discussed the techniques used for thermal, ridge, and wave soaring and all three types of lift for mountain soaring. Each provides a source of pure enjoyment and challenge. With practice and study, these sources of lift will take you to new heights and distances.

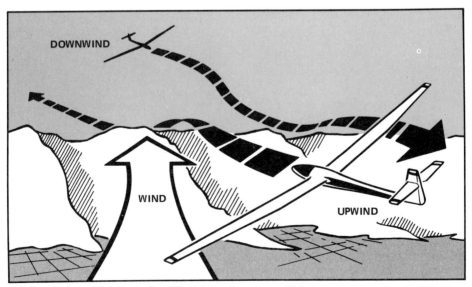

Fig. 15-12. Crossing a Ridge

Cross-Country Soaring

INTRODUCTION The greatest challenge for many soaring pilots is the first flight away from the local airport. Cross-country soaring requires a working knowledge of many chapters contained in the *Soaring Flight Manual*. The pilot should be familiar with medical factors, regulations, soaring computations, personal equipment, aeronautical charts, and the national airspace system, and be proficient in all flight operations.

This chapter is designed to highlight the factors which influence the successful completion of any cross-country flight. It includes flight preparation, FAI Soaring Awards, pretrip considerations, in-flight decisions, and off-field landings.

FLIGHT PREPARATION

Cross-country soaring is a safe and exhilarating sport. Like most other sports, it requires practice to attain the skill level necessary to accomplish it successfully. Two areas which require a high level of proficiency are spot landings and the ability to work a series of lift sources effectively. Dual instruction at the home airport will provide the needed flight experience.

SPOT LANDINGS

The home field can be used to practice spot landings. A simulated field, approximately 500 feet long and 100 feet wide, should be chosen for this purpose. If possible, it should be a sod area away from the normal landing area and laid out in a different direction.

Spot landings should be practiced within this area until they can be performed with accuracy, using short-field techniques such as slips and full dive brake approaches. The approaches should be fairly steep to simulate landing over the obstacles which commonly surround farm fields.

WORKING LIFT

Cross-country soaring consists basically of working a series of lift sources which are close enough together to be used as stepping stones toward a goal. Before any cross-country is attempted, however, it is necessary to be adept at recognizing the various sources of lift and to be able to work them with consistency.

An excellent tool to use for cross-country training is the 17-mile triangle, illustrated in figure 16-1. It affords the luxury of remaining within a safe gliding distance of the gliderport, while permitting practice in holding a heading, finding, entering, and leaving lift sources, and then proceeding on course to predetermined checkpoints. These are all prerequisites of a cross-country flight.

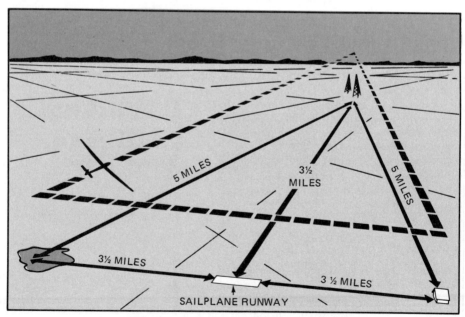

Fig. 16-1. Cross-Country Practice Triangle

Further practice increases the speed over the course and improves ability to judge how long to work any particular source of lift. Once proficiency is developed and the necessary confidence is gained, the instructor may sign off the pilot's logbook for cross-country flight. The next step is selecting a goal, and then planning and organizing the cross-country flight.

SOARING AWARDS

Goal selection is one of the most important aspects for any type of soaring. Every flight should have some particular goal in mind, since nothing leads to boredom faster than flying aimlessly around an airport at the top of a thermal. *Boredom also leads to the development of bad or careless habits.*

The Soaring Society of America has established a training program designed to provide goals for students prior to cross-country flight. Each level of achievement is recognized by an award. An "A pin" is presented after solo, a "B pin" is awarded for proficiency in basic soaring flight, and a "C pin" is presented when the student is ready for cross-country flight.

After the initial SSA training awards have been received, the next goal to strive for is the FAI awards. This badge system was established by the Federation Aeronautique Internationale, the world governing body of aeronautical competition and record keeping. The Soaring Society of America is a member of this organization and administers the FAI program in the United States. These awards and their specific requirements are depicted in figure 16-2.

The detailed rules for the FAI Awards are available from SSA. A current copy should be reviewed before a badge attempt, since occasionally the rules change and barograph and photo procedures are strictly enforced. The following conditions are a summary of the rules:

SILVER BADGE

1. A flight of at least 5 hours duration
2. A flight of at least 50 kilometers in a straight line (31.1 statute miles)
3. A height gain of at least 1,000 meters (3,281 feet)

GOLD BADGE

1. A flight of at least 5 hours duration (may be the same flight as for the Silver Badge)
2. A distance flight of 300 kilometers (186.4 statute miles)
3. A height gain of at least 3,000 meters (9,842 feet)

A Diamond may be added to the Gold Badge for each of the following tasks:
1. A flight of at least 300 kilometers over a triangular or out-and-return course.
2. A distance flight of 500 kilometers (311 statute miles)
3. A height gain of 5000 meters (16,400 feet)

Fig. 16-2. FAI Awards

1. An SSA Official Observer must supervise each flight.
2. The sailplane must be occupied solely by the pilot.
3. A sealed barograph must be carried on all altitude and distance flights and on most duration flights.
4. Distance flights with a turn point must have the turn around the point verified, usually by a photograph.
5. The 300- and 500-kilometer flight may be made in a straight line, a triangle, a goal-and-return, or a dog-leg with one turning point. All distance flights are subject to a penalty when the altitude lost between release and landing is over 1,000 meters (3,281 feet).

PRETRIP PLANNING

Accurate and complete pretrip planning contributes to the success of any cross-country flight. There are many steps to be taken and nothing should be left to chance. Most pilots develop a cross-country checklist to insure that every item is taken care of properly. Figure 16-3 is a sample checklist. Items may be added or deleted as necessary.

CROSS-COUNTRY CHECKLIST

PREPLANNING
1. Select goal
2. Obtain FAI application
3. Check weather
4. Arrange for crew
5. Plan the flight
6. Prepare two sets of maps (One for pilot, one for crew) Annotate checkpoints and restricted areas
7. Schedule sailplane and trailer (if necessary)
8. Personal items
   a. Warm clothing
   b. Cash for phone calls
   c. Food and water
   d. First aid kit
9. Equipment
   a. Tiedown kit
   b. Tools

CREW BRIEFING
1. Radio procedures (contact points)
2. Maps and map reading
3. Lost communications procedures
4. Telephone procedures
5. Miscellaneous items
   a. Car keys
   b. Cash
   c. Credit card
   d. Full gas tank
6. Trailer
   a. Proper ball for hitch
   b. Lights, safety chain, and spare parts
   c. Tools and tiedowns
7. Check out car radio

IN FLIGHT
1. Check oxygen system each time passing 10,000 feet MSL
2. Follow pre-briefed radio procedures
3. Check for possible landing areas continuously
4. Monitor sailplane's position

1. Attempt to contact crew
2. Begin searching for field at 2,000 feet AGL
3. Select a field at 1,500 feet AGL
4. Prepare for landing at 1,000 feet AGL
   a. Determine wind direction
   b. Check for obstacles
   c. Fly a good pattern at the proper airspeeds.
   d. Do not use the altimeter

AFTER LANDING
1. Note the time and turn off barograph
2. Tie down and secure the sailplane
3. Phone crew
   a. Your location coordinates
   b. Number of nearest phone
   c. Recommended route for crew
4. Have two witnesses sign landing card (if possible)
5. Let an SSA observer open the barograph

Fig. 16-3. Cross-Country Checklist

A good procedure is to plan the first cross-country under the supervision of a flight instructor who is familiar with the area. First, a call is made to the local flight service station or Weather Service Office to ensure the weather is conducive to a cross-country flight. Next, the pilot should select a goal and begin laying out the flight on a sectional chart. The charts should be prepared with enough detail so they may be used to navigate and keep track of inflight progress. Minimum altitudes should be calculated and marked on the chart. Some pilots prepare a profile view of a trip, as illustrated in figure 16-4, to aid in preparing for the flight.

PROFILE VIEW

The profile view permits determination of the minimum flight altitudes which will allow the sailplane to return to the departure airport or proceed to the next decision point. A safety margin is provided to allow for unexpected sink or other performance degradations by planning on half the published L/D

ratio. For example, with a published L/D of 30:1, assume a no-wind glide ratio of 15 to 1, 17 to 1 with a 10 m.p.h. tailwind, and 13 to 1 into a 10 m.p.h. headwind. The flight profile should allow the sailplane to arrive over either airport at 1,000 feet AGL, so a normal traffic pattern can be flown.

The glide table for each part of the flight is calculated as follows: Using a 13 to 1 ratio to return to the departure airport, the amount of altitude which will be lost per mile is computed by dividing 5,280 by 13, which equals 406 feet. Using a 17 to 1 ratio to proceed to the destination airport, the amount of altitude which will be lost per mile is computed by dividing 5,280 by 17, which equals 311 feet. Then, the values for each distance segment can be computed and plotted on the profile view. The go-ahead point falls where the two lines intersect.

The lines intersect at a point approximately 13.9 miles from the departure airport and 18.1 from the

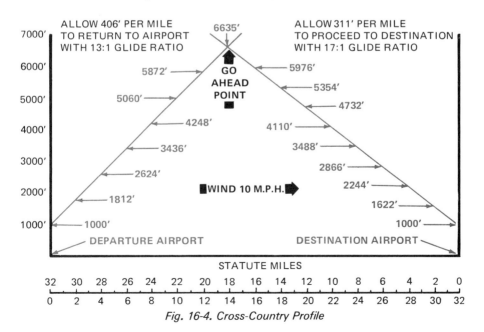

Fig. 16-4. Cross-Country Profile

destination airport, forming a go-ahead point at an approximate altitude of 6,635 feet above airport elevation. This altitude allows for a 1,000 foot pattern at each airport.

The profile chart can be used to determine the minimum enroute altitude at any particular point. The following procedures should be used any time the sailplane approaches a minimum altitude:

1. If the sailplane has not reached the go-ahead point at the minimum altitude, make an immediate turn and return to the departure airport. While returning, work any lift which may permit resuming course to the destination.
2. Enroute, work any lift above the minimum altitude for that point; otherwise, continue toward the next decision point or final goal.
3. After the go-ahead point is crossed, check progress and minimum altitudes periodically.
4. Get high and stay high. It is particularly important to be as high as possible toward the end of the thermal day.

The proper airspeed to use when flying with a tailwind on a cross-country is the best L/D. This airspeed should be increased by one-half of the estimated wind velocity when flying into a headwind.

Longer cross-country flights become a series of these profile charts. When used properly, the sailplane always remains within range of an airport or a suitable landing area.

EQUIPMENT

The next step in preflight planning is organizing the equipment needed for flight. Each item should be checked off the list and set aside for subsequent loading into the sailplane. The equipment recommended for specific

circumstances has been illustrated in the cross-country checklist earlier in the chapter.

CREW

Two or three people generally are enough for a good crewing team. It is up to the pilot to make sure the crew members are trained properly and know exactly what is expected during the flight. Again, a checklist should be used to make sure nothing is overlooked.

IN-FLIGHT DECISIONS

The motives for flying cross-country are different from those used near the airport. During initial training, staying up as long as possible is foremost, while in cross-country flying, speed becomes an all important factor. It is a race against time. In-flight decisions such as when to take off, when to release, when to leave the airport, how to find lift, how long to stay with a source of lift, how fast to fly between thermals, and when to begin looking for a place to land become all-important.

STARTING TIME

The answer to the question "When to take off?" depends on the goal, and weather. Longer flights need to begin as early as possible. The time varies daily and with locale and season, but experienced pilots in the area can give a good estimate.

The graph illustrated in figure 16-5 shows a trend in thermal height for a typical day. Thermal activity begins at about 10:30 in the morning and is maximum between 2:00 and 5:30 p.m.

TOW RELEASE

There is a great temptation for many pilots to release from the tow plane at the first sign of a good thermal. Many

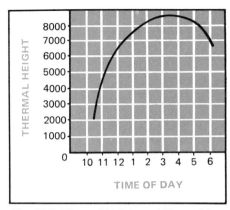

Fig. 16-5. Thermal Height and Time of Day

experts, however, feel it is best to stay on tow until a minimum altitude of 2,000 feet AGL is reached.

The first consideration after releasing is staying up, so it is wise to return to any known area of lift. As a general rule, the pilot should stay with any lift below 2,000 feet, unless the sailplane is drifting away from the gliderport.

LEAVING THE AIRPORT

The next decision to be made is whether to depart the airport and proceed on course. It should be made only when reasonably certain the sailplane can stay up. This decision should be based on the intensity of the lift in the vicinity of the airport, the sailplane's altitude, and how the weather looks in the direction of the destination.

SEARCHING FOR LIFT

Unless the pilot is fortunate enough to find a cloud street along the sailplane's course, a definite plan should be used in searching for lift. The best signs of thermal activity are cumulus clouds, dust columns, or smoke.

Finding a thermal is sometimes the result of a well-calculated guess. The closer the sailplane is to the cloud

bases, the easier it is to find thermals. The beginning wisp of a cumulus cloud usually has more intense thermal activity than small cumulus clouds, but, in the absence of these wisps, small cumulus in the growing stage usually provide acceptable lift. Clouds that appear firm around the edges are usually building, and should provide lift. Ragged, ill-defined clouds are usually dissipating, and may provide only sink.

The best policy when searching for a thermal is to experiment. When a thermal is found, the position that has the strongest lift relative to the cloud should be noted. The same position relative to other clouds also should provide strong lift. Generally, the best lift is found on the upwind side of a building cumulus cloud.

LEAVING LIFT

Speed is the all-important factor in cross-country flying since there is a limited amount of time for thermal activity. This becomes even more critical for long distance flights. For this reason, it is important to keep moving from thermal to thermal as rapidly as possible. This technique is illustrated in figure 16-6.

A rule-of-thumb used by many cross-country flyers to determine how long to remain with a thermal is to note the variometer when the thermal is giving the highest reading. When the lift drops to about 75 percent of the highest reading, it is advisable to leave and proceed on course if sufficient altitude has been achieved to easily reach the next thermal.

A good technique when leaving a thermal is to increase the airspeed until the variometer reads zero, while continuing to circle, and then roll out on

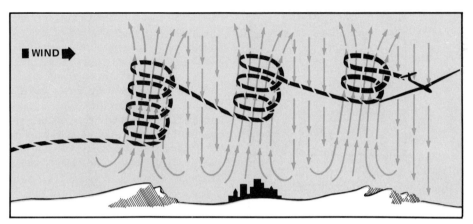

Fig. 16-6. Cross-Country Thermalling

course. This permits rapid penetration of the sinking air surrounding the thermal.

It is *not* advisable to stop and work another thermal if less than 1,000 feet of altitude has been used, unless it is considerably stronger than the last thermal. It is advisable to slow the sailplane to minimum sink airspeed while passing through lift, even if a decision is made not to circle. This technique is known as porpoising.

SPEED BETWEEN LIFT SOURCES

There are many ways to compute the speeds to fly between the various sources of lift. One emphasizes the use of the McCready speed ring mounted on the variometer's circular face.

Some pilots prefer to use general rules-of-thumb. A popular technique is to fly the variometer at a down reading equal to the last average climb rate when sufficient altitude is available. For example, if the variometer averaged a 400 f.p.m. rate of climb in the last thermal, a 400 f.p.m. rate of descent would be used while searching for the next thermal. The best L/D speed should be used at lower altitudes, or when conditions are weak.

Another technique which has been found effective for sailplanes with less sophisticated instruments is to increase speed to approximately 20 percent greater than the best L/D speed, depending on existing conditions. The higher speed would be used for good conditions while best L/D speed would be used for poor conditions.

Regardless of the method, a pilot should use good judgement when making inflight decisions on speed. In any case, pilots should remember to *speed up in sink* and *slow down in lift*. It is also wise to maintain interthermal speed until reaching the core of the next thermal, since high areas of sink usually exist on the edges of thermals.

OFF-FIELD LANDINGS

Every sailplane pilot should be adequately prepared to make an off-field landing. Off-field landings naturally cause some anxiety, but any time the sailplane descends to approximately 3,000 feet AGL, it is time to begin a serious search for a suitable area. The area should be narrowed down at 2,000 feet AGL; by 1,500 feet, a specific field should be selected. It should be long enough to accomodate the sailplane, considering obstructions and wind. Obstructions in the approach path reduce the available field length by at least ten times the height required to clear them. If the field slopes, it is usually best to land uphill, even with a tailwind. The following guidelines should be used to choose a landing area.

1. The first choice should be a newly-mowed field of even texture. These fields usually have the fewest surprises such as large rocks, stumps, ditches or holes.
2. The second choice would be a cultivated field.
3. A field with a short crop would be the next choice.
4. Pastures are often very hard; however, they can have holes, bushes, livestock, or other obstructions.
5. Higher crops should be well down the list of preferred landing sites because of destruction of crops, the possibility of a ground loop, and damage to the sailplane.

THE PATTERN AND LANDING

An ideal traffic pattern for an off-field landing is shown in figure 16-7. It contains an overhead leg, used to check field conditions and obstructions. On the crosswind leg, a continuing check of the landing area can be made while planning to enter the downwind leg at the proper distance from the field.

If it is necessary to approach over high obstacles, the base leg should be over or inside the obstructions. It is very important to maintain the proper approach speed, for precise glide path control.

A normal touchdown should be made just inside the landing area and the sailplane should be brought to a stop as quickly as possible. It should then be properly secured and tied down.

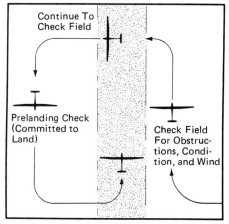

Fig. 16-7. Off-Field Landing Pattern

PILOT/FARMER RELATIONS

When a sailplane lands in a farmer's field, it is wise to remember that the pilot is a trespasser. The farmer is usually concerned about crops and livestock.

The pilot's attitude and concern toward the farmer's property will have a lot to do with the amount of cooperation received. The golden rule in this situation is to try to assume the farmer's viewpoint and conduct yourself as a guest.

After a good relationship has been established with the farmer, the next step is to notify the crew. The following items should be the minimum information given to the crew.

1. Telephone number at your present location

2. The coordinates of the field
3. Direction to the field or your location.

While the crew is enroute, the pilot should analyze all aspects of the flight and make notes on the good and bad decisions and what skills need improvement. These notes can be used to plan the next flight and establish future goals in cross-country soaring.

This chapter has highlighted the knowledge and skill areas to be developed before your first solo cross-country. Further instruction and study will equip you to enjoy one of the most gratifying experiences in soaring.

Introduction

The workbook section is designed to complement the text section of the manual. Each exercise relates to the corresponding chapter in the text.

A navigation plotter is necessary for some of the exercises in Chapter 9, and the time-speed-distance problems in that section can be solved more easily with the aid of a flight computer. No other supplemental materials are needed to complete the workbook exercises.

Several methods of answering questions are used in this workbook. Circle the correct choice on multiple choice questions, and fill in the blanks on the rest. An answer section follows the workbook to enable you to verify your answers.

Chapter 1 - Sailplane Aerodynamics

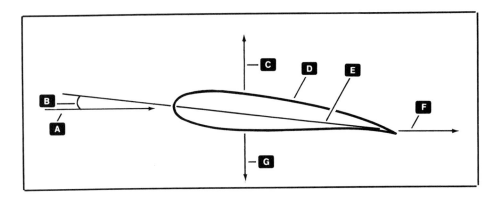

Identify the following items shown in the accompanying airfoil illustration.

1. Lift _____
2. Drag _____
3. Gravity _____
4. Camber _____
5. Chord line _____
6. Angle of attack_____
7. Relative wind _____

8. The angle at which the wings are attached to the fuselage is called the angle of
   1. deflection.
   2. attack.
   3. incidence.
   4. attachment.

9. If the airflow breaks away from the upper wing surface to the extent that adequate lift is no longer produced, the wing has exceeded its critical
   1. pitch angle.
   2. angle of incidence.
   3. lift angle.
   4. angle of attack.

10. A nearly vertical descent with the nose down and the sailplane descending in a helical, or cork screw path is a
    1. stall.
    2. spiral.
    3. auto-rotation.
    4. spin.

11. When a wing drops as the result of a stall, the higher wing continues to produce some lift. This induces a rolling movement called
    1. a barrel roll.
    2. spinning.
    3. spiraling.
    4. auto-rotation.

12. What action is necessary to break a stall in a sailplane?
    1. Stop the spin
    2. Reduce the angle of attack
    3. Reduce the airspeed
    4. Open the dive brakes

13. As air density increases, the amount of lift available at a constant airspeed and angle of attack _____ (increases, (decreases).

14. A drag force created as a by-product of lift is called
    1. lift drag.
    2. parasite drag.
    3. adverse drag.
    4. induced drag.

15. A drag force caused by the air's resistance to passage of the sailplane is called
    1. total drag.
    2. induced drag.
    3. parasite drag.
    4. friction drag.

16. As indicated airspeed decreases at a constant lift value, induced drag _____ (increases, decreases).

17. As indicated airspeed increases, parasite drag _____ (increases, decreases).

18. The airspeed at which the minimum total drag occurs is called the best
    1. L/D speed.
    2. total drag speed.
    3. glide speed.
    4. rate-of-climb speed.

19. The force that provides the forward movement of the sailplane through the air is
    1. total lift.
    2. reverse drag.
    3. gravity.
    4. pressure differential.

20. Which wing shape, or planform, is characterized by a rapid transition from maximum lift to a stall without the normal stall warning?
    1. Elliptical
    2. Rectangular
    3. Tapered
    4. Swept forward

21. A design feature that causes a stall to begin at the wing root instead of at the tip is called
    1. wing sweep.
    2. washout.
    3. taper.
    4. a stall indicator.

22. The relationship between the wing span and the wing chord is called the
    1. wing taper ratio.
    2. L/D ratio.
    3. aspect ratio.
    4. length-to-width ratio.

23. In what way are lift and drag affected by extending the flaps?
    1. Lift decreases and drag decreases.
    2. Lift increases and drag increases.
    3. Lift increases and drag decreases.
    4. Lift decreases and drag increases.

24. Which flap design is most efficient in terms of the least drag for the amount of lift produced?
    1. Plain flap
    2. Slotted flap
    3. Fowler flap
    4. Negative flap

25. When a slight upward, or negative, flap deflection is used, the result is
    1. increased drag.
    2. increased lift.
    3. decreased drag.
    4. decreased lift.

26. The flap design that increases the area of the airfoil is the
    1. plain flap.
    2. slotted flap.
    3. fowler flap.
    4. negative flap.

27. Spoilers are installed on the _____ (upper, lower) wing surfaces.

28. The primary purpose of spoilers is to
    1. decrease lift.
    2. increase lift.
    3. decrease drag.
    4. increase drag.

29. Dive brakes are installed on the _____ (upper, lower, upper and lower) wing surfaces.

30. The primary purpose of dive brakes is to
    1. increase lift and increase drag.
    2. increase lift and decrease drag.
    3. decrease lift and decrease drag.
    4. decrease lift and increase drag.

31. Movement about the vertical axis is controlled by the
    1. ailerons.
    2. rudder.
    3. elevator.
    4. flaps.

32. Movement about the lateral axis is controlled by the
    1. ailerons.
    2. rudder.
    3. elevator.
    4. flaps.

33. Movement about the longitudinal axis is controlled by the
    1. ailerons.
    2. rudder.
    3. elevator.
    4. flaps.

34. The roll axis is also known as the
    1. vertical axis.
    2. lateral axis.
    3. horizontal axis.
    4. longitudinal axis.

35. All movements of the sailplane in flight revolve around the
    1. geometric center.
    2. central axis.
    3. pilot's seat.
    4. center of gravity.

36. Fore and aft movement of the control stick will cause the sailplane to change its
    1. lateral direction.
    2. bank angle.
    3. angle of incidence.
    4. pitch attitude.

37. What is the reaction of the ailerons when the control stick is moved to the left?
    1. Left aileron deflects downward; right aileron deflects upward.
    2. Right aileron deflects downward; left aileron deflects upward.
    3. Left aileron deflects upward; right aileron deflects upward.
    4. Right aileron deflects upward; left aileron remains stationary.

38. When pressure is applied to the right rudder pedal, the nose of the sailplane moves to the _____ (left, right).

39. The tendency of a sailplane to maintain uniform flight and return to that condition when disturbed is called
    1. inertia.
    2. controllability.
    3. stability.
    4. positive trim.

40. Elevator control forces can be adjusted to maintain a desired pitch attitude by means of a
    1. control lock.
    2. horizontal stabilizer.
    3. stabilator.
    4. trim control.

41. If the sailplane's center of gravity exceeds the specified CG limits, the sailplane will lose its
    1. longitudinal stability.
    2. lateral stability.
    3. vertical stability.
    4. horizontal stability.

42. The tendency to return to wings-level flight is referred to as the sailplane's
    1. longitudinal stability.
    2. lateral stability.
    3. vertical stability.
    4. horizontal stability.

43. When the sailplane is turning in flight, the force that opposes the inward turning force is called
    1. counterforce.
    2. adverse yaw.
    3. gravity.
    4. centrifugal force.

44. At what bank angle will the resultant of gravity and centrifugal force equal twice the sailplane's weight?
    1. 15°
    2. 30°
    3. 45°
    4. 60°

45. A load factor of twice the sailplane's weight is expressed as

    _____ .

46. If a sailplane in a turn doubles its airspeed, the radius of the turn will be
    1. reduced by one-half.
    2. doubled.
    3. increased by one-half.
    4. quadrupled.

47. If airspeed is doubled at a constant bank angle, the rate of turn will be
    1. reduced by one-half.
    2. doubled.
    3. increased by one-half.
    4. quadrupled.

Chapter 2 - Performance Considerations

1. _____ (true, false) Density altitude can be read directly from the altimeter when 29.92 in. Hg. is set in the window.

2. As air temperature increases, air density _____ (increases, decreases).

3. When the density altitude is higher than indicated altitude, the true airspeed is _____ (higher, lower) than indicated airspeed.

4. _____ (true, false) The ratio of lift to drag will vary directly as a function of wind velocity.

5. A sailplane flying into a 20 m.p.h. headwind at a true airspeed of 60 m.p.h. would have a groundspeed of

   1. 20 m.p.h.
   2. 40 m.p.h.
   3. 60 m.p.h.
   4. 80 m.p.h.

6. Weight X Arm = _____

7. The location of the center of gravity is measured in inches from the

   1. moment.
   2. wings.
   3. datum.
   4. arm.

Use the following weight and arm data to complete items 8 through 11.

Item	Weight	Arm
Sailplane	710	96
Front Pilot	180	44
Rear Pilot	200	75

8. The empty sailplane CG moment is _____ .

9. The front pilot moment is _____ .

10. The rear pilot moment is _____ .

11. What is the actual flying center of gravity for this sailplane with two pilots?

    1. 71.67 in.
    2. 75.86 in.
    3. 79.27 in.
    4. 83.56 in.

12. Minimum sink speed may be defined as the airspeed that permits miminum altitude loss per unit of

    1. time.
    2. speed.
    3. distance.
    4. altitude.

13. If maximum distance over the ground is desired, the speed to fly in a calm wind is

1. maximum safe speed.
2. minimum sink speed.
3. best L/D speed.
4. minimum control speed.

14. _____ (true, false) A sailplane will always stall at the same indicated airspeed.

15. The ratio of the load supported by the wings to the actual weight of the sailplane is called the

1. G-factor.
2. load factor.
3. gross weight factor.
4. wing stress factor.

16. If a sailplane gains several thousand feet of altitude while maintaining a constant indicated airspeed, its true airspeed will

1. increase.
2. decrease.
3. fluctuate.
4. remain constant.

17. If a sailplane flying at minimum control airspeed were to increase the angle of attack, the result would be a

1. spin.
2. spiral.
3. pitch-up.
4. stall.

18. The maximum speed at which abrupt full control travel may be used without exceeding the load limits is called the

1. maximum control speed.
2. maneuvering speed.
3. never-exceed speed.
4. best L/D speed.

Chapter 3 - Flight Instruments

1. A magnetic compass can be used to follow a true course only if necessary corrections are made for magnetic _____ and compass _____.

2. The tendency of a compass to give erroneous indications when the sailplane is in a turn is due to a vertical attraction called magnetic _____.

3. A piece of yarn used as a slip/skid indicator is called a _____.

4. The metal ball used as an internally-mounted slip/skid indicator is called an _____.

5. The heart of the pitot-static system is a metal bellows called an _____.

6. The actual speed of a sailplane through the air is called
   1. calibrated airspeed.
   2. indicated airspeed.
   3. true groundspeed.
   4. true airspeed.

7. The sailplane's actual height above the terrain is called
   1. true altitude.
   2. absolute altitude.
   3. density altitude.
   4. pressure altitude.

8. The sailplane instrument that indicates the rate of climb or descent is the _____.

9. Around which axes does the attitude indicator show motion?
   1. Pitch and roll
   2. Roll and yaw
   3. Pitch and yaw

10. A pressure recording device used to provide a permanent record of pressure altitudes is the _____.

11. At an altitude of 5,000 feet AGL with no intervening obstructions, VHF radio waves can be received at a distance of approximately
    1. 40 miles.
    2. 80 miles.
    3. 120 miles.
    4. 160 miles.

12. The result of two radios transmitting simultaneously on the same frequency is a _____.

13. Fuzzy and indistinct transmissions are usually the result of
    1. holding the mike too far away.
    2. speaking directly into the mike.
    3. holding the mike too close.
    4. speaking across the mike.

14. When a turn is entered from a northerly heading, the magnetic compass initially indicates a turn in the _____ (same, opposite) direction.

15. In the accompanying illustration, the yaw string is indicating a _____ (skid, slip).

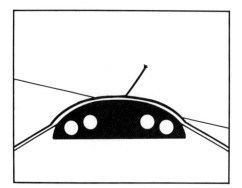

16. The inclinometer in the illustration is indicating a _____ (skid, slip).

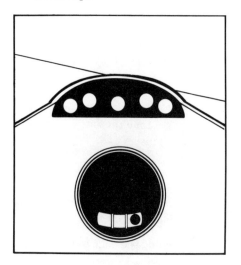

On the airspeed indicator pictured, identify the following items:

17. Never exceed speed _____

18. Flap operating range _____

19. Caution speed range _____

20. Normal operating range _____

21. Stall speed, flaps up _____

WHITE ARC

GREEN ARC

YELLOW ARC

RED LINE

Chapter 4 - Weather for Soaring

1. The force exerted by the weight of the atmosphere is called _____ _____.

2. As altitude increases, the weight of the air above _____ (increases, decreases).

3. Standard sea level atmospheric pressure is _____ in. Hg.

4. The general pattern of weather movement in the United States is

   1. east to west.
   2. west to east.
   3. north to south.
   4. south to north.

5. The amount of temperature drop for a specified increase in altitude is called the temperature _____ _____.

6. A station pressure reading of 24.92 in. Hg. on a standard day at 5,000 feet MSL would be converted to a sea level value of

   1. 19.92 in. Hg.
   2. 24.92 in. Hg.
   3. 24.97 in. Hg.
   4. 29.92 in. Hg.

7. Closely spaced isobars indicate that the pressure gradient is _____ (gentle, steep).

8. Light winds generally prevail when the pressure gradient is _____ (gentle, steep).

9. An atmospheric condition where temperature *increases* with altitude is caused by a temperature _____.

10. The total pattern of updrafts and downdrafts caused by sinking cold air forcing warm air to rise is called

    1. instability.
    2. lift and sink.
    3. thermal cycling.
    4. convective circulation.

11. Areas of lift, compared to areas of sink, generally cover a _____ (larger, smaller) portion of the total area of updrafts and downdrafts.

12. Thermal activity is possible only when the air is

    1. stable.
    2. moist.
    3. unstable.
    4. dry.

13. When a temperature inversion is present, soaring still may be possible _____ (above, beneath) the inverted layer.

14. What type of front sometimes develops when cool sea air moves inland to replace warm overland air?

    1. Cold front.
    2. Sea breeze front.
    3. Occluded front.
    4. Water front.

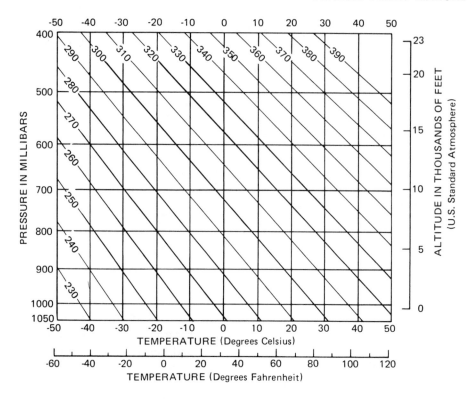

Use the accompanying pseudo-adiabatic chart to complete items 15 and 16.

15. Given:

    850-millibar temperature .... 20°C

    700-millibar temperature .... 10°C

    Forecast maximum .... 30°C

    Field elevation .... 2,000 feet

    Find:

    TI at 850 millibars _____

    TI at 700 millibars _____

16. Given:

    800-millibar temperature .... 15°C

    700-millibar temperature ..... 5°C

    600-millibar temperature .... -10°C

    Forecast maximum .... 35°C

    Field elevation .... 3,000 feet

Find:

TI at 800 millibars _____

TI at 700 millibars _____

TI at 600 millibars _____

17. Soaring conditions would probably be better in problem _____ (15, 16).

18. A positive TI for a given altitude indicates that thermal lift will probably be _____ at that altitude.

19. Lift produced by the upward deflection of the wind as it strikes the side of a hill is called

  1. shear lift.

  2. convective lift.

  3. wave lift.

  4. orographic lift.

20. The vertical oscillation created when high winds flow across a mountain range is called a

    1. valley wind.
    2. mountain wave.
    3. mountain wind.
    4. wind shear.

21. The amount of moisture in the air compared to the amount the air is capable of holding is called

    1. dewpoint.
    2. moisture factor.
    3. relative humidity.
    4. saturation.

22. The temperature at which moisture in the air begins to condense is the

    1. dewpoint.
    2. fog index.
    3. freezing point.
    4. chill factor.

23. If moisture is added to the air and the air temperature remains constant, the relative humidity will _____ (increase, decrease).

24. When moist, rising air is cooled to its dewpoint, visible moisture appears in the form of _____.

25. The most significant cloud type for finding thermal lift is the

    1. cirrus.
    2. cumulus.
    3. stratus.
    4. nimbostratus.

26. A small wisp of a cloud may indicate the start of a growing

    1. cumulus cloud.
    2. stratus cloud.
    3. squall line.
    4. cirrus cloud.

27. A cumulus cloud with a convex base and ragged outline is probably in the

    1. beginning stage.
    2. growth stage.
    3. mature stage.
    4. dissipating stage.

28. The cloud type that produces hazards such as hail, heavy rain, and violent updrafts is the

    1. nimbostratus.
    2. cumulus.
    3. cumulonimbus.
    4. stratus.

29. Lens-shaped clouds that mark the crests of mountain waves are called

    1. rotor clouds.
    2. roll clouds.
    3. fair weather cumulus clouds.
    4. lenticular clouds.

30. The zone of transition between two airmasses having different properties of moisture and temperature is referred to as a

    1. shear line.
    2. convergence.
    3. front.
    4. squall line.

31. A wedge of advancing cold air replacing warm air at the surface is a

    1. cold front.
    2. warm front.
    3. occluded front.
    4. stationary front.

32. The line of thunderstorms that often forms several miles ahead of a fast-moving cold front is called a

    1. shear line.
    2. prefrontal system.
    3. squall line.
    4. cloud street.

33. A front that has little or no movement is called a

    1. static front.
    2. stationary front.
    3. stable front.
    4. occluded front.

34. The term used to indicate the sky is completely hidden from the ground observer is

    1. solid overcast.
    2. total obscuration.
    3. zero ceiling.
    4. negative visibility.

35. Stratiform clouds that form at or near the surface are called

    1. low scud.
    2. haze.
    3. mist.
    4. fog.

36. Rain that falls through a layer of subfreezing air may form into

    1. ice pellets.
    2. hail.
    3. rime ice.
    4. snow.

37. The first stage in the development of a thunderstorm is the _____ stage.

38. The best course of action for a sailplane that encounters a cumulonimbus cloud is to

    1. circle downwind of the cloud.
    2. remain 1,000 feet below the base of the cloud.
    3. circle around the edges of the cloud.
    4. leave the area.

39. The type of turbulence found in the interior of cumulus and cumulonimbus clouds is usually _____ turbulence.

40. Hourly reports of weather observed at the reporting stations are called

_____

weather reports.

41. When upper air temperature soundings are not available, a forecast thermal index can be computed using temperature data from a

1. aviation routine weather report.
2. television weather forecast.
3. transcribed weather broadcast.
4. winds and temperatures aloft forecast.

42. Current information pertaining to tornadoes, severe thunderstorms, or large hail would be communicated to pilots by inclusion in a

1. convective SIGMET.
2. NOTAM.
3. SIGMET.
4. PIREP.

43. Weather conditions that are potentially hazardous only to aircraft with limited capabilities are reported in

1. a SIGMET.
2. an AIRMET.
3. the PATWAS.
4. a convective SIGMET.

44. A sailplane pilot who encounters unexpected weather conditions can aid other pilots by submitting a

1. SIGMET.
2. NOTAM.
3. TWEB.
4. PIREP.

45. The chart that gives such information as surface wind velocity and direction, temperature, humidity, dewpoint, and the general surface pressure pattern is the

1. low-level significant weather prognostic chart.
2. weather depiction chart.
3. surface analysis chart.
4. radar summary chart.

46. The overall current weather pattern, including frontal systems and areas of precipitation, is displayed on the

1. low-level significant weather prognostic chart.
2. weather depiction chart.
3. surface analysis chart.
4. radar summary chart.

47. If the winds aloft at 6,000 feet were forecast at 3512+10 and at 9,000 feet 3316+6, the wind at 7,500 feet should be from

1. 341° magnetic at 8 knots.
2. 340° magnetic at 14 knots.
3. 341° true at 8 knots.
4. 340° true at 14 knots.

Use the keys on pages 4-19 and 4-20 to decode the METAR and answer the following questions.

METAR KOKC 121955Z 01010KT 3SM -RA OVC020 13/17 A2975

48. The ceiling at the reporting station is
   1. 300 feet.
   2. 800 feet.
   3. 2,000 feet.
   4. 12,500 feet.

49. The visibility is
   1. 1.25 miles.
   2. 3 miles.
   3. 12.5 miles.
   4. 20 miles.

50. The weather reported in the observation is
   1. light rain.
   2. light showers.
   3. moderate rain.
   4. thunderstorms.

51. The observation was issued at
   1. 1955 ZULU.
   2. 1219 ZULU.
   3. 1955 local.
   4. 1219 local.

52. The temperature is
   1. 7°.   3. 17°.
   2. 13°.   4. 36°.

53. The dewpoint is
   1. 7°.   3. 17°.
   2. 13°.   4. 36°.

54. The altimeter setting is
   1. 29.45.   3. 31.25.
   2. 29.75.   4. 1012.5.

55. The wind direction and velocity are
   1. 000° at 11 knots.
   2. 010° at 10 m.p.h.
   3. 010° at 10 knots.
   4. 001° at 10 m.p.h.

56. The barometric pressure is
   _____ (above, below) standard.

Chapter 5 - Medical Factors

1. At sea level, the weight of the atmosphere is about
   1. 10 p.s.i.
   2. 15 p.s.i.
   3. 20 p.s.i.
   4. 25 p.s.i.

2. At high altitudes, the amount of oxygen that can be absorbed by the bloodstream is reduced because of the lower _____ _____.

3. Unless supplemental oxygen is used, some deterioration of physical and mental performance usually occurs after prolonged flight at
   1. 10,000 to 14,000 feet MSL.
   2. 15,000 to 18,000 feet MSL.
   3. 20,000 to 35,000 feet MSL.
   4. 35,000 to 40,000 feet MSL.

4. The *greatest* danger when flying at high altitudes is a condition known as
   1. dehydration.
   2. asphyxiation.
   3. hyperventilation.
   4. hypoxia.

5. Perhaps the most misleading aspect of hypoxia is that the pilot rarely recognizes a need for
   1. water.
   2. food.
   3. oxygen.
   4. warmth.

6. The surest way to avoid hypoxia is to
   1. jog every day.
   2. avoid smoking.
   3. hyperventilate.
   4. use supplemental oxygen.

7. The most serious hypoxia symptom normally occuring at 20,000 to 25,000 feet is
   1. cyanosis.
   2. dizziness.
   3. loss of coordination.
   4. loss of consciousness.

8. Rapid breathing, or hyperventilation, results in an inadequate supply of
   1. carbon dioxide.
   2. carbon monoxide.
   3. oxygen.
   4. nitrogen.

9. If a pilot is experiencing hyperventilation symptoms, the most effective cure is
   1. increased oxygen flow.
   2. decreased oxygen flow.
   3. deeper breathing.
   4. normal breathing.

10. As the sailplane rapidly gains altitude, the decreasing atmospheric pressure causes body gases to
    1. condense.
    2. vaporize.
    3. expand.
    4. contract.

11. The discomforts resulting from the expansion of trapped gases usually can be reduced by slowing the rate of _____.

12. Chewing gum should be avoided while ascending because it may result in
    1. swallowed air.
    2. digestive gases.
    3. ear pain.
    4. nitrogen bubbles.

13. A pain in the joints and muscles caused by nitrogen bubbles is called
    1. spasms.
    2. the chokes.
    3. the bends.
    4. gout.

14. Nitrogen bubble formation in the lung area is called
    1. the bends.
    2. the chokes.
    3. pulmonary edema.
    4. bronchitis.

15. The minimum time between scuba diving and flying should be
    1. 6 hours.
    2. 12 hours.
    3. 18 hours.
    4. 24 hours.

16. As the sailplane ascends and atmospheric pressure decreases, the middle ear equalizes pressure by expelling air through the
    1. ear drum.
    2. bronchial tubes.
    3. esophagus.
    4. eustachian tube.

17. The best way to relieve ear pain caused by a rapid decrease in altitude is to
    1. hold the nose and blow gently.
    2. chew gum.
    3. swallow several times.
    4. pull on the ear lobe.

18. Sudden acceleration or turning can cause a temporary state of spatial confusion called _____.

19. If a pilot continues a constant-rate turn for 30 to 45 seconds, the inner ear sensory organ will indicate a
    1. constant-rate turn.
    2. turn in the opposite direction.
    3. downward spiral.
    4. straight-and-level attitude.

20. The effects of vertigo can usually be overcome if the pilot is able to see the _____.

21. A condition of fatigue that persists over a long period of time is called _____ _____.

22. Short-lived fatigue, usually cured by rest, is called _____ _____.

23. A pilot having difficulty coordinating cockpit actions may be experiencing a type of acute fatigue called _____ _____.

24. Pilots suffering from chronic or acute fatigue just prior to a planned flight should

    1. take pep pills.
    2. drink plenty of coffee.
    3. eat a chocolate bar.
    4. stay on the ground.

25. The safest course of action for a pilot suffering from motion sickness is to

    1. drink some water.
    2. close the air vents.
    3. take a Dramamine tablet.
    4. land the sailplane.

26. Tranquilizers are well known in aviation because of their ability to

    1. relax the pilot.
    2. increase confidence.
    3. improve coordination.
    4. induce pilot error.

27. Most legitimate medications may be used safely as long as the pilot

    1. has a doctor's approval.
    2. gets plenty of sleep.
    3. avoids flying.
    4. takes only the prescribed dosage.

28. Non-prescription drugs, such as aspirin and cold remedies, are considered by aviators to be

    1. harmless in moderate amounts.
    2. safe for a healthy pilot.
    3. necessary if the pilot needs them.
    4. potentially dangerous when flying.

29. An analysis of aircraft accidents in the early 1960's revealed that alcohol was

    1. rarely a factor.
    2. a factor in 20 percent of the crashes.
    3. a factor in 40 percent of the crashes.
    4. a factor in 60 percent of the crashes.

30. Alcohol effects on the body are basically the same as the effects of

    1. mild tranquilizers.
    2. strong antihistamines.
    3. mild sedatives.
    4. general anesthetics.

31. According to the Federal Aviation Regulations, it is illegal to fly if as little as one alcoholic drink has been consumed within

    1. 4 hours.
    2. 8 hours.
    3. 12 hours.
    4. 16 hours.

32. Dehydration is caused by a critical loss of body _____.

33. If the body is unable to eliminate sufficient heat to maintain normal body temperatures, the result will usually be _____.

34. The best way to prevent both dehydration and heatstroke is to carry and use

    1. salt tablets.
    2. coffee.
    3. soft drinks.
    4. water.

35. Emotional disturbances such as anger, fear, and worry exert their *greatest* effect on the ability to

    1. concentrate.
    2. remember.
    3. maneuver.
    4. communicate.

36. _____ (true, false) The first noticeable effect of dehydration is a feeling of fatigue, followed by dizziness and nausea.

Chapter 6 - Regulations for Sailplane Pilots

Answer the following questions concerning FAR definitions using FAR Part 1 for reference.

1. _____ (true, false) The term "category" can be applied to a broad classification of aircraft (gliders, airplanes, etc.) or can be used as a grouping of aircraft (acrobatic, normal, etc.) based on intended use.

2. _____ (true, false) "Flight level" is based on the standard altimeter setting of 29.92.

3. _____ (true, false) FAR 1.1 defines "night" as the time between one hour after sunset to one hour before sunrise.

4. Navigation by visual reference to the ground is called

   1. VFR navigation.
   2. dead reckoning.
   3. pilotage.
   4. land navigation.

5. _____ (true, false) A glider is supported in flight by the dynamic reaction of air against its lifting surfaces.

6. _____ (true, false) Calibrated airspeed is the indicated airspeed of an aircraft, uncorrected for instrument position and/or error.

7. Controlled airspace means an airspace of defined dimensions within which _____ _____ _____ service is provided to IFR flights and to VFR flights in accordance with the airspace classification.

8. Load factor is the ratio of a specified load to the total _____ of the aircraft.

9. _____ (true, false) A medical certificate must be on a form prescribed by the Administrator.

10. Airspace that may not be transited at any time is designated as a (an)

    1. alert area.
    2. warning area.
    3. restricted area.
    4. prohibited area.

Answer the following questions using FAR Part 43 for reference.

11. The requirements for persons authorized to perform maintenance, preventive maintenance, and alterations are listed in FAR Part

    1. 43.
    2. 61.
    3. 71.
    4. 91.

12. _____ (true, false) Holders of a pilot certificate may perform preventive maintenance on any aircraft owned or operated by them that is not used in air carrier service. [43.3]

13. To perform maintenance, preventive maintenance, and alterations, the individual must hold a [43.3]

    1. mechanic certificate.
    2. repairman certificate.
    3. pilot certificate.
    4. commercial pilot certificate.

14. _____ (true, false) A change to the wings, tail surfaces or fuselage would be considered an airframe major alteration. [43 Appendix A]

15. _____ (true, false) The replacement, strengthening, or reinforcing of the monocoque or semimonocoque wings or control surfaces would be considered airframe major repairs. [43 Appendix A]

16. Pilots who own their own aircraft may perform the following types of preventive maintenance on the sailplane

    1. calibrate and repair instruments, paint the wings, replace a battery
    2. swing the compass, repair defective safety wire, repair a spar.
    3. replace safety belts, splice skin sheets, replace a seat.
    4. replace defective safety wiring or cotter keys, install a new tire. [43 Appendix A]

Answer the following questions using FAR Part 61 for reference.

17. _____ (true, false) A current pilot certificate must be in the pilot's possession or readily available when operating a sailplane.[61.3]

18. _____ (true, false) A local law enforcement officer may inspect a pilot's certificate at any time. [61.3]

19. Flight under IFR requires that the pilot in command have (a, an) _____ rating. [61.3]

20. _____ (true, false) A private pilot certificate expires at the end of the 24th month after the month in which it is issued. [61.19]

21. _____(true, false) The term glider refers to a class rating. [61.5]

22. _____ (true, false) A private pilot must hold a category, class, and type rating, if applicable, for the aircraft when carrying passengers. [61.31]

23. _____ (true, false) Flight time used to meet the recent flight experience requirements of [61.57] must be shown by a reliable record. [61.51]

24. _____ (true, false) A sailplane pilot may not act as pilot in command, or in any other capacity as required crew member with a known physical deficiency which would make that person unable to operate the aircraft in a safe manner.[61.53]

25. No person may act as pilot in command of a sailplane carrying passengers unless within the preceding _____ days at least _____ takeoffs and landings have been made in an aircraft of the same _____. [61.57]

26. _____ (true, false) Sailplane pilots must have a current medical certificate in their possesion to act as pilot in command of a sailplane. [61.3]

27. _____ (true, false) A private pilot may not pay less than the pro rata share of the operating expenses of a flight with passengers, provided the expenses involve only fuel, oil, airport expenditures, or rental fees.[61.113]

28. _____ (true, false) A flight review consists of a minimum of 1 hour of flight instruction and 1 hour of ground instruction. However, glider pilots may substitute a minimum of three instructional flights in a glider, each of which includes a flight to traffic pattern altitude, in lieu of the 1 hour of flight training.[61.56]

29. _____ (true, false) The act of selling marijuana is grounds for suspension or revocation of a pilot's certificate or rating. [61.15]

30. A *student pilot certificate* expires at the end of the _____ month after the month in which it was issued. [61.19]

31. _____ (true, false) A person who is caught cheating by the Administrator may not retake the test for one year. [61.37]

32. _____ (true, false) A written statement from a certificated flight instructor indicating flight instruction has been given in preparation for a flight test is a prerequisite to the flight test. [61.39]

33. An applicant for a knowledge or practical test who fails that test may reapply for the test only after receiving the necessary training and an _____ from the authorized instructor who gave the additional training.[61.49]

34. _____ (true, false) A student pilot certificate allows a pilot to act as pilot in command of an aircraft towing a glider. [61.69]

35. _____ (true, false) A person must be at least 16 years of age to be eligible for a student pilot certificate to operate a sailplane. [61.83]

36. _____ (true, false) A student pilot must have received instruction in stall recognition and recovery to be eligible for solo flight in a sailplane. [61.87]

37. _____ (true, false) The student pilot needs instruction on aeronautical charts, but not the magnetic compass for a solo cross-country in a sailplane. [61.93]

Answer the following questions using FAR Part 71 for reference.

38. _____ (true, false) Class E Airspace extends upward from 14,500 feet MSL, but does not include airspace less than 1,500 feet above the surface of the earth. [71.71]

39. Airspace which extends upward from 700 feet or more above the surface of the earth when designated in conjunction with an airport for which an approved instrument approach procedure has been prescribed is designated as _____ _____. [71.71]

40. When Class E airspace is designated in conjunction with airways or routes, the lateral extent is identical to that of a Federal airway and extends upward from ____ feet or higher unless otherwise specified. [71.71]

41. A Federal airway includes the airspace within parallel boundary lines _____ miles each side of the centerline. [71.75]

42. A Federal airway extends upward from _____ feet above the surface, to but not including _____ feet MSL. [71.75]

Answer the following questions using FAR Part 91 for reference.

43. _____ (true, false) The pilot in command of an aircraft is directly responsible for its operation. [91.3]

44. _____ (true, false) In an emergency, the pilot in command may deviate from any portion of Subpart A or B of FAR 91. [91.3]

45. _____ (true, false) A pilot in command who deviates from an FAR must write a report if requested by the Administrator. [91.3]

A pilot in command must become familiar with certain information prior to flight. Answer questions 46 through 70 with this in mind.

46. _____ (true, false) The pilot in command must be familiar with appropriate weather reports and forecasts prior to any flight not in the vicinity of an airport. [91.103]

47. _____ (true, false) It is legally permissible, although not advisable, for a sailplane passenger to be intoxicated provided the pilot in command is not under the influence of liquor or drugs. [91.17]

48. What is the prescribed time period prior to flight within which a chair-type parachute must have been repacked? [91.307]

   1. 30 days
   2. 60 days.
   3. 90 days.
   4. 120 days.

49. _____ (true, false) Anyone may legally repack a parachute if complete instructions are available. [91.307]

50. _____ (true, false) A pilot may not operate an aircraft in a careless or reckless manner which endangers life or property. [91.13]

51. No pilot may consume alcohol within _____ hours prior to flight. [91.17]

52. _____ (true, false) No pilot may fly while under the influence of alcohol or while using any drug that affects the faculties. [91.17]

53. Except for certain provisions, the wearing of a parachute is required if any intentional maneuver exceeds _____° of bank, or _____° nose-up or nose-down attitude. [91.307]

54. _____ (true, false) The hitch on the towplane requires only the towplane pilot's approval. [91.309]

55. The towline used to tow a sailplane should have a breaking strength of not less than _____ percent of the maximum certificated operating weight of the sailplane, and not more than _____ this operating weight. [91.309]

56. _____ (true, false) The towline may have a breaking strength of more than twice the operating weight of the sailplane if appropriate safety links are used. [91.309]

57. Whom should the pilot notify of planned towing operations within controlled airspace designated for an airport if there is no control tower in operation? [91.309]

1. Nearest UNICOM station
2. Regional ARTCC
3. FAA Administrator
4. Servicing FSS

58. Who is responsible for determining whether a sailplane is in a safe condition? [91.7]

1. Pilot in command
2. FAA Administrator
3. Gliderport operator
4. Ground crew

59. The flight crew must use supplemental oxygen during the entire flight above a cabin pressure altitude of _____ feet (MSL). [91.211]

60. Sailplane pilots must use supplemental oxygen between 12,500 and 14,000 feet MSL for that part of the flight more than _____ minutes duration. [91.211]

61. _____ (true, false) No person may operate an aircraft that has an experimental certificate for other than the purpose for which the certificate was issued. [91.319]

62. _____ (true, false) No person may operate an aircraft so close to another aircraft as to create a collision hazard. [91.111]

63. _____ (true, false) Formation flights are permissible only by arrangement between the pilots in command of each aircraft. [91.111]

64. _____ (true, false) All occupants must wear approved parachutes during formation flying. [91.111]

65. _____ (true, false) When weather conditions are above VFR minimums, it is the pilot's responsibility to see and avoid other aircraft, regardless of whether the flight is being conducted under IFR or VFR. [91.113]

66. The right-of-way over all other air traffic is given to an aircraft with an _____. [91.113]

67. When aircraft of the same category are converging at approximately the same altitude (except head-on, or nearly so), the aircraft to the other's _____ (left, right) has the right-of-way. [91.113]

68. When two aircraft are approaching head-on, each pilot will alter his course to the _____ (left, right) and pass well clear. [91.113]

69. _____ (true, false) Aircraft on final approach have the right-of-way over other aircraft in flight. [91.113]

70. _____ (true, false) If two aircraft are approaching an airport for landing, the aircraft at the lower altitude has the right-of-way. However, the pilot of the lower aircraft may not cut in front of the other aircraft if it is on final approach, or overtake it. [91.113]

Arrange the following in their order of right-of-way by numbering 1 through 6: [91.113]

71. Glider   _____

72. Airship   _____

73. Airplane or Rotorcraft   _____

74. Free balloon   _____

75. Aircraft in distress   _____

76. Aircraft towing a glider _____

77. A person may operate an aircraft in aerobatic flight [91.303]

    1. over any congested area of a city.
    2. above 1,500 feet A.G.L. with 3 miles visibility.
    3. within a control zone.
    4. over an open air assembly of persons.

78. Which light signal tells an aircraft in flight that the airport is unsafe for landing? [91.125]

    1. Steady red
    2. Flashing red
    3. Alternating red and green
    4. Flashing white

79. An alternating red and green light from the tower in respect to an aircraft on the surface or in flight means exercise _____ _____. [91.125]

Complete the following VFR table for minimum flight visibility and distance from clouds. [91.155]

Airspace/Altitude	Flight Visibility	Distance from Clouds
80. Class A		
Class B	_____ statute miles	
Class C .... ⎫	_____ statute miles	_____ feet below
Class D .... ⎭		_____ feet above
		_____ feet horizontal
81. Class E		
Less than 10,000 feet MSL	_____ statute miles	_____ feet below
		_____ feet above
		_____ feet horizontal
At or above 10,000 feet MSL	_____ statute miles	_____ feet below
		_____ feet above
		_____ s.m. horizontal
82. Class G.		
1,200 feet or less above the surface (regardless of MSL altitude) Day, except as provided in Section 91.155(b)	_____ statute miles	
Night, except as provided in Section 91.155(b)	_____ statute miles	_____ feet below
		_____ feet above
		_____ feet horizontal
More than 1,200 feet above the surface but less than 10,000 feet MSL		
Day	_____ statute miles ⎫	_____ feet below
Night	_____ statute miles ⎭	_____ feet above
		_____ feet horizontal
More than 1,200 feet above the surface and at or above 10,000 feet MSL	_____ statute miles	_____ feet below
		_____ feet above
		_____ s.m. horizontal

83. While flying over a city, town, or settlement, an aircraft should be _____ feet above the highest obstacle within a horizontal radius of _____ feet of the aircraft. [91.119]

84. _____ (true, false) Except for takeoff or landing, an aircraft must be flown at an altitude from which an emergency landing can be made without undue hazard to persons or property. [91.119]

85. An aircraft may not be operated closer than _____ feet to any person. [91.119]

86. The current reported altimeter setting should be used when below _____ feet MSL. [91.121]

87. _____ (true, false) Each pilot operating an aircraft departing an airport in Class C airspace must comply with any traffic pattern established for that airport in Part 93. [91.127]

88. Aircraft operations at airports with control towers require the use of two-way radios when within _____ _____ _____. [91.129]

89. _____ (true, false) No pilot operating under VFR may land an aircraft at an airport with an operating control tower if the aircraft radio fails in flight. [91.129]

90. _____ (true, false) Temporary flight restrictions do not apply to sailplanes. [91.137]

91. _____ (true, false) A sailplane may enter a prohibited area if permission has been obtained from the controlling agency. [91.133]

_____ (true, false) Notices to
92. Airmen are issued when designating an area within which temporary flight restrictions apply. [91.137]

93. Except for special VFR, VFR flight is not allowed within the lateral boundaries of the surface areas of Class B, C, D, or E airspace designated for an airport beneath the ceiling when the ceiling is less than _____ feet. [91.155]

94. When flying under VFR, takeoff, landing, or entering the traffic pattern of an airport within the lateral boundaries of the surface areas of Class B, C, D, or E airspace is not permissible (except for special VFR) unless the ground visibility at that airport is at least _____ statute mile(s). If the ground visibility is not reported, the flight visibility must be at least _____ statute mile(s). [91.155]

Use NTSB Part 830 to answer the following questions.

95. _____ (true, false) If an aircraft is involved in an accident and receives substantial damage, this situation would be considered as an "aircraft accident" which must be reported. [830.2]

96. _____ (true, false) Immediate notification to the National Transportation Safety Board (NTSB) is required if an emergency landing is made. [830.5]

97. Within what time period after an accident must a report be filed? [830.15]
   1. 5 days
   2. 7 days
   3. 10 days
   4. 14 days

98. _____ (true, false) A report on an accident shall be filed with the Administrator of the NTSB. [830.15]

99. _____ (true, false) A report on an incident should be filed only if requested by the NTSB representative. [830.15]

Chapter 7 - Flight Publications and Airspace

1. _____ (true, false) All aircraft operating within the boundaries of Class B airspace are subject to certain rules and equipment requirements.

2. Basic flight information and ATC procedures are covered in the _____ _____ _____.

3. _____ (true, false) The aeronautical chart is the primary method used to provide aeronautical information for navigation within the National Airspace System.

4. Data which may affect the safety of flight, such as a runway which is closed for maintenance, can be found in the _____ _____ _____.

5. Communications frequencies, such as ground control, may be found in the _____ _____ _____.

6. Information concerning the locations of parachute jumping areas is included in the

   1. Aeronautical Information Manual.
   2. Notices to Airmen.
   3. Airport/Facility Directory.
   4. Federal Aviation Regulations.

7. The highest vertical limit of Class G airspace is _____ feet MSL, excluding the airspace within 1,500 feet AGL.

8. The area within 10 statute miles of an uncontrolled airport on which a flight service station is located is termed

   1. transition area.
   2. Class D airspace.
   3. airport advisory area.
   4. Class C surface area.

Match the airspace classification on the left with the appropriate characteristics on the right. Characteristics may apply to more than one class of airspace.

9. Class A _____

10. Class B _____

11. Class C _____

12. Class D _____

13. Class E _____

14. Class G _____

A. Begins at the surface

B. Uncontrolled by ATC

C. Operating control tower

D. 18,000 feet to FL600

E. Two-way radio communication with ATC

F. May begin at surface or 700 or 1,200 feet AGL

15. Anytime the pilot is flying above 10,000 feet MSL (and more than 1,200 feet above the surface), the visibility required for VFR flight is

    1. 1/2 mile.
    2. 1 mile.
    3. 3 miles.
    4. 5 miles.

16. With a special VFR clearance, aircraft operations can be conducted in Class D airspace if the visibility is at least _____ _____ _____ and the aircraft can remain clear of clouds.

17. _____ (true, false) The ceiling of Class D airspace usually extends to 2,500 feet above the airport surface.

Questions 17 through 21 deal with special use airspace. List the type of airspace associated with each of the following conditions.

CONDITION   TYPE OF AIRSPACE

18. Flight of aircraft not permitted.   _____

19. Use of airspace is subject to limitations.   _____

20. Hazards of flight exist such as artillery firing, aerial gunnery.   _____

21. Numerous high speed jet aircraft operating in the area.   _____

22. High volume of pilot training being conducted. _____

Chapter 8 - Aeronautical Charts and Navigation

1. The distance a point lies north or south of the equator is expressed as degrees of _____.

2. Lines of longitude, or meridians, measure distance east and west of the _____ _____.

3. Any point on the earth's surface can be identified by its latitude and longitude values which are expressed as _____ _____.

4. The angular difference between the direction to true north and magnetic north is called magnetic
   1. deviation.
   2. declination.
   3. error.
   4. variation.

5. If an aircraft is to fly a true course of 270° and there is a magnetic variation of 8°E, what magnetic heading must be flown?
   1. 262°
   2. 270°
   3. 278°

6. _____ (true, false) An easterly variation is subtracted from the true heading and a westerly variation is added to determine magnetic heading.

7. A compass direction of 315° also may be expressed as
   1. northeast.
   2. northwest.
   3. southeast.
   4. southwest.

8. One inch on a sectional chart represents a ground distance of about _____ statute miles.

9. Contour lines on a chart connect points of equal _____.

10. Isogonic lines on a chart connect points of equal _____ _____.

11. The airport symbol Ⓡ means the airport is _____.

12. A navigation procedure that uses a map or chart to identify an aircraft's position relative to the ground is called
   1. pilotage.
   2. dead reckoning.
   3. land navigation.
   4. time and distance.

13. The navigation method of computing time and distance between checkpoints is called
   1. pilotage.
   2. dead reckoning.
   3. instrument navigation.

14. If a sailplane is on a VOR radial of 270°, the magnetic bearing from the sailplane to the station is
   1. 90°.
   2. 180°.
   3. 270°.
   4. 360°.

15. If the course selector on a VOR is set at 330° and the sailplane heading is also 330°, a left CDI indication means the sailplane
    1. must turn right.
    2. is right of the selected course.
    3. is left of the selected course.
    4. has a VOR malfunction.

16. The difference between a magnetic bearing and its reciprocal is
    1. 0°.
    2. 90°.
    3. 180°.
    4. 270°.

Match the annotations on the accompanying chart excerpt with the feature identifications below by placing the appropriate letters in the spaces provided.

17. _____ Four lane highway

18. _____ Power line with tower

19. _____ CTAF frequency

20. _____ Obstruction less than 1,000 feet AGL

21. _____ Restricted airport, not open to public

22. _____ Man-made dam

23. _____ Outdoor theater

24. _____ Oil well

25. _____ Class C airspace

26. _____ Control tower frequency

27. _____ VOR

28. _____ Maximum elevation figure

29. _____ Airport with paved runways

30. _____ Railroad

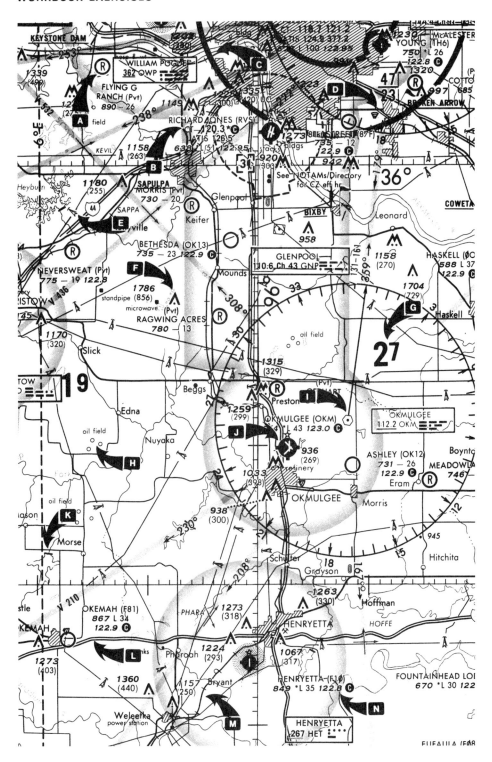

Chapter 9 - Computations for Soaring

1. How long will it take a sailplane to fly 120 miles at an average speed of 90 miles per hour?

    1. 45 minutes
    2. 1 hour
    3. 1 hour 20 minutes
    4. 1 hour 30 minutes

2. A sailplane flying at an average speed of 70 m.p.h. for 43 minutes will cover a distance of about

    1. 37 miles.
    2. 43 miles.
    3. 50 miles.
    4. 62 miles.

3. The average airspeed of a sailplane that travels 25 miles in 43 minutes is

    1. 18 m.p.h.
    2. 35 m.p.h.
    3. 43 m.p.h.
    4. 52 m.p.h.

4. At a pressure altitude of 12,000 feet, with an outside air temperature of -10°C, and indicated airspeed of 70 m.p.h., the computed true airspeed is

    1. 70 m.p.h.
    2. 80 m.p.h.
    3. 84 m.p.h.
    4. 87 m.p.h.

5. A sailplane flying at a true airspeed of 85 m.p.h. with a 25 m.p.h. headwind has a groundspeed of _____.

6. How many feet of altitude will a sailplane lose in 15 nautical miles (6,000 feet per mile) if its L/D ratio is 22:1?

    1. 4,100
    2. 4,600
    3. 5,500
    4. 8,090

Use the accompanying sectional chart excerpt and a navigation plotter to complete items 7-11.

7. The distance from Stigler Airport to Tahlequah Airport, in statute miles, is_____.

8. How long would it take to fly from Wagoner Airport to Stigler Airport at an average speed of 35 miles per hour?_____.

9. What is the true course from Stigler Airport to Sequoyah Park Airport?_____.

10. What true course should be flown from Tahlequah Airport to Stigler Airport?_____.

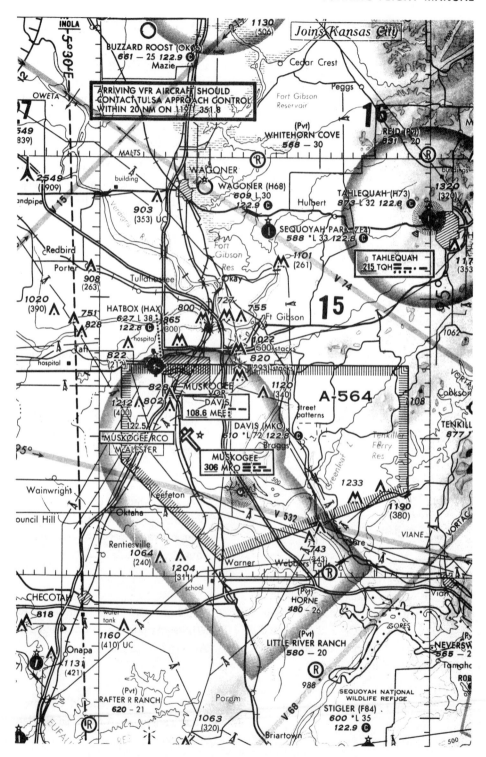

Complete a wind triangle on the chart excerpt and solve the following problem.

Given:

    Departure Airport

        . . . . Sequoyah Park

    Destination. . . . . Stigler

    True airspeed . . . . 45 m.p.h.

    Wind direction . . . . 120°

    Wind velocity . . . . 15 m.p.h.

Determine:

11. True Course_____

12. True heading_____

13. Magnetic variation_____

14. Magnetic heading_____

15. Groundspeed_____

16. Time enroute_____.

Chapter 10 - Personal Equipment

1. High-pressure oxygen cylinders normally are filled to a pressure of_____p.s.i.

2. The oxygen flow system needed above 35,000 feet is the _____ system.

3. The continuous-flow oxygen system is adequate for altitudes up to about_____feet.

4. The component of the continuous-flow system that helps to conserve oxygen is the

   1. pressure regulator.
   2. flow regulator.
   3. high-pressure cylinder.
   4. rebreather bag.

5. The system that automatically mixes oxygen with atmospheric air is the_____ system.

6. Which oxygen flow system is the minimum requirement for a flight altitude of 32,000 feet?
   1. Continuous-flow
   2. Diluter-demand
   3. Pressure-demand

7. What device alerts the pilot when oxygen is not flowing?
   1. Warning light
   2. Flow meter
   3. Blinker flag
   4. Pressure gauge

8. The duration of an oxygen supply_____(increases, decreases) as altitude increases.

9. The best thing to do if the oxygen system fails or the oxygen supply becomes exhausted at high altitude is to

   1. breathe more rapidly.
   2. use the bailout bottle until it is empty, then begin a normal descent to a lower altitde.
   3. Use the bailout bottle while rapidly descending to 10,000 feet or lower.
   4. remain at altitude for 30 minutes, then use the bailout bottle while descending.

List the five elements of the "price" checklist.

10. P_____

11. R_____

12. I_____

13. C_____

14. E _____

15. The parachute should be fitted while the wearer is

   1. standing straight.
   2. crouching slightly.
   3. seated in a chair.

16. In the event of a parachute landing in a remote or wilderness area, the most useful contingency equipment is a good

  1. pair of shoes.
  4. hunting knife.
  3. flashlight.
  4. survival kit.

17. _____ (true, false) If aviation breathing oxygen is not available, either hospital or welder's oxygen is an acceptable substitute.

18. Immediately prior to a parachute landing, the body should be_____.

Chapter 11 - Preflight and Ground Operations

1. If the sailplane flight handbook does not contain an assembly/-disassembly checklist, the pilot may assume that a checklist will be

   1. unnecessary.
   2. on a cockpit placard.
   3. developed by the pilot.
   4. stamped on the fuselage.

2. Prior to assembly, all spar pins and control connections should be cleaned with a solvent and then

   1. inventoried.
   2. lubricated.
   3. assembled.
   4. tested

3. The best way to ensure that the controls are properly connected is to perform a _____ _____ _____.

4. After the trailer is parked for loading or unloading, the wheels should be

   1. blocked.
   2. removed.
   3. deflated.
   4. raised.

5. _____ (true, false) In unsheltered high wind areas, the tail of the sailplane should be on the ground and tied down securely.

6. Ropes, chains, and ground anchors used for tiedown should be capable of holding two to three times the sailplane's

   1. basic weight.
   2. empty weight.
   3. net weight.
   4. gross weight.

7. To protect the rudder from high wind conditions, it should be secured with a _____.

8. If control locks are not used, the control stick should be secured with the _____ _____.

9. When moving the sailplane by hand, structural damage to the wing could occur if pressure is applied to the _____ _____.

10. The minimum rope length for ground towing is half the wing span plus _____ feet.

11. A ground towing vehicle should never move the sailplane at a speed faster than a

    1. slow running pace.
    2. fast running pace.
    3. slow walking pace.
    4. fast walking pace.

12. When towing downwind or crosswind during high wind conditions, there should be two wingwalkers plus a third crewmember at the

    1. upwind wing.
    2. downwind wing.
    3. tail.
    4. towline.

13. A thorough preflight inspection should be accomplished each day before the _____ _____.

14. To ensure that the parachute has been repacked within the prescribed time period, the pilot should check the_____ _____.

15. The parachute ripchord pins should be in place and safetied with a thread and

    1. safety wire.
    2. lead seal.
    3. cotter key.
    4. safety pins.

16. The oxygen mask must fit properly to prevent_____.

17. Proper clothing is an important consideration

    1. in the summer.
    2. in the winter.
    3. for long flights.
    4. for all flights.

18. The airworthiness of the sailplane rests solely with the

    1. owner.
    2. pilot.
    3. ground crew.
    4. FAA inspector.

19. The sailplane preflight inspection should begin with a check of the

    1. control surfaces.
    2. launch equipment.
    3. oxygen system.
    4. cockpit area.

20. _____ (true, false) The preflight checklist is used only for the first inspection after assembly.

Chapter 12 - Aero Tow Launch Procedures

Match the ground/launch signals given in column A with the description given in column B.

Column A	Column B
1. _____ Connect towline	A. Crewmember places wingtip on ground.
2. _____ Open tow hitch	B. Crewmember levels the sailplane's wings
3. _____ Close tow hitch	C. Pilot interlocks index fingers and thumbs of both hands
4. _____ Take up slack	D. *Tow pilot* waggles rudder
5. _____ Towplane ready	E. *Sailplane pilot* waggles rudder in wings-level position
6. _____Hold	F. Crewmember holds open hand vertically
7. _____Begin takeoff	G. Crewmember repeatedly moves arms from vertical to lateral positions
8. _____Emergency	H. Crewmember signals with cutting motion across throat
9. _____Release towline	I. Crewmember closes hand held vertically

---

Match the airborne/airborne emergency signals in column A with the description given in column B.

Column A	Column B
10. _____ Turn right	A. Rocking of sailplane's wings
11. _____ Turn left	B. Rocking of towplane's wings
12. _____ Increase speed	C. Fishtailing sailplane with rudder
13. _____ Decrease speed	D. Fishtailing towplane with rudder
14. _____ Immediate release	E. Maneuver sailplane to left and pull towplane's tail gently
15. _____ Sailplane cannot release	F. Rocking of sailplane's wings when positioned to the side of the towplane
16. _____ Towplane cannot release	G. Maneuver sailplane to right and pull towplane tail gently

17. The most common tow rope length used for normal towing operations is

    1. 100 to 150 feet.
    2. 150 to 200 feet.
    3. 200 to 250 feet.
    4. 250 to 300 feet.

18. Splices are used rather than knots to attach tow ropes to tow rings because they preserve the _____ of the tow ropes.

19. The breaking strength of a towline must be at least _____ percent of the maximum certificated operating weight of the sailplane and no more than _____ times the maximum operating weight of the sailplane.

20. If safety links are used in conjunction with the towline, the safety links at the towplane end of the towline must have _____ (greater, lesser) strength than the safety link at the sailplane end of the towline.

21. The tow hitch used for aero tow operations is usually located

    1. near the center of gravity.
    2. aft of the center of gravity.
    3. just forward of the center of gravity.
    4. well forward of the center of gravity.

Name the prelaunch checklist items which are part of the ABCCCD check.

22. A_____
23. B_____
24. C_____
25. C_____
26. C_____
27. D_____

28. Two advantages of the high tow postion are _____ _____ and the ability to make an immediate release without the chances of becoming entangled in the towline.

29. The wake generated by the towplane is caused by

    A_____
    B_____
    C_____

30. When transitioning through the wake from the high to low tow position, care should be taken not to accomplish it too rapidly or _____ _____ can develop.

31. During a normal shallow to medium banked turn on tow, the sailplane's nose should be pointed toward the

    1. inside of the turn.
    2. outside of the turn.
    3. towplane's fuselage.
    4. "greenhouse" area.

32. The tow release should be made from the _____ tow position.

33. After confirming a tow release, the sailplane pilot should initiate a

1. descending left turn.
2. level right turn.
3. level right left turn.
4. shallow climb.

34. The *primary* cause of slack in the towline is

1. deceleration of the sailplane.
2. turbulent air.
3. Wake turbulence.
4. acceleration of the sailplane.

35. The greatest danger of slack line is

1. an increased chance of towline breakage.
2. becoming entangled in the line.
3. knotting.
4. an inadvertent release.

36. Which tow position should be used for beginning the wake boxing maneuvers? _____

37. If the towplane should lose power during the take off roll, what action should be taken by the sailplane pilot?

1. An immediate release and turn to the left.
2. A straight ahead stop.
3. An immediate release and turn to the right.

38. If an emergency occurs during the launch below 200 feet AGL, the sailplane pilot should release and

1. turn back toward the runway.
2. turn only to avoid obstacles.
3. fly a normal pattern.
4. fly a modified pattern.

39. _____ (true, false) The correct position for a normal takeoff is directly behind the towplane and no higher than the top of the towplane's fuselage.

40. If a large uncontrollable loop develops in the towline, or it appears that the towline is about to become entangled on the sailplane, the sailplane pilot should immediately

1. pull up.
2. release.
3. turn away from the loop.
4. descend.

Chapter 13 - Ground Launch Procedures

Match the ground launch signals in column A with the description given in column B.

Column A

1. _____ Not ready
2. _____ Take up slack
3. _____ Ready for takeoff
4. _____ Increase speed
5. _____ Decrease speed
6. _____ Take up slack (paddles)
7. _____ Slack removed (paddles)
8. _____ Stop operations (paddles)

Column B

A. Rocking the wings (air)
B. Leveling the wings (ground)
C. Crossing paddles overhead
D. Yawing the sailplane (air)
E. Raising and lowering wing (ground)
F. Crossing paddles below waist
G. Holding both paddles above head
H. Holding wing down (ground)

---

9. _____ (true, false) a safety link in the towline is optional for ground launches.

10. The length of the safety link should be

   1. 2 to 3 feet.
   2. 3 to 5 feet.
   3. 5 to 10 feet.
   4. 10 to 15 feet.

11. A safety link must be directly attached to the

   1. release mechanism.
   2. towplane.
   3. sailplane.
   4. parachute.

12. The preferred location for a tow hitch used for ground launch is

   1. near the nose.
   2. between the nose and wing.
   3. near the center of gravity.
   4. at the aerodynamic center.

13. What type of vehicle is preferred for an auto tow?

   1. Compact car
   2. tractor
   3. full-sized sedan
   4. pickup truck

14. When two tow hitches are installed on a sailplane, they should

   1. both be interconnected.
   2. have a common release.
   3. be used at the same time.
   4. have separate releases.

15. What type of instrument is used to measure the pull on a towline?

   1. Micrometer
   2. Tensiometer
   3. Tension gauge
   4. Master brake cylinder

16. What is the preferred type of towline to be used for ground launches?

    1. manila rope
    2. nylon
    3. wire
    4. cable

17. What is the *minimum* acceptable towline length which should be used for ground launch?

    1. 600 feet
    2. 1,000 feet
    3. 1,500 feet
    4. 2,000 feet

18. What is the *minimum* runway length to be used for an auto tow?

    1. 2,000 feet
    2. 2,500 feet
    3. 3,000 feet
    4. 4,000 feet

19. Under the listed conditions, compute the proper towspeed for the launch vehicle after the sailplane reaches 200 feet of altitude.

    Sailplane's maximum
      auto/winch tow speed . . 75 m.p.h.
    Surface wind. . . . . 6 m.p.h.
    Wind gradient. . . . . 10 m.p.h.

20. What is the maximum climb angle that should be used by the pilot during a ground launch?

    1. 15°
    2. 30°
    3. 45°
    4. 60°

21. How many ground crewmembers should be involved in an auto tow?

    1. two
    2. three
    3. five
    4. seven

22. What type of tool should be kept in the automobile and near the anchor during an auto-pulley launch in case of an emergency?

    1. Hacksaw
    2. Screwdriver
    3. Hammer
    4. Boltcutters

23. What is the *maximum* towline length recommended for winch launches?

    1. 3,000 feet
    2. 4,000 feet
    3. 5,000 feet
    4. 6,000 feet

24. _____ (true, false) The best course of action should porpoising occur during the launch is to increase back pressure on the control stick to place tension on the towline.

Chapter 14 - Basic Flight Maneuvers and Traffic Patterns

1. Airspeed is controlled primarily through use of the
   1. ailerons.
   2. rudder.
   3. elevator.
   4. variometer.

2. The purpose of clearing turns is to
   1. check the flight controls.
   2. reduce airspeed.
   3. search for thermals.
   4. check for other traffic.

3. The path of the sailplane over the ground is the sailplane's
   1. track.
   2. heading.
   3. course.
   4. bearing.

4. The direction in which the sailplane is pointing is the sailplane's
   1. track.
   2. heading.
   3. course.
   4. bearing.

5. Crab, or wind correction angle, is the angle between
   1. wind direction and true course.
   2. wind direction and magnetic north.
   3. the wind's true and magnetic direction.
   4. the sailplane's heading and track.

6. Which flight controls must be used when entering properly coordinated turns?
   1. Rudder and elevator only
   2. Ailerons and rudder only
   3. Elevator and rudder only
   4. Ailerons, rudder, and elevator

7. The sideward motion of a sailplane due to wind effect is called
   1. displacement.
   2. drift.
   3. crab angle.
   4. skid.

8. The pilot can determine whether a turn is coordinated by referring to the
   1. horizon.
   2. magnetic compass.
   3. yaw string.
   4. airspeed indicator.

9. The *first* step in recovering from an excessive bank angle that has caused the nose to drop is to
   1. increase rudder pressure.
   2. increase back pressure.
   3. apply opposite rudder and roll out.
   4. shallow the bank angle.

10. At minimum control speed, a stall could result from a decrease in
    1. the load factor.
    2. airspeed.
    3. angle of attack.
    4. pitch attitude.

List six indicators of a potential stall condition.

11. _____

12. _____

13. _____

14. _____

15. _____

16. _____

17. Recovery from a turning stall is accomplished by

    1. lowering the nose and applying opposite rudder.
    2. shallowing the bank angle and raising the nose.
    3. lowering the nose and steepening the bank angle.
    4. neutralizing all controls.

18. Recovery from a spin is accomplished by applying full opposite

    1. aileron and rudder pressure.
    2. aileron and aft control stick pressure.
    3. rudder and forward control stick pressure.
    4. aileron and forward control stick pressure.

19. To perform a forward slip, one wing is lowered, opposite rudder is applied, and the nose is slightly_____ (raised, lowered) with respect to the normal approach attitude.

20. When a side slip is performed into the wind during a crosswind landing, the ground track should be

    1. sideways in the direction of the low wing.
    2. in the opposite direction of the crosswind.
    3. a gentle curve toward the runway centerline.
    4. straight and parallel to the sailplane's longitudinal axis.

21. The sailplane's altitude at the point of entry into a landing traffic pattern should be approximately _____ feet AGL.

22. The turn to downwind should be made between _____ and _____ feet AGL.

23. If too much altitude is lost on the base leg to permit a safe turn to final, the best course of action is to

    1. continue the pattern and land short.
    2. land out of the base leg.
    3. raise the nose to conserve altitude.
    4. increase flap extension to stretch the glide.

24. If, on final approach, the aim point appears to move down the canopy, the glide path is too _____ (high, low).

25. The landing flare should be initiated at an altitude of approximately _____ feet.

26. Directional control is maintained after a crosswind touchdown by applying

    1. downwind rudder
    2. upwind rudder.
    3. downwind aileron.
    4. upwind aileron.

27. The sailplane's groundspeed during a downwind landing, as compared to a normal upwind landing, is normally

    1. higher.
    2. lower.
    3. about the same.

28. The first step in any stall recovery is to

    1. lower the nose.
    2. level the wings.
    3. close the dive brakes.
    4. raise the flaps.

29. Practice spins should be entered at an altitude no lower than

    1. 1,500 ft. AGL.
    2. 2,000 ft. AGL.
    3. 3,500 ft. AGL.
    4. 5,000 ft. AGL.

30. If back pressure is relaxed during a spin, the sailplane may enter

    1. a straight glide.
    2. level flight.
    3. a gliding turn.
    4. a spiral dive.

31. The purpose of a forward slip is to

    1. shallow the gliding angle.
    2. steepen the gliding angle.
    3. reduce airspeed.
    4. correct for a crosswind.

On the accompanying traffic pattern diagram, identify the following items

32. Aim point _____

33. Base leg _____

34. Entry leg _____

35. Touchdown point _____

36. Final approach _____

37. Downwind leg _____

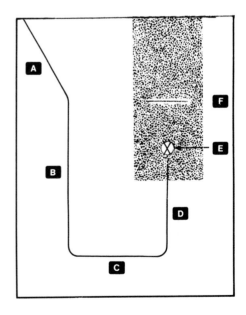

Chapter 15 - Soaring Techniques

1. A rising body of warm air is known as a _____.

2. _____ (true, false) Convection currents are most likely to occur in a stable atmosphere.

3. The cloud type which is the best indicator of thermal activity is the

   1. stratus.
   2. cirrus.
   3. cumulus.
   4. nimbo-stratus.

4. Areas covered with vegetation usually produce _____ (more, less) thermal activity than brown fields.

5. _____ (true, false) The presence of a temperature inversion indicates the probability of good soaring.

6. _____ (true, false) When more than one sailplane is circling in a thermal, direction of turn is determined by the highest sailplane.

7. The best airspeed to use while thermalling is

   1. maneuvering speed.
   2. best L/D speed.
   3. minimum control speed.
   4. minimum sink speed.

8. While searching for a thermal, the recommended speed to maintain is

   1. maneuvering speed.
   2. best L/D speed.
   3. minimum control speed.
   4. minimum sink speed.

9. When a thermal is first encountered, the sailplane may tend to roll _____ (toward, away from) the side with the stronger lift.

10. Shortly after a thermal is entered, a turn is started, and the lift disappears after turning 60°, which indicates

    1. a turn in the wrong direction.
    2. a late turn.
    3. an early turn.
    4. a proper turn.

11. When a loss of lift occurs immediately after starting the turn in a thermal, it indicates

    1. a turn in the wrong direction.
    2. a late turn.
    3. an early turn.
    4. a proper turn.

12. A decrease in lift between 90° and 180° of turn is an indication of

    1. a turn in the wrong direction
    2. a late turn.
    3. an early turn.
    4. a proper turn.

13. _____ (true, false) When a turn has been made in the wrong direction, a good technique is to roll out after 270° of turn, wait a few seconds after lift is regained, and then turn in the original direction.

14. The best possibility for finding lift above a potential lift source on the ground should exist _____ (upwind, downwind) from the source.

15. When overtaking another sailplane along a ridge, it should be passed on the

    1. left.
    2. right.
    3. side toward the ridge.
    4. side away from the ridge.

16. For a mountain wave to form, the wind across the mountain tops should have a speed of at least

    1. 15 m.p.h.
    2. 25 m.p.h.
    3. 40 m.p.h.
    4. 55 m.p.h.

17. The crests of mountain waves may be marked by

    1. cumulus clouds.
    2. cirrus clouds.
    3. lenticular clouds.
    4. rotor clouds.

18. The turbulent area beneath the wave crests may contain

    1. cumulus clouds.
    2. cirrus clouds.
    3. lenticular clouds
    4. rotor clouds.

19. A low release in the rotor area should be made toward the _____ (upwind, downwind) side.

20. Near the downwind side of a ridge, you should expect to find an area of _____ (lift, sink).

Chapter 16 - Cross-Country Soaring

1. The first consideration in planning a cross-country flight is

    1. to check the weather.
    2. the sailplane preflight.
    3. briefing the crew.
    4. goal selection.

2. All altitude and distance claims must be verified by

    1. a photographic record.
    2. an observer in the cockpit.
    3. a sealed barograph.
    4. ground observation.

3. A cross-country profile view helps ensure a safe return-or-proceed altitude by providing a series of
    1. glide ratios.
    2. decision points.
    3. speeds to fly.
    4. sink rates.

4. A safety margin is incorporated into the profile view by reducing the published L/D ratio by

    1. 10 per cent.
    2. 25 per cent.
    3. 50 per cent.
    4. 75 per cent.

5. A properly computed flight profile should allow the sailplane to arrive over either the departure or destination airport at an altitude of at least

    1. 500 feet AGL.
    2. 1,000 feet AGL.
    3. 1,500 feet AGL.
    4. 2,000 feet AGL.

6. Any lift encountered after passing the go-ahead point with sufficient altitude should be _____ (worked, by-passed).

7. Regardless of thermal indications, the sailplane normally should remain on tow to a minimum altitude of

    1. 1,000 feet AGL.
    2. 1,500 feet AGL.
    3. 2,000 feet AGL.
    4. 3,000 feet AGL.

8. If the highest variometer reading obtained in a thermal is 400 f.p.m., the decision to leave the thermal and proceed on the cross-country course should be made when the variometer reading drops to approximately

    1. 150 f.p.m.
    2. 225 f.p.m.
    3. 300 f.p.m.
    4. 350 f.p.m.

9. The proper speed to fly when passing through lift with no intention to stop and work the lift is

    1. best L/D speed.
    2. minimum sink speed.
    3. minimum control speed.
    4. maximum safe speed.

10. A serious search for an off-field landing area should be started any time the altitude has dropped to

    1. 1,000 feet AGL.
    2. 2,000 feet AGL.
    3. 3,000 feet AGL.
    4. 4,000 feet AGL.

11. The first choice of an off-field landing site normally should be a

    1. pasture.
    2. cultivated field.
    3. field with a short crop.
    4. newly-mowed field.

12. In the event of an off-field landing, the first action after establishing good relations with the property owner should be to

    1. notify the crew.
    2. analyze the flight.
    3. plan the next flight.
    4. prepare for a ground launch.

13. The best lift is usually found on the _____ (upwind, downwind) side of a _____ (building, dissipating) cumulus cloud.

14. The best speed to fly between thermals when conditions are weak and there is no headwind is

    1. minimum controllable airspeed.
    2. minimum sink speed.
    3. best L/D speed.
    4. best L/D speed plus 20 m.p.h.

15. _____ (true, false) As a general rule, it is good practice to speed up in lift and slow down in sink.

16. Obstructions in the aproach path reduce available landing length by at least _____ times the height required to clear them.

17. _____ (true, false) It is usually better to land on a field with a short crop than in a plowed field.

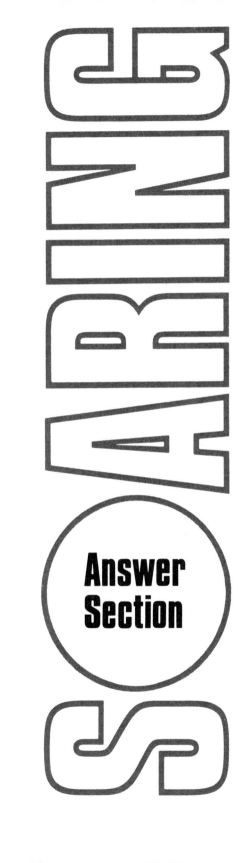

SOARING

Answer
Section

CHAPTER 1

1. C	17. increases	33. 1
2. F	18. 1	34. 4
3. G	19. 3	35. 4
4. D	20. 1	36. 4
5. E	21. 2	37. 2
6. B	22. 3	38. right
7. A	23. 2	39. 3
8. 3	24. 3	40. 4
9. 4	25. 3	41. 1
10. 4	26. 3	42. 2
11. 4	27. upper	43. 4
12. 2	28. 1	44. 4
13. increases	29. upper and lower	45. 2Gs
14. 4	30. 4	46. 4
15. 3	31. 2	47. 1
16. increases	32. 3	

CHAPTER 2

1. false	7. 3	13. 3
2. decreases	8. 68,160 lb./in.	14. false
3. higher	9. 7920 lb./in.	15. 2
4. false	10. 15,000 lb./in.	16. 1
5. 2	11. 4	17. 4
6. moment	12. 1	18. 2

CHAPTER 3

1. Variation, deviation	8. variometer	15. slip
2. dip	9. 1	16. skid
3. yaw string	10. barograph	17. red line
4. inclinometer	11. 2	18. white arc
5. aneroid	12. loud squeal	19. yellow arc
6. 4	13. 4	20. green arc
7. 2	14. opposite	21. bottom of green arc

CHAPTER 4

1. atmospheric pressure
2. decreases
3. 29.92
4. 2
5. lapse rate
6. 4
7. steep
8. gentle
9. inversion
10. 4
11. smaller
12. 3
13. beneath
14. 2
15. -2
    +5
16. -10
    -7
    -10
17. 16

18. weak
19. 4
20. 2
21. 3
22. 1
23. increase
24. clouds
25. 2
26. 1
27. 4
28. 3
29. 4
30. 3
31. 1
32. 3
33. 2
34. 2
35. 4
36. 1
37. cumulus

38. 4
39. thermal
40. aviation routine
41. 4
42. 1
43. 2
44. 4
45. 3
46. 2
47. 4
48. 3
49. 2
50. 1
51. 1
52. 2
53. 3
54. 2
55. 3
56. below

CHAPTER 5

1. 2
2. atmospheric pressure
3. 1
4. 4
5. 3
6. 4
7. 4
8. 1
9. 4
10. 3
11. ascent
12. 1
13. 3
14. 2
15. 4
16. 4
17. 1
18. vertigo

19. 4
20. horizon
21. chronic fatigue
22. acute fatigue
23. skill fatigue
24. 4
25. 4
26. 4
27. 3
28. 4
29. 3
30. 4
31. 2
32. water
33. heatstroke
34. 4
35. 1
36. true

CHAPTER 6

1. true	36. true	72. 5
2. true	37. false	73. 6
3. false	38. true	74. 2
4. 3	39. Class E	75. 1
5. true	40. 1,200	76. 4
6. false	41. 4	77. 2
7. air traffic control	42. 1,200, 18,000	78. 2
8. weight	43. true	79. extreme caution
9. true	44. true	80. N/A, N/A
10. 4	45. true	3, clear of clouds
11. 1	46. true	3, 500, 1,000, 2,000
12. true	47. false	81. 3, 500, 1,000, 2,000
13. 1	48. 4	5, 1,000, 1,000, 1
14. true	49. false	82. 1, clear of clouds
15. true	50. true	3, 500, 1,000, 2,000
16. 4	51. 8	Day 1, 500, 1,000, 2,000
17. true	52. true	Night 3, 500, 1,000, 2,000
18. true	53. 60, 30	5, 1,000, 1,000, 1
19. instrument	54. false	83. 1,000, 2,000
20. false	55. 80, twice	84. true
21. false	56. true	85. 500
22. true	57. 4	86. 18,000
23. true	58. 1	87. true
24. true	59. 14,000	88. Class D airspace
25. 90, 3, category	60. 30	89. false
26. false	61. true	90. false
27. true	62. true	91. true
28. true	63. true	92. true
29. true	64. false	93. 1,000
30. 24th	65. true	94. 3, 3
31. true	66. emergency	95. true
32. true	67. right	96. false
33. endorsement	68. right	97. 3
34. false	69. true	98. false
35. false	70. true	99. true
	71. 3	

CHAPTER 7

1. true	8. 3	16. 1 statute mile
2. Aeronautical Information Manual	9. D, E	17. true
3. true	10. A, C, E	18. prohibited area
4. Notices to Airmen	11. A, C, E	19. restricted area
5. Airport/Facility Directory	12. A, C, E	20. restricted area
6. 3	13. F	21. military operations area
7. 14,500	14. B	22. alert area
	15. 4	

CHAPTER 8

1. latitude
2. prime meridian
3. geographic coordinates
4. 4
5. 1
6. true
7. 2
8. 8
9. elevation
10. magnetic variation
11. restricted
12. 1
13. 2
14. 1
15. 2
16. 3
17. L
18. E
19. N
20. F
21. A
22. K
23. D
24. H
25. C
26. B
27. I
28. G
29. J
30. M

CHAPTER 9

1. 3
2. 3
3. 2
4. 3
5. 60 m.p.h.
6. 1
7. 44
8. 1 hr. 22 min.
9. 349°
10. 187°
11. 169°
12. 155°
13. 5°30'E
14. 149°
15. 34 m.p.h.
16. 1 hr. 17 min.

CHAPTER 10

1. 1800
2. pressure-demand
3. 25,000
4. 4
5. diluter-demand
6. 2
7. 3
8. decreases
9. 3
10. pressure
11. regulator
12. indicator
13. connections
14. emergency
15. 1
16. 4
17. false
18. relaxed

CHAPTER 11

1. 3
2. 2
3. positive control check
4. 1
5. false
6. 4
7. rudder lock
8. seatbelt
9. trailing edge
10. 5
11. 3
12. 3
13. first flight
14. inspection card
15. 2
16. leakage
17. 4
18. 2
19. 4
20. false

CHAPTER 12

1. C
2. F
3. I
4. B
5. D
6. A
7. E
8. G
9. H
10. E
11. G
12. A
13. C
14. B
15. F
16. D
17. 2
18. strength
19. 80, 2
20. greater
21. 4
22. Altimeter
23. Seat belts and shoulder harness
24. Canopy
25. Control
26. Cable
27. Direction of wind
28. better visibility
29. wing down wash wingtip vortices propeller slipstream
30. slack line
31. 2
32. high
33. 2
34. 4
35. 2
36. high or normal tow
37. 3
38. 2
39. true
40. 2

CHAPTER 13

1. H	7. C	13. 4	19. 44 m.p.h.
2. E	8. G	14. 2	20. 3
3. B	9. false	15. 2	21. 2
4. A	10. 3	16. 4	22. 4
5. D	11. 3	17. 2	23. 4
6. F	12. 3	18. 4	24. false

CHAPTER 14

1. 3	20. 4
2. 4	21. 1,000
3. 1	22. 700, 800
4. 2	23. 2
5. 4	24. high
6. 4	25. 5
7. 2	26. 1
8. 3	27. 1
9. 4	28. 1
10. 2	29. 3
The answers to questions 11-16 may occur in any order.	30. 4
11. nose-high attitude	31. 2
12. decreasing airspeed	32. E
13. reduced control effectiveness	33. C
14. vibration or buffeting	34. A
15. decreasing wind noise	35. F
16. aft control stick	36. D
17. 1	37. B
18. 3	
19. raised	

CHAPTER 15

1. thermal	6. false	11. 1	16. 2
2. false	7. 4	12. 3	17. 3
3. 3	8. 2	13. true	18. 4
4. less	9. away from	14. downwind	19. upwind
5. false	10. 2	15. 3	20. sink

CHAPTER 16

1. 4	7. 3	13. upwind, building
2. 3	8. 3	14. 3
3. 2	9. 2	15. false
4. 3	10. 3	16. 10
5. 2	11. 4	17. false
6. worked	12. 1	

SOARING

Glossary of Terms

Accelerated Stall — A stalled angle of attack of the wing at an airspeed above the minimum for that condition. Also called a high-speed stall.

Adverse Yaw — Movement about the yaw axis opposite to the desired direction of turn caused by increased lift and induced drag on the rising wing and decreased lift and induced drag on the descending wing.

AGL — Above ground level (altitude).

Aileron — A hinged portion of the trailing edge of the wing near the tip used to provide a banking or rolling force around the longitudinal axis.

Aircraft — A device that is used or intended to be used for flight in the air.

Airfoil — Any part of an aircraft (primarily the wing and tail surfaces) which deflects the air through which it moves to produce a desired reaction.

Airspeed — The speed of an aircraft in relation to the air through which it is flying. *Indicated* airspeed (IAS) is the reading of the airspeed indicator. *True* airspeed (TAS) is the IAS corrected for air density.

Airworthiness Certificate — Issued by the FAA to each aircraft implying that, having met certain criteria, the aircraft is airworthy. It is normally issued to a make and model of aircraft and is valid as long as required inspections are attested to in the aircraft log.

Angle of Attack — The angle between the chord line of the wing and the direction of the relative wind.

Angle of Incidence — The angle between the chord line of the wing and the longitudinal axis of the glider.

ASL — Above sea level (altitude).

Aspect Ratio — The ratio between the span and the mean chord of the wings.

Attitude — The inclination of the axes of the sailplane relative to the horizontal.

Axis — The theoretical line extending through the center of gravity in each major plane. The three axes are longitudinal, lateral, and vertical.

Bank — To roll about the longitudinal axis.

Barograph — A recording aneroid barometer. A recording of a flight is called a barogram.

Best Glide Speed — The indicated airspeed that results in the flattest glide obtainable in perfectly still air.

Buffeting — The beating effect on the rear of a sailplane caused by the turbulent wake of the wing as the angle of attack nears the stalling point.

Camber — The cross-sectional curvature of the wing.

Center of Gravity — The point through which, for balance purposes, the total force of gravity is considered to act.

Checklist — A list of items usually carried or posted in the sailplane which require the attention of the pilot during various flight operations.

Checkpoint — In aerial navigation, an easily identifiable spot on the ground, (and on the map) used to mark the progress of a flight.

Chord Line — An imaginary straight line from the leading edge to the trailing edge of an airfoil.

Clean — The condition of a sailplane after reducing parasitic drag to the lowest possible value.

Clear (the area) — To verify that the nearby airspace is clear of other aircraft.

Coefficient of Drag — A mathematical determinant of the amount of drag that is generated by a given airfoil at a given angle of attack.

Coefficient of Lift — A mathematical determinant of the amount of lift that can be generated by a given airfoil section at a given angle of attack.

Convection — The up or down movement of a limited portion of the atmosphere due to thermal action.

Convergence — The area where two bodies of air that have relative motion meet. A likely area of lift.

Coordination — The use of aileron and rudder in such a way that the glider neither slips nor skids so the slip-skid ball and the yaw string remain centered.

Course — The ground path over which the pilot intends to fly. *True* course is measured by reference to true north. *Magnetic* course is TC corrected for variation. *Compass* course is MC corrected for deviation.

Crabbing — Pointing up-wind to counteract for wind drift. Crab angle is also called wind correction angle.

Crossed Controls — Simultaneous application of right rudder and left aileron or vice versa.

Cumulonimbus (CuNim) — The thunderstorm cloud.

Cumulus — A cloud whose origin is in upward-moving air.

Decay — The stage in the life cycle of a cumulus cloud when the lift has changed to sink.

Deviation — The compass error caused by local magnetic forces in the sailplane.

Dive Brakes — Devices whose prime purpose is to create drag; most dive brakes also reduce lift.

Diving Tendency — The tendency in a turn for the nose to fall and the airspeed to increase.

Downwash — The downward thrust imparted to the air by a wing, whose "equal and opposite reaction" supports a portion of the aircraft's weight.

Drag — The force opposing forward motion.

Drift — The angle between heading and track.

Drogue Chute — A deployable parachute attached to the tail of a sailplane which, when deployed, increases drag to permit steeper landing approaches and shorter landing rolls.

Elevator — The horizontal movable surface at the tail used to control the pitch attitude.

Empennage — The entire tail group of an aircraft, consisting of fixed and movable elements.

Fairing — A member or structure whose primary purpose is to smooth the airflow over the aircraft to reduce drag.

Federal Aviation Administration (FAA) — The Governing body of civil aviation in the U.S. Its responsibility in the field of soaring includes the airworthiness of gliders, licensing of pilots and gliders, air traffic rules, and many other matters.

Federation Aeronautique Internationale (FAI) — The world governing body of aeronautical contests and custodian of world records.

Fin — The fixed vertical tail surface, used to provide directional stability.

Flaps — Hinged portions of the trailing edge of both wings between the ailerons and the fuselage, whose purpose is to alter the lift and drag characteristics of the wing.

Flare (out) — In landing, to change the final approach flight path from descending to parallel with the landing surface. *Round out* is also used with the same meaning.

Foehn Gap — In a mountain wave system marked by clouds, the foehn gap is an area of blue sky between the mountain's cap clouds and the lenticular cloud over the first lee wave.

Foehn Wind — A warm dry wind blowing down the slope of a mountain. The Chinook, of the Rocky Mountains, is one of many local names given to foehn winds.

Fuselage — The body to which the wings and tail are attached.

"G" Gravity — The load on a glider's structure is stated in terms of multiples of the force of gravity. A 4G load on a wing would be four times the load applied by gravity alone.

Glide — Sustained forward flight in which speed is maintained by descending in the surrounding air. A sailplane gains altitude only by descending in upward-moving air that is rising faster than the sailplane's rate of descent.

Glider (Sailplane) — Any wing-supported aircraft with no power source of its own. Glider and sailplane are usually used synonymously. When a distinction is intended, sailplanes are meant for soaring whereas gliders are primarily for descent.

Glide Ratio — The ratio of forward to downward motion, numerically the same as the ratio of lift to drag, L/D.

Ground Effect — The gain in lift during flight close to the ground that is caused by compression of the air between the wings and the ground, by interference of the ground with the airflow patterns about the wing, and other factors. It is greatest as close to the ground as possible, but is measurable up to an altitude equal to the wingspan.

Ground Loop — An uncontrollable violent turn on the ground.

Groundspeed — The speed with reference to the earth. It is the true airspeed plus or minus the effect of the wind.

Hang-glider — A lightweight glider in which the pilot is suspended below the wing.

Heading — The direction the sailplane is pointed. In navigation, the course corrected for wind drift. Heading may be true, magnetic or compass.

High Tow (Normal Tow) — In aero tow, the position slightly above the towplane's wake.

Horizontal Wind Shear — A change in wind velocity or direction with altitude.

IFR Conditions — Weather conditions below the minimum for flight under visual flight rules.

Inclinometer (also called slip-skid ball) — A ball in a fluid-filled, curved glass tube which indicates whether the aircraft is slipping or skidding.

Induced Drag — The rearward acting component of lift. Increases with decreasing airspeed.

Isogonic Line — On maps, a line connecting points of equal magnetic variation; used when computing magnetic course from true course.

Knot — A unit of speed equalling one nautical mile (6,080 feet) per hour.

Landing Speed — The indicated airspeed at the moment of touchdown.

Lapse Rate — In the atmosphere, the rate of change of temperature and pressure with altitude.

L/D (spoken L over D) — Lift divided by drag. This significant ratio is numerically the same as the glide ratio.

Lazy Eight — A mild aerobatic maneuver developed from a pair of 180° turns in opposite directions. Climbs and dives alternate.

Leading Edge — The forward edge of an airfoil — the opposite of trailing edge.

Lenticular Cloud (Lennie) — The characteristic lens-shaped cloud of a mountain wave.

Lift — (1) Upward currents strong enough to carry a sailplane up. (2) The supporting force of a wing.

Load — The forces acting on the structure of a sailplane. *Static* load is the weight of the sailplane. *Gross* load is the ready-to-fly weight, pilot included. *Maneuvering* loads are those imposed by use of the controls, and *gust* loads are those imposed by air currents. The *useful* load is the difference between the empty weight and the maximum authorized weight.

Load Factor — The sum of the loads on a structure, expressed in G units. The *limit* load factor is the *never-exceed* value beyond which structural damage may occur.

Log — A required record of pilot or sailplane flight time. Details are covered by FAA regulations.

Loop — An aerobatic maneuver as nearly as possible a perfect circle in a vertical plane.

Low Tow — In aero tow, the position of the glider slightly below the towplane's wake.

MacCready Speed Ring — A rotatable bezel around the variometer marked with the indicated airspeeds suitable to various rates of climb or descent.

Maneuvering Speed — The maximum speed at which the wings are capable of developing sufficient lift to impose the limit load factor. Below this speed, neither control inputs nor gust loads can result in damaging structural loads.

Minimum Controllable Airspeed — Flight at an airspeed just above the stall, when any reduction of airspeed or increase in load factor would result in indications of a stall.

Minimum Sink Speed — The indicated airspeed at which the glider loses altitude most slowly.

National Aeronautic Association (NAA) — The U.S. National Aero Club. The body delegated by the FAI to govern aeronautical contests and process record claims in the U.S. For soaring, this work has been redelegated to SSA, a division of NAA.

Netto — A system which indicates only the vertical movement of the air, regardless of the sailplane's rate of climb or descent.

Open-class Gliders — Unrestricted, within the competitive definition of the term *glider*.

Overbanking Tendency — In a turn, the effect of the outer wing going faster than the inner wing and thus having more lift, steepening the angle of bank.

Overdevelopment — An increase in the extent of cumulus cloud cover which significantly reduces the sun's heating of the earth, slowing or even stopping thermal activity.

Overshoot — To land beyond the intended spot — The opposite of undershoot.

Parasite Drag — Resistance to the sailplane's passage through the air. Increases with increasing airspeed.

Penetrate — To make progress against an adverse wind. Good penetration requires the glider to have a good glide ratio in the upper speed range.

Pitch Attitude — The angle of the longitudinal axis of the glider to the horizontal. Nose high or low.

Pitot Tube — An open-ended tube exposed to the air in front of the glider for measuring impact air pressure. The pitot tube is the source of dynamic pressure for the airspeed indicator and the constant energy device of the variometer.

Placard — A required statement of operation limitations that is permanently affixed where it can be seen by the pilot during flight.

Porpoising — Repeated dynamic pitching of the sailplane when being ground launched.

Red Line — A warning red mark on the airspeed indicator that corresponds to the maximum airspeed given on the placard.

Registration Certificate — Statement of ownership and assigned identity numbers of the sailplane. It must be displayed where it can be seen when the sailplane is on the ground.

Relative Wind — The direction of the airflow in respect to an airfoil.

Release — The device for, or the act of, disengaging the tow rope.

Roll — Displacement around the longitudinal axis of an aircraft.

Roll-out — The path of a landing sailplane after it touches down until it comes to a full stop.

Rotor — The swirling circulation under the crest of a mountain wave. The rotor is sometimes marked by ragged wispy clouds and is an area of severe turbulence.

Roundover — In a ground launch, the period just before release, when the rate of climb is diminishing and the glider is resuming a normal gliding attitude.

Rudder — The hinged vertical control surface used to induce or overcome yawing moments about the vertical axis.

Sailplane — A glider whose performance is high enough to permit soaring flight.

Sea Breeze Front — The zone of convergence between warm inland air and the moist cool air from over the ocean.

Separation — Turbulence over the top of an airfoil. Burble.

Shear Line — The plane of separation between airmasses moving at different speeds or in different directions. The shear may be vertical, horizontal, or inclined.

Sink — Descending currents in which the glider loses altitude faster than in still air.

Skid — Sideways motion of a glider with wings level; or in a turn, away from the low wing.

Slip — Sideways motion of a glider toward the lowered wing.

Slip-skid Ball — See Inclinometer.

Slow Flight — See Minimum Controllable Airspeed.

Soar — To fly without engine power and without loss of altitude.

Soaring Society of America (SSA) — A division of the National Aeronautic Association. The SSA is the delegated governing body for soaring contests and record flights in the U.S.; it publishes SOARING Magazine and other publications, and represents the interests of the sport before the regulatory agencies of government. Acts as coordinator, supporter and friend to all segments of soaring, both private and commercial. SSA operates with a small paid staff and a vast amount of volunteer effort from its more dedicated members.

Solo — A flight during which the pilot is the sole occupant of the aircraft.

Span — The maximum distance from wingtip to wingtip of an aircraft.

Speed Ring — A movable bezel around a variometer to assist the pilot in deciding at what speed to fly between thermals or on the final glide.

Speed-to-Fly — The indicated airspeed which produces the flattest glide in any situation of convection.

Spin — An aerobatic maneuver in which the glider spirals tightly downward in a nose-low attitude.

Spiral — All gliding turns are generally spiral in form. The unintended and uncontrolled high-speed spiral can be dangerous.

Spoilers — Devices that disturb the airflow across the wing to *spoil* the lift and increase drag, resulting in a steeper glide path.

Stability — The tendency to maintain normal straight flight and to return to this condition if the attitude is disturbed.

Stable Air — An atmosphere with a lapse rate such that a parcel of air which is displaced up or down will tend to return to its original level.

Stabilizer — The fixed horizontal tail surface used to provide pitch stability.

Stall — The loss of lift at the angle of attack at which the flow of air separates significantly from the top of the wing. An aircraft can be stalled in any attitude, and the only way to recover it is to reduce the angle of attack.

Stalling Speed — The airspeed at which the wing stalls.

Static Source — A source of air at the surrounding atmospheric pressure, unaffected by dynamic forces.

Stick — The control within the cockpit that actuates the ailerons and elevator.

Terminal Velocity — The highest speed attainable in a prolonged vertical dive. Drag producing devices may be used to hold terminal velocity below placard maximum.

Thermal — Air heated by the underlying surface rising through surrounding cooler air. Thermals may also be triggered when unstable air is lifted by other means, for example, by cold fronts. *Thermalling* is climbing in a thermal.

Total Energy Variometer — A variometer compensated to respond only to changes in the total energy of the sailplane; thus a change in airspeed due to stick deflection does not register as lift or sink on the variometer.

Track — The ground path over which the sailplane actually flies.

Trim Control — A small auxilary control on the elevator or a spring device bearing on the elevator control system for the purpose of relieving the pilot of the need to hold a pressure on the stick to maintain the desired airspeed.

Variation — The angular difference in the direction to the true and magnetic north poles.

Variometer — A sensitive and fast-responding instrument showing rate of climb or descent. The basic instrument of soaring.

VFR Conditions — Weather conditions equal to or better than the minimum for flight under visual flight rules.

Wake — The disturbed and mostly downward moving air behind an aircraft.

Weak Link — A section of rope of a breaking strength specified by the FAA that is incorporated into stronger tow ropes and cables as a safety device.

Weathervane — The tendency of an aircraft to face into the wind due to its effect on the vertical surfaces of the tail group.

Wind Shadow — An area of calm in the lee of windbreaks such as hills, buildings and rows of trees. Such spots, when sunny, are likely sources of thermals on windy days.

Wind Shift — An abrupt change in the surface wind that can pose a serious problem for any landing aircraft but, especially, for gliders.

Wind Sock — A cloth sleeve mounted aloft and used to estimate the speed and direction of the wind.

Wind Velocity Gradient — The horizontal wind shear close to the ground caused by the frictional effect of the terrain. The gradient can be a hazard to landing gliders.

Wing — An airfoil whose major function is to provide lift by dynamic reaction to the air flowing over it.

Yaw — Rotation of the glider around its vertical axis. *Adverse yaw* is against the direction of banking and is caused by the difference in drag of the down and up wings.

Yaw String — A few inches of yarn tied to the centerline of the sailplane in front of the pilot. When it blows to one side, it indicates a slip or a skid.

a

b

e

f

g

U

V

W

Y